ELEMENTS OF
English 9

Douglas Hilker

Sue Harper

Harcourt Canada

Orlando Austin New York San Diego Toronto London

Canadian Cataloguing in Publication Data

Main entry under title:

Elements of English 9

Includes index..
ISBN 0-7747-0575-2

1. Readers (Secondary). 2. Reading comprehension — Problems, exercises, etc. I. Hilker, Douglas. II. Harper, Sue, 1952-

PE1121.E38 1999   428'.6   C99-930552-2

Authors

Douglas Hilker
Writing Team Leader for the Ontario Curriculum Policy Document for English and Lead Developer for the Ontario Secondary School Grade 10 Literacy Test

Sue Harper
Head of English, John Fraser Secondary School, Mississauga, ON

Reviewers

Anne Carrier, Head of English, North Toronto Collegiate Institute, Toronto, ON
Sue Clarke, Assistant Deputy Head, Walkerville Secondary School, Windsor, ON
Susan King, Head of English, Weston Collegiate Institute, Weston, ON
Rocky Landon, Limestone District School Board, Kingston, ON
Nancy Polack, Program Leader: English, Lasalle Secondary School, Sudbury, ON
Michael Rossetti, Head of English, Father Henry Carr Catholic High School, Rexdale, ON

Project Manager: Gaynor Fitzpatrick
Supervising Editor: Su Mei Ku
Editorial Assistant: Ian Nussbaum
Senior Production Editor: Margot Miller
Production Coordinator: Tanya Mossa
Permissions Coordinator: Patricia Buckley
Cover and Interior Design: Sharon Foster Design
Page Composition: Sharon Foster Design
Cover Illustration: Jamie Hogan
Printing and Binding: Friesen Printers

 Printed in Canada on acid-free paper

3 4 5 6   07 06 05 04

Table of Contents

UNIT 3 MEDIA

UNIT 4 THE REFERENCE SHELF

Section One: The English Language

Section Two: Reading and Researching

Section Three: Writing

Section Four: Oral Communication Skills

Section Five: The Media

What can you—the student who reads the selections in this textbook and works through the activities—expect for your efforts?

You require a high level of literacy for success in all your high school subjects. Literacy is the key to success whether you continue on to university or college or enter the world of work and society after graduation. This textbook invites you first and foremost to develop a full range of skills and knowledge related to both the use of language for effective communication, and to the study of literature, language, and media. The reading passages and the activities that accompany them will engage you in high-level critical and creative thinking skills.

The literary and informational selections invite you to explore diverse topics and points of view from different countries, cultures, and time periods with an emphasis on themes and issues relevant to contemporary young Canadians.

The activities give you practice in

- developing reading strategies appropriate to a variety of topics, styles, and forms
- writing clearly and effectively in a variety of forms for a wide range of audiences and purposes
- listening and speaking in both formal and informal situations
- analyzing and creating media works
- working independently
- working with a partner, a small group, or the whole class in a cooperative and collaborative manner

Unit 1—Language and Form invites you to think about how language is used in the present and has been used in the past to communicate information and ideas accurately, clearly, and effectively.

Unit 2—Literature introduces you to authors of short stories, expositions, poetry, and drama from Canada and around the world that will enrich your understanding of yourself, your community, your country, and your world.

Unit 3—Media focuses on understanding the pervasive influence and impact of the media on individuals and society in the modern technological world.

Unit 4—The Reference Shelf provides you with information, rules, and tips for using language in written, oral, and media forms of communication correctly, effectively, and creatively.

It is important for you to understand the range of knowledge and skills that you are expected to be able to demonstrate by the end of the year. Ask your teacher or guidance counsellor for the curriculum expectations you will be evaluated on in all of your subjects this year. Find out about how you will be expected to demonstrate the knowledge and skills described in those expectations. Preparation is the first step to success.

Your teachers' ongoing evaluation of your performance in class and on assignments, projects, tests, and exams will provide you with valuable information on your strengths and weaknesses. However, your own self-evaluation will help you track your progress towards meeting the expected standards of the curriculum as well as your personal goals. An excellent way of tracking your progress is to keep a personal learning log. Once a week or at the end of each set of activities answer some of the following questions in your log:

- What do I know now that I didn't know before?
- What evidence can I give that I have become a better reader, viewer, writer, speaker, listener, researcher, and/or group member?
- What have I found out about the way I learn best?
- What are my strengths and weaknesses in the development of the knowledge and skills emphasized in the past week or unit of study?
- What are my immediate and long-term goals for improvement?

Enjoy the book.

Good luck extending and improving your literacy skills.

Douglas Hilker
Sue Harper

Some books are to be tasted, others to be swallowed, and some few to be chewed and digested; that is, some books are to be read only in parts; others to be read, but not curiously;[1] and some few to be read wholly and with diligence and attention.

From Francis Bacon, "Of Studies"

---

[1] curiously: too carefully

UNIT I
Language and Form

The Page

MARGARET ATWOOD

"The page waits . . ."

Before Reading

1. Every job has a certain amount of stress. Imagine that you are a professional writer. Make a list of stresses you might face trying to do your job.

2. Write about the part of the writing process you find most challenging. Follow this by writing about the part of the writing process you like the best.

1. The page waits, pretending to be blank. Is that its appeal, its blankness? What else is this smooth and white, this terrifyingly innocent? A snowfall, a glacier? It's a desert, totally arid, without life. But people venture into such places. Why? To see how much they can endure, how much dry light?

2. I've said the page is white, and it is: white as wedding dresses, rare whales, seagulls, angels, ice and death. Some say that like sunlight it contains all colours; others, that it's white because it's hot, it will burn out your optic nerves; that those who stare at the page too long go blind.

3. The page itself has no dimensions and no directions. There's no up or down except what you yourself mark, there's no thickness and weight but those you put there, north and south do not exist unless you're certain of them. The page is without vistas and without sounds, without centres or edges. Because of this you can become lost in it forever. Have you never seen the look of gratitude, the look of joy, on the faces of those who have managed to return from the page? Despite their faintness, their loss of blood, they fall on their knees, they push their hands into the earth, they clasp the bodies of those they love, or, in a pinch, any bodies they can get, with an urgency unknown to those who have never experienced the full horror of a journey into the page.

4. If you decide to enter the page, take a knife and some matches, and something that will float. Take something you can hold onto, and a prism to split the light and a talisman that works, which should be hung on a chain around your neck: that's for getting back. It doesn't matter what kind of shoes, but your hands should be bare. You should never go into the page with gloves on. Such decisions, needless to say, should not be made lightly.

There are those, of course, who enter the page without deciding, without meaning to. Some of these have charmed lives and no difficulty, but most never make it out at all. For them the page appears as a well, a lovely pool in which they catch sight of a face, their own but better. These unfortunates do not jump: rather they fall, and the page closes over their heads without a sound, without a seam, and is immediately as whole and empty, as glassy, as enticing as before.

5. The question about the page is: what is beneath it? It seems to have only two dimensions, you can pick it up and turn it over and the back is the same as the front. Nothing, you say, disappointed.

But you were looking in the wrong place, you were looking *on the back* instead of *beneath. Beneath the page* is another story. Beneath the page is a story. Beneath the page is everything that has ever happened, most of which you would rather not hear about.

The page is not a pool but a skin, a skin is there to hold in and it can feel you touching it. Did you really think it would just lie there and do nothing?

Touch the page at your peril: it is you who are blank and innocent, not the page. Nevertheless you want to know, nothing will stop you. You touch the page, it's as if you've drawn a knife across it, the page has been hurt now, a sinuous wound opens, a thin incision. Darkness wells through.

After Reading

1. a) In part 1 of this **prose poem**, Margaret Atwood compares a writer to an adventurer who likes to go places, such as the desert. Explain how a writer is like an adventurer.

    b) Using print or electronic resources, research a famous Canadian adventurer.

2. In part 2 of the poem, Atwood compares the whiteness of the page to several other white things. In a small group, brainstorm a list of reasons why each of these images is an effective comparison to the blank page. Be prepared to share your list with the class.

3. a) Find the words that Atwood uses in part 3 to create a negative feeling about the journey into the page. In your **journal**, describe a time when you had writer's block.

    b) As a class, make a list of strategies you can use when faced with writer's block. This could happen with an assignment, in an exam, or when you are writing for yourself.

    c) Write an **article** for a school newspaper or a teen magazine in which you give advice about getting past writer's block. Try to include some humour, **anecdotes**, and quotations from friends and experts (real or imagined) to make your article lively and interesting. Take your writing through several drafts and peer editings before submitting or posting your article. (See The Reference Shelf, page 268.)

4. Using print and electronic resources, research the Greek **myth** of Narcissus. Show how the second paragraph of part 4 is an **allusion** to this famous myth. In your notebook, explain why this is an effective allusion to use when talking about people "losing themselves" in their own writing.

The Speling Konferens

KEN WEBER

"... English spelling is a mess ..."

Before Reading

1. Make a list of spelling rules you remember from elementary school.

2. What types of spelling errors do you commonly make? Can you put your errors into categories (e.g., homophones, doubling consonants, *-ent/-ant* endings)? (See The Reference Shelf, pages 243–247.)

Lights come up very slowly to a dim level. They remain dim throughout the play. A purple glow in the lighting creates a sense of strangeness.

Everything about the set is old, and solid, and massive, and rich. The centre of the room is dominated by the kind of huge, oak, rectangular table that no one could afford to buy today. Around it, in perfect, rigid order, sit eleven very wide, high-backed, chairs. On the table, in front of each chair, a dull brass plate identifies a different province.

Along the thick stone walls hang larger-than-life portraits of the Fathers of Confederation. Above the table, a round, iron chandelier hangs from a single chain that goes up into the blackness.

The atmosphere must reek of importance. This is a room somewhere in the Parliament buildings. The audience might imagine itself in the last century, were it not for one corner of the stage. Underneath the fire alarm is a security guard sound asleep. His regular, gentle snores are the only sound on the set. Above him, a small, frayed sign hangs crookedly:

These Premises Patrolled by Ever-Alert Security Ltd

Below this sign hangs another one equally small, but far more imposing:

The Ministers of Education
for the
Provinces and Territories of
Canada
Annual Conference
DO NOT ENTER

The door creaks open. A girl of about twelve takes several steps into the room. She is casually dressed: jeans, running shoes, and a sweater—in sharp contrast to the set. There is a school bag over her shoulder. She gives the guard a quick glance, then walks to the chair marked Alberta and slides into it. Then a second head pokes through the doorway.

Alberta: It's OK. We can start.
The second person enters. She too is about twelve and is also casually dressed. With a wary eye on the guard she walks to the New Brunswick chair.
New Brunswick: What about him?
Alberta: Forget him. He was here all day with the adults. He'll *never* wake up!
New Brunswick: (*Nodding at the doorway*) Let's go! *Nine more young people come in. They are a mixture of boys and girls. All of them look like they have just come from school.*

Alberta: All right. There's no time to waste. Do you all have your recommendations ready? (*There are general nods*) Good. New Brunswick, will you read the mandate again please?
New Brunswick: (*In a town-crier voice*) Whereas it is agreed that English spelling is a mess, and whereas it is agreed that we students are more confused by spelling than by any other subject, this august council shall proclaim the Canadian Easy Spelling Charter, according to the following rules. . . . That's it, we don't have any rules yet.
Alberta: That's what this meeting is all about. By the time we're finished here, spelling in Canada will be changed forever. Prince Edward Island, you are first. From you, we go around the table.

Prince Edward Island: We propose the elimination of the soft "c." We'll use "s" instead. Sertainly the sitizens of Canada would selebrate this change. Prinse Edward Island would for sure, and every other provinse too, I'll bet.

Manitoba: There's no need to have a "c" at all. We propose eliminating the hard "c." The letter "k" will do just nisely. And think of the konfusion this change kould take kare of. At any rate we'd have kloser kontrol of our language. Do you agree Nova Skotia?

Nova Scotia: There'd be konsiderable exsitement among the kids at skhool. That's for sure. There's no doubt your rekommendation would be a suksess. However, we've got another problem in Nova Skotia. It's the "sh" sound. You can spell that sound in English with a "t," with an "s," with a "c," even with "sh!" No wonder students go round in sirkles.

We suggest keeping the letter "c" and using it for "sh." Those of us who live by the seacore—not just in Nova Skocia, but on the west koast in Britic Kolumbia—would have a much easier time.

Alberta: Curely no one kould objekt to that?

There are nods of agreement.

Yukon and Northwest Territories: I think our rekommendacion is possible now. The letter "x" has always seemed rather useless to us. Now it's unnecessary. With "k" and "s" doing real duty, the sensible thing is to take out "x"—just eksklude it from the language.

Ontario: If I may go nekst, Yukon, your komment leads right into ours. We propose to eliminate silent "e" and . . .

A chorus of objections drowns out Ontario. Alberta raps on the table, as the guard shifts slightly in his chair. They all look up and are silent.

Alberta: Wiping out silent "e" is opening a real kan of worms, Ontario.

Newfoundland: Yes. Think of the difference between *kar* and *kare*, and *not* and *note*. Curely, you kan't ekspekt the nacion to aksept so great a change! We'll be in a worse mess than before!

Ontario: But think about words like *simple* and *sinse* and *sentre*, or is it *senter?* Do we really need the silent "e"? Or words like *sensible* and *before?* Does the silent "e" really change anything?

British Columbia: I think he's got something there. Just what is your rekommendacion, Ontario?

Ontario: To eliminate silent "e" when it is unnesessary, in words like *maskulin* and *feminin*. And, when the vowel is *long*, just double it. Instead of *pale*, we'd wriit *paal;* instead of *flute*, we'd wriit *fluut!*

Newfoundland: Riight! Ii see! Wee'd hav Kaap Fortuun in our provins; there'd bee the Kaap of Good Hoop in Afrika. . . .

Saskatchewan: I wonder if Regina will hav to becom Regiina? Ooh well, wee kan work that out. I liik the proopoosal.

Alberta: Ii taak it everyon is agreed? Good! This is really Konfederaacion at work!

A few of them glance up at the portrait of Sir John A. Macdonald.

British Columbia: Ii beeleev my iideea should bee nekst sins it follows logikally. Ii doon't knoow a singl person who liiks the "ie" and "ei" business. Wee proopoos they bee reeplaasd with double "ee" and doubl "aa." Then wee won't hav to worry how to spell words liik *konseet*, or *naabor*, or *beeleev*, or *deesel*.

Quebec: Hear, hear! Britic Kolumbia. That "ei-ie" business has to bee the weerdest ruul in any languaag. And Ii hav another to deal with. Let's reeplaas soft "g" with "j." Alsoo, whenever the "j" sound appears in a "tion" word, liik *question*, let's uus "j" ther too. After all, "j" is a very underuusd letter. This sugjesjion will lead to som positiv chaanjes.

Alberta: Noo quesjion of that, Quebek. Wee hav to mov mor quikly now. New Brunswik, your sugjesjion is nekst.

New Brunswick: A simpl but uusful proopoosal. Reeplaas "ph" with "f." Who needs "ph"? Do you knoow that words liik foonoograf will bee twenty persent shorter . . . hey—wait a minut. Foonoograf *would hav been* twenty persent shorter without Ontarioo's chaanj . . .

Noise level goes up as arguments begin. Alberta raps for silence.

Alberta: Too laat. Tiim's waasting. Newfoundland, you're nekst; let's hurry!

Newfoundland: Doubl konsonants. Our languaaj wil get by just fiin without thees odbals. They maak akuuraat speling imposibl. And whiil wee'r at it, let's taak out siilent leters. They'r dum. Wee al noow that!

Saskatchewan: Egsaktly Newfoundland, thank you! My sugjesjion foloows the saam liin of thinking. It's the "gh" nonsens that wee'r konsernd about. Look at words liik *ghost*, and *laugh*, and *slaughter*. Why woud wee uus "gh"? Speling is touf eenouf as it is.

Alberta: Riit, Saskatchewan. Out goos "gh." (*She stands up and clears her throat*) Laadees and jentlmen, wee hav maad som jenuuinly inteelijent progres heer. Our Konferens wil bee judjd a sukses. Now, in konkluuding, Ii hav two duutees left. On is to reemiind you that the chair movs east on provins a year, soo that means you'r on nekst, Saskatchewan. (*There is polite applause*) Two, you know the chairperson maaks noo proopoosals, but gets to pik nekst year's topik . . .

Newfoundland: Yes, hav you thout about this, Alberta? Wee'v hardly skratchd the surfas in speling. Ther's such a long waay to goo. What do wee do about "s" that sounds liik "z"? Wee dumpd "gh," soo why not dump "wh"? Then there's "y" that sounds liik "ii" and liik "ee." And ther's al that "ir," "er," "ar" konfusion. And "ou" proonounsd diferent waays in words such as "thout," and "kour," and "bou." And ther's . . .

Alberta: Point aksepted, Newfoundland. Personaly, Ii'd maak the ruul that every word bee speld the waay it sounds—if Ii had mii waa. Then Inglish miit bee eezeer for Kanaadeeanz frum kost too kost. But wee'd beter maak haast sloolee. It tuk Inglish speling a long tiim to get miksd up; let's fiks it at the saam paas. Noo. Ii proopoos that at the nekst konfrens wee trii too doo som reepairs on this metrik stuf . . .

Shaking their heads and with serious expressions, the boys and girls file out. Last out is Quebec. He stops by the guard whose hat has fallen askew. Quebec straightens it for him. The guard continues to snore as the lights go out.

After Reading

1. Based on information in the story, create a chart in which you list the suggested spelling changes and examples of those changes. In a third column, place a check mark beside the rules you agree with. In small groups, compare your charts and discuss the pros and cons of making the changes you believe are good ones.

2. What would some of the problems be if we changed the spelling rules as each of the provinces has suggested? Discuss with the class.

3. Explain one major difference between American and Canadian spellings. As a class, **debate** the advantages and disadvantages of having different systems. (See The Reference Shelf, page 283.)

4. a) List the types of spelling errors not caught by an electronic spell-checker.

   b) Write a **business letter** to a major software company suggesting improvements it needs to make to its spell-checker program. See the Glossary, page 295, for a description of a business letter.

5. With a partner, write a list of strategies you can use when you don't know how to spell a word. Then, with your partner, create posters based on these spelling strategies. Display them where they can be used as reminders when you write.

Talk

AN ASHANTI FOLK TALE

"Fantastic, isn't it?" his stool said. "Imagine a talking yam!"

Before Reading

1. Find the city of Accra and look up the word "Ashanti".
2. Share with a partner a favourite childhood story.

Once, not far from the city of Accra on the Gulf of Guinea, a country man went out to his garden to dig up some yams to take to market. While he was digging, one of the yams said to him, "Well, at last you're here. You never weeded me, but now you come around with your digging stick. Go away and leave me alone!"

The farmer turned around and looked at his cow in amazement. The cow was chewing her cud and looking at him.

"Did you say something?" he asked.

The cow kept on chewing and said nothing, but the man's dog spoke up.

"It wasn't the cow who spoke to you," the dog said. "It was the yam. The yam says leave him alone."

The man became angry because his dog had never talked before, and he didn't like his tone, besides. So he took his knife and cut a branch from a palm tree to whip his dog.

Just then the palm tree said, "Put that branch down."

The man was getting very upset about the way things were going, and he started to throw the palm branch away, but the palm branch said, "Man, put me down softly!"

He put the branch down gently on a stone, and the stone said, "Hey, take that thing off me."

This was enough, and the frightened farmer started to run for his village. On the way he met a fisherman going the other way with a fish trap on his head.

"What's the hurry?" the fisherman asked.

"My yam said, 'Leave me alone!' Then the dog said, 'Listen to what the yam says!' When I went to whip the dog with a palm branch, the tree said, 'Put that branch down!' Then the palm branch said, 'Do it softly!' Then the stone said, 'Take that thing off me!'"

"Is that all?" the man with the fish trap asked. "Is that so frightening?"

"Well," the man's fish trap said, "did he take it off the stone?"

"Wah!" the fisherman shouted. He threw the fish trap on the ground and began to run with the farmer, and on the trail they met a weaver with a bundle of cloth on his head.

"Where are you going in such a rush?" he asked them.

"My yam said, 'Leave me alone!'" the farmer said. "The dog said, 'Listen to what the yam says!' The tree said, 'Put that branch down!' The branch said, 'Do it softly.' And the stone said, 'Take that thing off me!'"

"And then," the fisherman continued, "the fish trap said, 'Did he take it off?'"

"That's nothing to get excited about," the weaver said, "no reason at all."

"Oh, yes it is," his bundle of cloth said. "If it happened to you, you'd run too!"

"Wah!" the weaver shouted. He threw his bundle on the trail and started running with the other men.

They came panting to the ford in the river and found a man bathing.

"Are you chasing a gazelle?" he asked them.

The first man said breathlessly, "My yam talked to me, and it said, 'Leave me alone!' And the dog said, 'Listen to your yam!' And when I cut myself a branch the tree said, 'Put that branch down!' And then the branch said, 'Do it softly!' And the stone said, 'Take that thing off me!'"

The fisherman panted, "And my trap said, 'Did he?'"

The weaver wheezed, "And my bundle of cloth said, 'You'd run too!'"

"Is that why you're running?" the man in the river asked.

"Well, wouldn't you run if you were in their position?" the river said.

The man jumped out of the water and began to run with the others. They ran down the main street of the village to the house of the chief.

The chief's servants brought his stool out, and he came and sat on it to listen to their complaints. The men began to recite their troubles.

"I went to my garden to dig yams," the farmer said, waving his arms. "Then everything began to talk! My yam said 'Leave me alone!' My dog said, 'Pay attention to your yam!' The tree said, 'Put that branch down!' The branch said, 'Do it softly!' And the stone said, 'Take it off me!'"

"And my fishtrap said, 'Well, did he take it off?'" the fisherman said.

"And my cloth said, 'You'd run too!'" the weaver said.

"And the river said the same," the bather said hoarsely, his eyes bulging.

The chief listened to them patiently, but he couldn't refrain from scowling.

"Now this really is a wild story," he said at last. "You'd better all go back to your work before I punish you for disturbing the peace."

So the men went away, and the chief shook his head and mumbled to himself, "Nonsense like that upsets the community."

"Fantastic, isn't it?" his stool said. "Imagine a talking yam!"

After Reading

1. Write a continuation of this story.

2. Most **folk tales** have a moral or message. State the **moral** and the **theme** of this story and give reasons for your choice.

3. The **repetition** of what each animal or object says in this story provides it with a kind of **incremental refrain**. With a partner, describe the effect of the repetition in this passage. Identify other stories, folk tales, or songs that have similar repetition. Record your findings in your notebook.

4. Select one line as the funniest in the story and give reasons for your choice. Be prepared to share your choice with the class.

5. Children's stories and animated films often use the device of animals or inanimate objects that speak. Write a short **opinion piece** that accounts for the popularity of this device.

6. Using print and electronic resources, prepare a short **research report** on animal communication, such as that of dolphins, dogs, or ants.

12

Listen Up!
Enhancing Our Listening Skills

WARREN SHEPELL CONSULTANTS

". . . despite all of our attempts at improving communications, we often neglect the communication skill which is used the most—listening."

Before Reading

1. With your classmates, make a list on the board of signs that show a person is not listening to you.

2. Make up a very **short story** about something that happened to you last night. Tell the story to someone in the class and then have him or her tell it to another person who, in turn, relates it to someone else. Do this until a chain of about five or six people have heard the story. See what happens to the story by the end of the chain. Why does this happen?

3. As a class, discuss the difference between hearing and listening.

Have you ever thought about how important listening can be? Just consider that we spend 80 percent of our waking hours communicating and over 45 percent of that time listening to others—spouses, children, friends, co-workers, and acquaintances.

What is listening? Many of us think that listening is what we do while waiting for our turn to talk. Listening is more than being quiet and hearing. Dr. Lyman K. Steil, a well-known authority on the subject of listening, explains that listening involves four stages. First, we hear the message, then, we interpret it, evaluate it, and respond to it.

Studies have shown that most of us understand, evaluate, and retain approximately 50 percent of what is said. And after two days, we remember only half of that. The end result is that we comprehend and retain only 25 percent of what is said.

In the workplace, the cost of poor listening adds up to dollars and cents. It can involve the cost of additional time spent in repeating instructions and having to redo assignments that were carried out incorrectly. Further, some workplace accidents involving physical harm to workers are the result of an individual not listening to directions or warnings prior to acting.

On a personal front, our relationships with people can suffer if we do not listen effectively, or if we do not have people in our lives who will actively listen to us from time to time. We all need someone with whom to share our ideas, thoughts and feelings. If we do not have a listener in our lives, we can begin to feel lonely and isolated.

How would you rate your best friend as a listener? The magic of a warm and sincere friendship is usually one of the rewards of good listening. We are attracted to people who listen. They calm us and support us.

If listening is really this important, then why aren't we better listeners? There's actually a physiological reason for our listening difficulties. Our capacity to listen ranges from 400 to 600 words a minute, while the average speaking rate is about 125 words per minute.

This can give us plenty of time to think about other things while a person is talking to us.

A major reason for our poor listening habits may be lack of training. We teach reading, writing, and speaking in our schools. Adults take courses in speed reading, business writing, and public speaking. Yet, despite all of our attempts at improving communications, we often neglect the communication skill which is used the most—listening.

Another reason for poor listening is that we may be too busy to focus exclusively on another individual. Have you ever been too busy to lend a sympathetic ear to a child who has had a tough day at school or to really listen to your mate discuss his or her frustrations?

Sometimes we don't listen to others because we think that they expect us to solve their problems. Yet, few of our friends and relatives really want us to organize their finances, find them new mates, or solve their work frustrations. Oftentimes they are wanting to share their thoughts and feelings with us and want only for us to understand and appreciate what they are going through.

Being able to put ourselves into "someone else's shoes," or someone else's experience, so that we can understand how another may feel, is known as empathic listening. We can let people know that we are listening and do understand them by reflecting back to them how we think they must feel. "You must be so excited" might be communicated to someone who is enthusiastically telling you about a promotion they have just received.

We should be aware that empathic listening is the kind of first aid that many people seek. Leo Buscaglia, a well-known psychologist and author, puts it this way: "When I ask you to listen to me and you start giving advice, you have not done what I asked." Remember, there are times when people want us to listen to them and nothing more.

Before you can become a good listener, you must become a flexible listener. In other words, it's crucial to vary your listening style to suit the speaker, the subject, and the occasion.

Consider your reason for listening. More often than not, your reason for listening will help decide your style of listening. Are you listening for pleasure, to receive ideas and information, to evaluate information, or to show empathy? These are the four basic reasons for listening.

If you listen to a business seminar the same way you listen to a TV comedy, you may not retain much from the seminar. And it stands to reason that the critical listening style that you would use to evaluate information regarding a major purchase you are about to make is not the style you would use when listening to a friend's troubles.

Taking a look at your listening habits is the first step towards becoming a better listener. Most of us have a number of listening faults. So don't be surprised if you identify yourself in more than one of these illustrations.

The biased listener

Usually, the biased listener isn't listening. The biased listener has tuned out and is planning what to say next based on some fixed ideas they have about the subject.

When bias becomes prejudice, we may even tune out a person because of his or her age, accent, or occupation.

Ask yourself: Are my biases a barrier to listening? The road to tuned-in listening begins with a deliberate effort to get rid of preconceived ideas and to give others a fair hearing.

The distracted listener

All of us fit into this category at one time or another. Distracted listeners allow internal or external distractions to prevent them from giving others their undivided attention.

Unfortunately, a lot of distracted listeners don't realize that it's important to get ready to listen. You can't turn yourself into an attentive listener unless you make a deliberate effort to tune out internal distractions and concentrate on what the speaker is saying. If this is not possible, it may be better to set another time to meet with and listen to that person so that he or she can have your undivided attention.

For the most part, external distractions can be eliminated simply by finding a quiet place for your important conversations—one where you'll be free from interruptions.

The impatient listener

The impatient listener is one who interrupts and seldom lets people finish what they have to say. It can be easy to slip into this habit.

If you find it extremely frustrating to listen to people who, perhaps, talk slowly, you are probably an impatient listener. Becoming a patient listener involves making an effort not to interrupt. At first, you'll find it difficult to listen without interrupting. But you'll be pleasantly surprised when the lines of communication open up. Remember, if you have been courteous enough to listen to others, more often than not, they'll listen to you.

The passive listener

The passive listener does not realize that listening is an active process. When we are engaged in conversation with this listener, we are never sure if our message is understood. Why? Simply because we receive little or no feedback. Obviously, this can cause plenty of communication problems.

A telephone conversation with a passive listener is even more difficult than a face-to-face conversation. More often than not, a speaker's words are met with stony silence. That's why people often wonder if their call has been disconnected. If you are having a telephone conversation and have the person on the other end of the line ask "Are you still there?" it may be because you have not been communicating to him or her that you are listening.

If you have a tendency to be a passive listener, try turning yourself into a responsive listener by providing people with more feedback. Just lean slightly forward, establish eye contact, and nod or smile when appropriate. An occasional remark such as "I see," "uh-huh," or "yes" can be used when the conversation is either face-to-face or by telephone.

You may realize that your listening skills need some improvement. Although you're not going to change a lifetime of listening habits overnight, you can, with a little time and effort, learn to become a better listener.

Remember that listening is an important communication skill. It should not be taken for granted. You'll find that your family, business, and social interactions will improve—thanks to better listening!

After Reading

1. State the **topic** of this **essay**. In one well-written sentence, state the **thesis** of this essay. (See the Glossary, page 303, for definitions of topic and thesis.)

2. a) From the essay, make point-form notes on each type of listener.

   b) For each type, create an **icon** to represent that listener. Be prepared to explain your designs to the class.

3. In a **journal** entry, write about a time you demonstrated one of the poor listening habits described in the essay. Be sure to include what happened as a result.

4. Examine the way the information is presented in this essay. Describe the techniques that have been used to make the essay clear and easy to understand.

5. a) In your notebook, write a short essay on the usefulness of learning about listening. Consider different occasions when you need good listening skills: at home, school, and work.

   b) Trade your work with a classmate and edit the essay, focusing your comments on rearranging, adding, deleting, and substituting ideas. With your partner, discuss each other's essays using the written suggestions as the basis for your discussion.

   c) Have a different classmate edit your work for spelling and grammar.

6. In pairs or threes, **role play** a situation that might happen at work, home, or school in which you demonstrate one listening problem. Present your role play to the class and have them identify which listening type you were acting out.

7. Make a list of strategies you could use to become a good listener. With your classmates, create a combined list on chart paper or Bristol board and post it in your classroom.

The Seven Ages of Man

An Excerpt From *As You Like It*, Act II, Scene 7

WILLIAM SHAKESPEARE

Before Reading

Historically, the term "man" has been used to represent both genders. Make
a list of words that have changed to reflect gender equality (e.g., *mailman*
has become *letter carrier*).

Jacques: All the world's a stage,
And all the men and women merely players;
They have their exits and their entrances,
And one man in his time plays many parts,
His acts being seven ages. At first the infant,
Mewling and puking in the nurse's arms.
Then the whining schoolboy, with his satchel
And shining morning face, creeping like snail
Unwillingly to school, And then the lover,
Sighing like furnace, with a woeful ballad
Made to his mistress' eyebrow. Then a soldier,
Full of strange oaths and bearded like the pard,
Jealous in honour, sudden and quick in quarrel,
Seeking the bubble reputation
Even in the cannon's mouth. And then the justice,
In fair round belly with good capon lined,
With eyes severe and beard of formal cut,
Full of wise saws and modern instances;
And so he plays his part. The sixth age shifts

Into the lean and slipper'd pantaloon,
With spectacles on nose and pouch on side,
His youthful hose, well saved, a world too wide
For his shrunk shank; and his big manly voice,
Turning again toward childish treble, pipes
And whistles in his sound. Last scene of all,
That ends this strange eventful history,
Is second childishness and mere oblivion,
Sans teeth, sans eyes, sans taste, sans everything.

After Reading

1. List "the seven ages of man" as presented by Shakespeare in this passage.

2. Select a word to describe the **tone** of this passage and explain why you do or do not agree with the playwright.

3. Select one line that you think is the funniest in the passage and give reasons for your choice.

4. Find an example of a **simile**, a **metaphor**, **alliteration**, and **onomatopoeia** in the passage.

5. This passage was written about four hundred years ago. With a partner, identify aspects of the writing that relate the passage to its own time period.

6. The meaning of some words in this passage have changed since Shakespeare's time. Check a dictionary to find modern-day equivalents of the following: *mewling*, *pard*, *saws*, *pantaloon*, and *mere*. (See also The Reference Shelf, pages 226–229.)

7. Prepare a **dramatic reading** of the passage to present to the class.

8. Write an updated version of the passage: A Modern Seven Ages of Man or Woman.

9. Write an **essay** agreeing or disagreeing with this statement: Adolescence is the best time of a person's life.

Great Expectations

An Excerpt

CHARLES DICKENS

"A fearful man, all in coarse grey, with a great iron on his leg . . . seized me by the chin."

Before Reading

1. As a class, read the opening paragraph of this story aloud. Discuss the differences between nineteenth-century and modern writing.

2. In a **journal** entry, write about a time you were terrified as a child.

My father's family name being Pirrip, and my Christian name Philip, my infant tongue could make of both names nothing longer or more explicit than Pip. So I called myself Pip, and came to be called Pip.

I give Pirrip as my father's family name on the authority of his tombstone and my sister—Mrs. Joe Gargery, who married the blacksmith. As I never saw my father or my mother, and never saw any likeness of either of them (for their days were long before the days of photographs), my first fancies regarding what they were like were unreasonably derived from their tombstones. The shape of the letters on my father's gave me an odd idea that he was a square, stout, dark man, with curly black hair. From the character and turn of the inscription, *"Also Georgiana Wife of the Above,"* I drew a childish conclusion that my mother was freckled and sickly. To five little stone lozenges, each about a foot and a half long, which were arranged in a neat row beside their grave, and were sacred to the memory of five little brothers of mine—who gave up trying to get a living exceedingly early in that universal struggle—I am indebted for a belief I religiously entertained that they had all been born on their backs with their hands in their trouser pockets, and had never taken them out in this state of existence.

Ours was the marsh country, down by the river, within, as the river wound, twenty miles of the sea. My first most vivid and broad impression of the identity of things seems to me to have been gained on a memorable raw afternoon towards evening. At such a time I found out for certain that this bleak place overgrown with nettles was the churchyard; and that Philip Pirrip, Late of this Parish, and Also Georgiana Wife of the Above, were dead and buried; and that Alexander, Bartholomew, Abraham, Tobias, and Roger, infant children of the aforesaid, were also dead and buried; and that the dark flat wilderness beyond the church-yard, intersected with dikes and mounds and gates, with scattered cattle feeding on it, was the marshes; and that the low leaden line beyond was the river; and that the distant savage lair from which the wind was rushing was the sea; and that the small bundle of shivers growing afraid of it all and beginning to cry was Pip.

"Hold your noise!" cried a terrible voice, as a man started up from among the graves at the side of the church porch. "Keep still, you little devil, or I'll cut your throat!"

A fearful man, all in coarse grey, with a great iron on his leg. A man with no hat, and with broken shoes, and with an old rag tied round his head. A man who had been soaked in water, and smothered in mud, and lamed by stones, and cut by flints, and stung by nettles, and torn by briars; who limped, and shivered, and glared, and growled; and whose teeth chattered in his head, as he seized me by the chin.

"Oh! Don't cut my throat, sir," I pleaded in terror. "Pray don't do it, sir."

"Tell us your name!" said the man. "Quick!"

"Pip, sir."

"Once more," said the man, staring at me. "Give it mouth!"

"Pip. Pip, sir."

"Show us where you live," said the man. "Pint out the place!"

I pointed to where our village lay, on the flat in-shore among the alder-trees and pollards, a mile or more from the church.

The man, after looking at me for a moment, turned me upside down, and emptied my pockets. There was nothing in them but a piece of bread. When the church came to itself—for he was so sudden and strong that he made it go head over heels before me, and I saw the steeple under my feet—when the church came to itself, I say, I was seated on a high tomb-stone, trembling, while he ate the bread ravenously.

"You young dog," said the man, licking his lips, "what fat cheeks you ha' got."

I believe they were fat, though I was at that time undersized, for my years, and not strong.

"Darn me if I couldn't eat 'em," said the man, with a threatening shake of his head, "and if I han't half a mind to't!"

I earnestly expressed my hope that he wouldn't, and held tighter to the tomb-stone on which he had put me; partly to keep myself upon it; partly to keep myself from crying.

"Now lookee here!" said the man. "Where's your mother?"

"There, sir!" said I.

He started, made a short run, and stopped and looked over his shoulder.

"There, sir!" I timidly explained. "Also Georgiana. That's my mother."

"Oh!" said he, coming back. "And is that your father alonger your mother?"

"Yes, sir," said I; "him, too; late of this parish."

"Ha!" he muttered then, considering. "Who d'ye live with—supposin' ye're kindly let to live, which I han't made up my mind about?"

"My sister, sir—Mrs. Joe Gargery—wife of Joe Gargery, the blacksmith, sir."

"Blacksmith, eh?" said he. And looked down at his leg.

After darkly looking at his leg and at me several times, he came closer to my tombstone, took me by both arms, and tilted me back as far as he could hold me, so that his eyes looked most powerfully down into mine, and mine looked most helplessly up into his.

"Now lookee here," he said, "the question being whether you're to be let to live. You know what a file is?"

"Yes, sir."

"And you know what wittles is?"

"Yes, sir."

After each question he tilted me over a little more, so as to give me a greater sense of helplessness and danger.

"You get me a file." He tilted me again. "And you get me wittles." He tilted me again. "You bring 'em both to me." He tilted me again. "Or I'll have your heart and liver out." He tilted me again.

I was dreadfully frightened, and so giddy that I clung to him with both hands, and said, "If you would kindly please let me keep upright, sir, perhaps I shouldn't be sick, and perhaps I could attend more."

He gave me a most tremendous dip and roll, so that the church jumped over its own weathercock. Then he held me by the arms in an upright position on the top of the stone, and went on in these fearful terms:

"You bring me, to-morrow morning early, that file and them wittles. You bring the lot to me at that old battery over yonder. You do it, and you never dare to say a word or dare to make a sign concerning your having seen such a person as me, or any person sumever, and you shall be let to live. You fail, or you go from my words in any partickler, no matter how small it is, and your heart and your liver shall be tore out, roasted, and ate. Now, I ain't alone, as you may think I am. There's a young man hid with me, in comparison with which young man I am a angel. That young man hears the words I speak. That young man has a secret way pecooliar to himself of getting at a boy, and at his heart, and at his liver. It is in wain for a boy to attempt to hide himself from that young man. A boy may lock his door, may be warm in bed, may tuck himself up, may draw the clothes over his head, may think himself comfortable and safe, but that young man will softly creep and creep his way to him and tear him open. I am a-keeping that young man from harming of you at the present moment with great difficulty. I find it wery hard to hold that young man off of your inside. Now, what do you say?"

I said that I would get him the file, and I would get him what broken bits of food I could, and I would come to him at the battery, early in the morning.

"Say, Lord strike you dead if you don't!" said the man.

I said so, and he took me down.

"Now," he pursued, "you remember what you've undertook, and you remember that young man, and you get home!"

"Goo-good night, sir," I faltered.

"Much of that!" said he, glancing about him over the cold wet flat. "I wish I was a frog. Or a eel!"

At the same time, he hugged his shuddering body in both his arms—clasping himself, as if to hold himself together—and limped towards the low church wall. As I saw him go, picking his way among the nettles, and among the brambles that bound the green mounds, he looked in my young eyes as if he were eluding the hands of the dead people, stretching up cautiously out of their graves to get a twist upon his ankle and pull him in.

When he came to the low church wall, he got over it like a man whose legs were numbed and stiff, and then turned round to look for me. When I saw him turning, I set my face towards home, and made the best use of my legs. But presently I looked over my shoulder, and saw him going on again towards the river, still hugging himself in both arms, and picking his way with his sore feet among the great stones dropped into the marshes here and there for stepping-places when the rains were heavy, or the tide was in.

The marshes were just a long black horizontal line then, as I stopped to look after him; and the river was just another horizontal line, not nearly so broad nor yet so black; and the sky was just a row of long angry red lines and dense black lines intermixed. On the edge of the river I could faintly make out the only two black things in all the prospect that seemed to be standing upright; one of these was the beacon by which the sailors steered—like an unhooped cask upon a pole—an ugly thing when you were near it; the other a gibbet, with some chains hanging to it which had once held a pirate. The man was limping on towards this latter, as if he were the pirate come to life, and come down, and going back to hook himself up again. It gave me a terrible turn when I thought so, and as I saw the cattle lifting their heads to gaze after him, I wondered whether they thought so, too. I looked all round for the horrible young man, and could see no signs of him. But now I was frightened again, and ran home without stopping.

After Reading

1. Find the meaning of the following words and add them to your list of new and unfamiliar words: *derived, lozenges, vivid, nettles, lair, pollards, battery, eluding, gibbet.* Choose the definition closest to the meaning in the selection.

2. You are a director filming the graveyard scene. Draw a **storyboard** of the first four shots you would use to create suspense for your audience. Underneath each one, write the words and the sounds the audience would hear with each shot. (See The Reference Shelf, pages 288–289.)

3. Find five examples of **dialect** in this story. Record the words in your notebook and write down the meaning of the words in **Standard Canadian English**. How does the use of dialect enrich the **atmosphere** of the story?

4. a) Using examples from the selection, describe the difference between Pip's language and that of the convict.

   b) Explain the impression the writer creates of each of the **characters** by the differences in their speech.

5. a) Analyze the function of the fifth paragraph of the selection.

   b) Defend the writer's use of repetition and incomplete sentences here.

6. a) Choose your favourite **image** from the selection. Record the words or phrases that create that picture in your mind.

   b) Imagine you are creating an **advertising** campaign for a product. What product would best be represented by your favourite image? Create a slogan for the product that would match the feeling in the image.

7. a) Dickens first wrote *Great Expectations* in **serial** form for a magazine, with each episode appearing in subsequent issues. List the advantages and disadvantages of reading a novel in serial form.

   b) In a well-developed paragraph, evaluate how good this excerpt would be as the first episode. Be sure to use quotations from the selection wherever possible to support your opinion.

8. In your notebook, explain how your background as a reader interferes or helps with your understanding of Dickens' writing. With your classmates, discuss the ease or difficulty of reading *Great Expectations*, making some generalizations about who might find the story easiest or hardest to read.

The Highwayman

ALFRED NOYES

Before Reading

In your **journal**, write about a book you've read or a movie or television show you've seen where two young people were kept apart. How did it end?

Part One

The wind was a torrent of darkness among the gusty trees,
The moon was a ghostly galleon tossed upon cloudy seas,
The road was a ribbon of moonlight over the purple moor,
And the highwayman came riding—
5   Riding—riding—
The highwayman came riding, up to the old inn-door.

He'd a French cocked-hat on his forehead, a bunch of lace at his chin,
A coat of the claret velvet, and breeches of brown doeskin;
They fitted with never a wrinkle: his boots were up to the thigh!
10   And he rode with a jewelled twinkle,
          His pistol butts a-twinkle,
His rapier hilt a-twinkle, under the jewelled sky.

Over the cobbles he clattered and clashed in the dark inn-yard,
He tapped with his whip on the shutters, but all was locked and barred;
15   He whistled a tune to the window, and who should be waiting there
But the landlord's black-eyed daughter,
          Bess, the landlord's daughter,
Plaiting a dark red love-knot into her long black hair.

And dark in the dark old inn-yard a stable-wicket creaked
20 Where Tim the ostler listened; his face was white and peaked;
His eyes were hollows of madness, his hair like mouldy hay;
But he loved the landlord's daughter,
    The landlord's red-lipped daughter;
Dumb as a dog he listened, and he heard the robber say—

25 "One kiss, my bonny sweetheart, I'm after a prize tonight,
But I shall be back with the yellow gold before the morning light;
Yet, if they press me sharply, and harry me through the day,
Then look for me by moonlight,
    Watch for me by moonlight,
30 I'll come to thee by moonlight, though hell should bar the way."

He rose upright in the stirrups; he scarce could reach her hand,
But she loosened her hair i'the casement! His face burnt like a brand
As the black cascade of perfume came tumbling over his breast;
And he kissed its waves in the moonlight,
35   (Oh, sweet black waves in the moonlight!)
Then he tugged at his reins in the moonlight, and galloped way to the West.

Part Two

He did not come in the dawning; he did not come at noon;
And out o'the tawny sunset, before the rise o'the moon,
When the road was a gypsy's ribbon, looping the purple moor,
40 A red-coat troop came marching—
    Marching—marching—
King George's men came marching, up to the old inn-door.

They said no word to the landlord, they drank his ale instead;
But they gagged his daughter and bound her to the foot of her narrow bed;
45 Two of them knelt at her casement, with muskets at their side!
There was death at every window;
    And hell at one dark window;
For Bess could see, through her casement, the road that *he* would ride.

They had tied her up to attention, with many a sniggering jest;
50 They had bound a musket beside her, with the muzzle beneath her breast!
"Now keep good watch!" and they kissed her.

She heard the doomed man say—
Look for me by moonlight;
   Watch for me by moonlight;
55   *I'll come to thee by moonlight, though hell should bar the way!"*

She twisted her hands behind her; but all the knots held good!
She writhed her hands till her fingers were wet with sweat or blood!
They stretched and strained in the darkness, and the hours crawled by like years,
Till, now, on the stroke of midnight,
60   Cold on the stroke of midnight,
The tip of one finger touched it! The trigger at least was hers!

The tip of one finger touched it; she strove no more for the rest!
Up, she stood up to attention, with the muzzle beneath her breast;
She would not risk their hearing: she would not strive again;
65   For the road lay bare in the moonlight;
      Blank and bare in the moonlight;
And the blood of her veins in the moonlight throbbed to her love's refrain.

Tlot-tlot; tlot-tlot! Had they heard it? The horse-hoofs ringing clear;
Tlot-tlot, tlot-tlot, in the distance? Were they deaf that they did not hear?
70   Down the ribbon of moonlight, over the brow of the hill,
The highwayman came riding,
      Riding, riding!
The red-coats looked to their priming! She stood up straight and still!

Tlot-tlot, in the frosty silence! *Tlot-tlot* in the echoing night!
75   Nearer he came and nearer! Her face was like a light!
Her eyes grew wide for a moment; she drew one last deep breath,
Then her finger moved in the moonlight,
      Her musket shattered the moonlight,
Shattered her breast in the moonlight and warned him—with her death.

80   He turned, he spurred to the West; he did not know who stood
Bowed, with her head o'er the musket, drenched with her own blood!
Not till the dawn he heard it, and his face grew grey to hear
How Bess, the landlord's daughter,
      The landlord's black-eyed daughter,
85   Had watched for her love in the moonlight, and died in the darkness there.

Back, he spurred like a madman, shrieking a curse to the sky,
With the white road smoking behind him, and his rapier brandished high!
Blood-red were his spurs in the golden noon; wine-red was his velvet coat,
When they shot him down on the highway,
90   Down like a dog on the highway,
And he lay in his blood on the highway, with a bunch of lace at his throat.

And still of a winter's night, they say, when the wind is in the trees,
When the moon is a ghostly galleon tossed upon cloudy seas,
When the road is a ribbon of moonlight over the purple moor,
95 *A highwayman comes riding—*
   Riding—riding—
A highwayman comes riding, up to the old inn-door.

Over the cobbles he clatters and clangs in the dark inn-yard;
He taps with his whip on the shutters, but all is locked and barred;
100 *He whistles a tune to the window, and who should be waiting there*
But the landlord's black-eyed daughter,
  Bess, the landlord's daughter,
Plaiting a dark red love-knot into her long black hair.

After Reading

1. As a class, clap the **rhythm** of the first **stanza** to identify the stressed and unstressed syllables in the poem. Explain how the rhythm imitates the sound of a galloping horse.

2. Write a **synopsis** of the story in the poem using twenty-five words or less.

3. In your notebook, write a paragraph explaining why some sections of the poem are in italics.

4. If you were making a movie of this poem, who would you cast as Bess, as the Highwayman, and as Tim, the ostler? Explain your reasons.

5. Explain how the poet uses **foreshadowing** to prepare the reader for later events in the poem. Assess whether the foreshadowing increases the reader's interest and **suspense** or undermines the impact of the final events in the poem.

6. This poem is famous for its use of **metaphor**, **simile**, rhythm, **onomatopoeia**, and repetition. Find an effective example of each of these poetic devices in the poem and explain your choices.

7. With a partner, find all the apostrophes in the poem. For each, identify if the apostrophe indicates possession or a contraction. In the case of contractions, write down the letters replaced by the apostrophe. (If the contraction is one that you and your partner do not ordinarily use in your writing, explain why the poet may have chosen to replace the letters with an apostrophe.) (See The Reference Shelf, page 250.)

8. With a partner, count the number of exclamation marks in the poem. Prepare a one- or two-paragraph **report** to the class on whether you and your partner feel the poet has overused exclamation marks in this poem or has used them to good effect. (See The Reference Shelf, page 249.)

9. Make a list of words that are new to you, or unfamiliar to you as used in the poem, and check their meaning in a dictionary.

10. In a group of four, prepare a choral reading of the poem for the class.

11. Write a short story about lovers kept apart by events beyond their control.

The Cremation of Sam McGee

ROBERT SERVICE

Before Reading

In your **journal**, write about a time when you were extremely cold. Include **similes**, **metaphors**, and exaggeration to get your point across.

> There are strange things done in the midnight sun
>   By the men who moil for gold;
> The Arctic trails have their secret tales
>   That would make your blood run cold;
> 5 The Northern Lights have seen queer sights,
>   But the queerest they ever did see
> Was that night on the marge of Lake Lebarge
>   I cremated Sam McGee.

Now Sam McGee was from Tennessee, where the cotton blooms and blows.
10 Why he left his home in the South to roam 'round the Pole, God only knows.
He was always cold, but the land of gold seemed to hold him like a spell;
Though he'd often say in his homely way that "he'd sooner live in hell."

On a Christmas Day we were mushing our way over the Dawson trail.
Talk of your cold! through the parka's fold it stabbed like a driven nail.
15 If our eyes we'd close, then the lashes froze till sometimes we couldn't see;
It wasn't much fun, but the only one to whimper was Sam McGee.

And that very night, as we lay packed tight in our robes beneath the snow,
And the dogs were fed, and the stars o'erhead were dancing heel and toe,
He turned to me, and "Cap," says he, "I'll cash in this trip, I guess;
20 And if I do, I'm asking that you won't refuse my last request."

Well, he seemed so low that I couldn't say no; then he says with a sort of moan:
"It's the cursèd cold, and it's got right hold till I'm chilled clean through to the bone.
Yet 'tain't being dead—it's my awful dread of the icy grave that pains;
So I want you to swear that, foul or fair, you'll cremate my last remains."

25 A pal's last need is a thing to heed, so I swore I would not fail;
And we started on at the streak of dawn; but God! he looked ghastly pale.
He crouched on the sleigh, and he raved all day of his home in Tennessee;
And before nightfall a corpse was all that was left of Sam McGee.

There wasn't a breath in that land of death, and I hurried, horror-driven,
30 With a corpse half hid that I couldn't get rid, because of a promise given;
It was lashed to the sleigh, and it seemed to say: "You may tax your brawn and
    brains,
But you promised true, and it's up to you to cremate those last remains."

Now a promise made is a debt unpaid, and the trail has its own stern code.
35 In the days to come, though my lips were dumb, in my heart how I cursed that load.
In the long, long night, by the lone firelight, while the huskies, round in a ring,
Howled out their woes to the homeless snows—Oh God! how I loathed the thing.

And every day that quiet clay seemed to heavy and heavier grow;
And on I went, though the dogs were spent and the grub was getting low;
40 The trail was bad, and I felt half mad, but I swore I would not give in;
And I'd often sing to the hateful thing, and it hearkened with a grin.

Till I came to the marge of Lake Lebarge, and a derelict there lay;
It was jammed in the ice, but I saw in a trice it was called the "Alice May."
And I looked at it, and I thought a bit, and I looked at my frozen chum;
45 Then "Here," said I, with a sudden cry, "is my cre-ma-tor-eum."

Some planks I tore from the cabin floor, and I lit the boiler fire;
Some coal I found that was lying around, and I heaped the fuel higher;
The flames just soared, and the furnace roared—such a blaze you seldom see;
And I burrowed a hole in the glowing coal, and I stuffed in Sam McGee.

50 Then I made a hike, for I didn't like to hear him sizzle so;
And the heavens scowled, and the huskies howled, and the wind began to blow.
It was icy cold, but the hot sweat rolled down my cheeks, and I don't know why;
And the greasy smoke in an inky cloak went streaking down the sky.

I do not know how long in the snow I wrestled with grisly fear;
55 But the stars came out and they danced about ere again I ventured near;
I was sick with dread, but I bravely said: "I'll just take a peep inside.
I guess he's cooked, and it's time I looked"; . . . then the door I opened wide.

And there sat Sam, looking cool and calm, in the heart of the furnace roar;
And he wore a smile you could see a mile, and he said: "Please close that door.
60 It's fine in here, but I greatly fear you'll let in the cold and storm—
Since I left Plumtree, down in Tennessee, it's the first time I've been warm."

There are strange things done in the midnight sun
By the men who moil for gold;
The Arctic trails have their secret tales
65 *That would make your blood run cold;*
The Northern Lights have seen queer sights,
But the queerest they ever did see
Was that night on the marge of Lake Lebarge
I cremated Sam McGee.

After Reading

1. Write a **synopsis** of the **poem** in twenty-five words or less.

2. Describe the **tone** created by the **rhythm** and **rhyme scheme** of the poem and explain how the tone softens the grisly nature of the events being described.

3. Find examples of **slang** words and **colloquial expressions** in the **direct speech** portions of the poem and assess whether they enhance or undermine the literary merit of the poem.

4. In a small group, rewrite the poem as a script. Rehearse and present your dramatized version of "The Cremation of Sam McGee" to the class.

5. With a partner, write a new **stanza** for the poem following the rhythm and rhyme scheme used by the poet.

6. Create an illustrated version of one or two stanzas of the poem.

7. Prepare a short research **report** on Robert Service or on the Gold Rush.

The Creator of Anne of Green Gables Writes

An Excerpt From Lucy Maud Montgomery's Journal

"[Anne] is so real that, although I've never met her, I feel quite sure I shall do so some day . . ."

Before Reading

Discuss the purpose of keeping a **journal** and the level of language and formality you would expect to find in another person's journal.

Friday, Jan. 27, 1911
Cavendish, P.E.I.

Margaret and I had a delightful walk down the road this evening in the twilight. It was a very still, breathless evening—a storm evidently brewing. The world was white and dim and windless.

I cannot get used to the pleasantness of having a congenial friend near me. It seems rather unnatural. I have never had living near me a friend with whom I could talk freely on subjects near to my heart. Even long ago, when I regarded Amanda and Lucy as friends, there was never any real communion of spirit or mind between us. Lucy could talk of nothing but dress and petty gossip and Amanda was little better. And of late years there has been no one near me with whom I could, or cared to, go any deeper than the surface. But now I have Margaret with whom I can discuss many—not all—subjects, understanding and understood. It means much to me. A little congenial companionship goes a long way to sweeten life.

After Margaret went in I prowled about a bit by myself. There were no stars out but there were shadowy woods and white spaces and dim tree-lands. I looked on them and loved them. How I love

33

Cavendish! I love it for its beauty—I love it for its old associations, as I will never love any other spot on earth.

To-day I was again annoyed and amused—with the annoyance distinctly uppermost—to be asked, as I so constantly am, "Was So-and-So the original of This-or-That in your books"?

This annoys me because I have *never* drawn any of the characters in my books "from life", although I may have taken a quality here and an incident there. I have used real places and speeches freely but I have never put any person I knew into my books. I may do so some day but hitherto I have depended wholly on the creative power of my own imagination for my book folk.

Nevertheless I have woven a good deal of reality into my books. Cavendish is to a large extent *Avonlea*. *Mrs. Rachel Lynde's* house, with the brook below, was drawn from Pierce Macneill's house. I also gave Mrs. Pierce's name to *Mrs. Lynde* but beyond that there was no connection whatever between them. *Green Gables* was drawn from David Macneill's house, now Mr. Webb's—though not so much the house itself as the situation and scenery, and the truth of my description of it is attested by the fact that everybody has recognized it. Had they stopped there it would be well, but they went further and insist that David and Margaret Macneill figure as *Matthew* and *Marilla*. They do not. The *Matthew* and *Marilla* I had in mind were entirely different people from David and Margaret. I suppose the fact that David is a notoriously shy and silent man makes people think I drew *Matthew*

from him. But I made *Matthew* shy and silent simply because I wished to have all the people around *Anne* as pointedly in contrast with her as possible.

In connection with this there was one odd coincidence which probably helped to establish the conviction that David was *Matthew*. *Green Gables* was illustrated by an artist unknown to me and to whom Cavendish and David were alike unknown. Nevertheless, it cannot be denied that the picture of *Matthew* when he brings *Anne* home, has a very strong resemblance to David Macneill.

The brook that runs below the *Cuthbert* place and through *Lynde's Hollow* is, of course, my own dear brook of the woods which runs below Webb's and through "Pierce's Hollow".

Although I had the Webb place in mind I did not confine myself to facts at all. There are, I think, willows in the yard but there are no "Lombardies", such as *Anne* heard talking in their sleep. Those were transplanted from the estates of my castle in Spain. And it was by no means as tidy as I pictured *Green Gables*—at least, before the Webbs came there. Quite the reverse in fact, David's yard was notoriously *untidy*. It was a local saying that if you wanted to see what the world looked like on the morning after the flood you should go into David's barnyard on a rainy day!

They had a good cherry orchard but no apple orchard. However, I can easily create an apple orchard when I need one!

Marilla is generally accredited to Margaret. This is absurd. Whatever accidental resemblance there may be between

David and *Matthew* there is none whatever between Margaret and *Marilla*. The former is a very intelligent, broad-minded woman, which poor *Marilla* certainly was not. Others imagine *Marilla* was drawn from grandmother. This is also false. There are certain qualities common to *Marilla* and grandmother—and to many others—but those qualities I put into *Marilla* for the same reason I made *Matthew* silent and shy—to furnish a background for *Anne*.

When I am asked if *Anne* herself is a "real person" I always answer "no" with an odd reluctance and an uncomfortable feeling of not telling the truth. For she is and always has been, from the moment I first thought of her, so real to me that I feel I am doing violence to something when I deny her an existence anywhere save in Dreamland. Does she not stand at my elbow even now—if I turned my head quickly should I not see her—with her eager, starry eyes and her long braids of red hair and her little pointed chin? To tell that haunting elf that she is not *real*, because, forsooth, I never met her in the flesh! No, I cannot do it! She *is* so real that, although I've never met her, I feel quite sure I shall do so some day—perhaps in a stroll through Lover's Lane in the twilight—or in the moonlit Birch Path—I shall lift my eyes and find her, child or maiden, by my side. And I shall not be in the least surprised because I have always known she was *somewhere*.

The idea of getting a child from an orphan asylum was suggested to me years ago as a possible germ for a story by the fact that Pierce Macneill got a little girl from one, and I jotted it down in my note book. There is no resemblance of any kind between *Anne* and Ellen Macneill who is one of the most hopelessly commonplace and uninteresting girls imaginable. But I may mention here another odd coincidence. Although Ellen Macneill never crossed my mind while I was writing the book, yet a stranger who was in Cavendish two years ago, boarding at Pierce's, told Ellen that her profile was exactly like the *Anne* profile on the cover of *Green Gables*! And when I heard this I agreed that it was, although her profile on the book has distinction while Ellen's is hopelessly common. This picture was also drawn by an artist who had never seen Cavendish or Ellen!

Bright River is Hunter River. *Anne's* dislike of being laughed at because she used big words is a bitter remembrance of my own childhood. *The White Way of Delight* is practically pure imagination. Yet the idea was suggested to me by a short stretch of road between Kensington and Clinton, which I always thought very beautiful. The trees meet overhead for a short distance but they are beech trees, not apple trees.

Anne's habit of naming places was an old one of my own. The *Lake of Shining Waters* is generally supposed to be the Cavendish Pond. This is not so. The pond at Park Corner is the one I had in mind. But I suppose that a good many of the effects of light and shadow I have seen on the Cavendish pond figured unconsciously in my descriptions; and certainly the hill from which *Anne* caught her first glimpse of it was "Laird's Hill", where I have often stood at sunset, enraptured with the beautiful view of shining pond and crimson-brimmed harbor and dark blue sea.

White Sands was Rustico and the "shore road" has a real existence, and is a very beautiful drive. I remember one moonlight drive I had around that road. I shall never forget the starry, sparkling, shimmering beauty of sky and sea.

The house in which *Anne* was born was drawn from my own little birthplace at Clifton. The *Katie Maurice* of *Anne* was *my Katie Maurice*—that imaginary playmate of the glass bookcase door in our sitting room. The idea of the *Haunted Wood* was of course taken from the old Haunted Wood of the Nelson boys and myself. But the wood I had in mind as far as description went was the spruce-clad hill across the brook hollow from Webb's. The *Dryad's Bubble* was purely imaginary but the "old log bridge" was a real thing. It was formed by a single large tree that had blown down and lay across the brook. As far back as I can remember it lay there and must have served as a bridge for a generation before that for it was hollowed out like a shell from the tread of hundreds of passing feet. Earth had blown into its crevices and ferns and grasses had found root in it and fringed it luxuriantly. Velvet moss covered its sides. Below was a clear, sun-flecked stream.

A year or two ago the old log-bridge became so worn and slender that it was quite unsafe. So Mr. Webb put a little bridge of longers across the brook and we use that now.

Anne's tribulations over puffed sleeves were an echo of my old childish longing after "bangs". "Bangs" came in when I was about ten. In the beginning they figured as a straight, heavy fringe of hair cut squarely across the forehead. A picture of "banged" hair of course looks absurd enough now; but, like all fashions, "bangs" looked all right when they were "in". And to anybody with a high forehead they were very becoming.

Well, bangs were "all the rage". All the girls in school had them. I wanted a "bang" terribly. But grandfather and grandmother would never hear of it. This was unwise and unjust on their part. Whatever the present day taste may think of "bangs" it would not have done me or anyone any harm to have allowed me to have one and it would have saved me many a bitter pang. How I did long for "bangs"! Father wanted me to have them—he always wanted me to have any innocent thing I desired. Oh, how well he understood a child's heart! I often pleaded with him when he came to see me (that was the winter he was home from the west) to cut a "bang" for me, but he never would because he knew it would offend grandmother. I was often tempted to cut one myself but I dreaded their anger too much. I knew that if I did I would be railed at as if I had disgraced myself forever and that I would never set down to the table that grandfather would not sneer at them.

"Bangs" remained in a long time—nearly twenty years. When I was fifteen and went out west I got my long-wished for "bang" at last. Grandfather sneered at it when I went home, of course, but the thing was done and he had to reconcile himself to it. Besides, the "bang" had changed a good deal in that time. The heavy straight bang was gone and the accepted fashion was an upward curling fluff, not unlike the pompadour of today in general effect, with only a loose curl or two downwards. How I did envy girls with naturally curly hair! My hair was very straight. I had to curl my poor fringe constantly and even then the last dampness would reduce it to stringy dismalness. It is only about six years since bangs went hopelessly out. It is not likely they will ever come in again—in my time at least. But I shall never forget them. I longed for them and how humiliated I felt when I could not have them.

I had beautiful hair when I was a child—very long, thick, and a golden brown. It turned very dark when I grew up—much to my disappointment. I love fair hair.

The *Spectator*, in reviewing *Green Gables*—*very* favorably, I might say—said that possibly *Anne's* precocity was slightly overdrawn in the statement that a child of eleven would appreciate the dramatic effect of the lines,

"Quick as the slaughtered
squadrons fell
In Midian's evil day."

But I was only nine years old when those lines thrilled my very soul as I recited them in Sunday School. All through the following sermon I kept repeating them to myself. To this day they give me a mysterious pleasure.

I remember that Maggie Abbott and I swore eternal friendship as *Anne* and *Diana* did. Only we did not do it in a garden but standing on a high loft beam in Uncle John Montgomery's barn at Malpeque. Amanda and I also once wrote out two "Notes of Promise", vowing everlasting faith, had them witnessed by two of the schoolgirls, and finished them up with a red seal. I have mine yet somewhere. I think I was true to *my* vow. But if Amanda thinks she was, her ideal of friendship must be very different from mine. Still, she *was* my friend once in childhood and early girlhood. Perhaps she could not help—or did not know how to help—the strange temperamental change which came over her at the threshold of womanhood. These things are bound up with physiological mysteries beyond our penetration. In early life Amanda was her mother's child. When she grew up her dormant inheritance from her father developed and she changed into an altogether different being. To me, the Amanda who was my girlhood friend is as one dead. I think of her lovingly and regretfully. I can never feel that the Amanda of to-day is the same person as my friend of long ago. . . .

Anne's idea that diamonds looked like amethysts was once mine. I did not know there were such stones as amethysts but I had read of diamonds. I had never seen one nor heard one described, and I pictured to myself a beautiful stone of living purple. When Uncle Chester brought Aunt Hattie to see us after their marriage I saw the little diamond in her ring and I was much disappointed. "It wasn't my idea of a diamond"—well, many things in life and in the world have not been like my idea of them! I love diamonds now—I love their pure, cold, dewlike sheen and glitter. But once they were a bitter disillusion to me.

Lover's Lane was of course *my* Lover's Lane. *Willowmere* and *Violet Vale* were compact of imagination. But the Birch Path exists somewhere, I know not where. I have a picture of it—the reproduction of a photo which was published in the *Outing* magazine one year. Somewhere in America that lane of birches is. *Avonlea* school was the Cavendish school, but the teachers were mythical. *Miss Stacey* resembled Miss Gordon in some respects but I cannot say she was drawn from her. The episode of the mouse falling into the pudding sauce once happened to a friend of mine—Mrs. George Matheson; old Literary concerts furnished forth the description of the concert in *Avonlea Hall*. The scene where *Anne* and *Diana* jump into bed on poor *Miss Barry* was suggested to me by a story father told me of how he and two other boys had jumped into bed on an old minister in the spare room at Uncle John Montgomery's long ago. I worked it up into a short story, published early in my career in *Golden Days*; then used the idea later on in my book. The old "Mayflower" picnics of Miss Gordon's devising were used. The affecting farewell speech of James MacLeod was used also although, to do Jim justice, he was not in any respect like *Teddy Phillips*, being a very fair teacher. We used to make balsam Rainbows in the school spring, just as *Anne* and *Diana* made them in the *Dryad's Bubble*.

As for the notable incident of the liniment cake—when I was teaching in Bideford Mrs. Estey flavored a layer cake with anodyne liniment just as it happened in the story. Never shall I forget the taste of that cake. What fun we had over it! A strange minister was there to tea that night—a Mr. Kirby—and *he* ate all his piece of cake. What he thought of it we never knew. Possibly he imagined it was simply some new-fangled kind of flavoring. The dialogues which the girls had in their concerts "The Society for The Suppression of Gossip" and "The Fairy Queen" were old stand-bys of schooldays. We had the former at our first school concert in which I personated the amiable "Miss Wise", and the latter at a school examination. I was the *Fairy Queen*, being thought fitted for the part by reason of my long hair which I wore crimped and floating over my shoulders from a wreath of pink tissue roses. I "appeared" suddenly through the school door, in answer to an incantation, in all the glory of white dress, roses, hair, kid slippers and wand—and I enjoyed my own dramatic appearance quite as much as anybody! That really was one of the most *satisfying* moments of my life.

The Story Club was suggested by a little incident of one summer long ago when Jamie Simpson, Amanda Macneill, and I all wrote a story on the same plot. I furnished the plot and I remembered only that it was a very tragic one and the heroine was drowned. I haven't the stories now—I wish I had—but they were very sad. It was the first, and probably the last, time that Jamie and Amanda attempted fiction but I had already quite a little library of stories—in which almost everybody died! I do wish I had kept them. I burned them in exasperation on the day I realized what trash they were. They *were* trash—but they would have been quite valuable trash to me now, because they were so enormously funny. One was entitled "My Graves" and was a long tale of the various peregrinations of a minister's wife. I made her a Methodist minister's wife so that she would have to peregrinate frequently. She buried a child in every place she lived in! All Canada, from Newfoundland to Vancouver, was peppered with "her" graves. I wrote the story in the first person, described the children, pictured out their death-beds and described their tombstones and epitaphs! That story was never finished. After having killed off about seven children—she was to have thirteen altogether—I wearied of so much infanticide and ceased from my slaughter of the innocents.

Then there was "The History of Flossie Brighteyes"—the autobiography of a doll. I couldn't kill a doll but I dragged her through every other tribulation. However, I allowed her to have a happy end with a good little girl who loved her for the dangers she had passed and did not mind a few legs and eyes missing.

But what dazzlingly lovely heroines I had! And how I dressed them! Silks—satins—velvets—laces—they never wore anything else! And I literally poured diamonds and rubies and pearls over them. But what booted beauty and rich attire? "The paths of glory lead but to the grave". They must either be murdered or die of a broken heart. There was no escape for them.

The incident of *Anne's* dyeing her hair was purely imaginary. Oddly enough, however, after *Green Gables* was written, but before it was published, Sadie Macneill, a Cavendish girl who had fiery tresses dyed her hair black. I was appalled when I heard of it for I felt sure that everyone, when the book came out, would think that I had made use of this fact. And they did! And probably always will! And her family are furious with me! Yet am I innocent.

The entrance examination of *Queen's* was "drawn from life" as well as the weeks of suspense that followed. *Matthew's* death was not, as some have supposed, suggested by grandfather's. Poor *Matthew* must die so that there might arise the necessity for self-sacrifice on *Anne's* part. So he joined the long procession of ghosts that haunt my literary past.

There was less of "real life" in *Avonlea* than in *Green Gables*, and much more of invention. Some of my experiences in school-teaching were reflected in it, but in the atmosphere only, not in the incidents. I felt exactly as *Anne* felt when she opened school the first day—and I was as woefully tired and discouraged at night. My Bideford pupils used to drive crickets. A Bideford pupil gave the same definition of "freckles" as *Jimmy Andrews* did—"George Howell's face, ma'am", and several other answers were genuine.

The scene of the walk in the *Golden Picnic* was laid through the woods and fields back of Lover's Lane but *Hester's* garden is purely imaginary. *Davy's* idea that heaven was in "*Simon Fletcher's* garret" was suggested by a belief of my own childhood. One Sunday when I was very small—I could not, I think have been more than four—I was with Aunt Emily in Clifton church—the old church with its square box pews. I heard the minister say something about heaven. "Where is heaven?" I whispered to Aunt Emily. She simply pointed upward. With childhood's literal and implicit belief I took it for granted that this meant the attic of Clifton church. For a long time I firmly believed that heaven was there! As mother was "in heaven" she must be there, too. Now, why could we not get up there and see her? There was a square hole in the ceiling. Surely it was quite possible. It was a great puzzle to me that nobody ever seemed to think of doing it. I resolved that when I grew older *I* would find some way of getting to Clifton and getting up into heaven anyhow. Alas! Hood wrote in his delightful "I Remember" that he was further off from heaven than when he was a boy. I can echo that. When I was a child heaven was only seven miles away. But now! Is it not beyond the furthest star?

Kilmeny reflects very little out of my own experience. *Jack Reid's* sentence, "Courting is a very pleasant thing which a great many people go too far with" was the *bona fide* opening sentence Jack Millar wrote in a composition in Bideford school. The view of *Lindsay Harbor* and the gulf, with the revolving light, is drawn from the view I have so often gazed on over New London Harbor. "Old Charlie's" Latin prayer was really delivered by old Professor Macdonald at a Dalhousie convocation. James Laird's place up on the hill was my model of the *Williamson* place—but James and Mrs. Laird are most decidedly *not* the *Williamsons*. The woods through which Eric walked to meet his fate are the woods beyond Lover's Lane.

After Reading

1. Make a list of words you do not know in this selection. Using a dictionary, write out the most appropriate meaning for each word based on its context.

2. Using human, print, and/or electronic sources, find out all you can about the **plot** and **characters** of *Anne of Green Gables*. For any character names mentioned in the **journal**, write a brief **character description** based on your research.

3. Describe how Lucy Maud Montgomery feels about people believing her writing is based on real life. Show how this feeling comes across in the **tone** of her journal entry.

4. a) Make a chart like the one below for paragraph 12 ("When I am asked if *Anne* herself . . .").

Sentence Number	First Four Words	Verbs	Special Sentence Features	Number of Words

   b) Describe Montgomery's writing **style**.

   c) With a partner, discuss how this differs from your expectations of journal writing and explain the differences you've found.

5. Think back to when you were a child. Did you have an imaginary friend or a dream about the way you would live some day? Did you have a favourite place to hide? In your journal, write about the way you imagined your future during your childhood.

Cats

NORMA HARRS

". . . people are like cats."

Before Reading

1. As a class, produce a list of words and ideas that you associate with the word *cats*.

2. Find out how many people in your class write letters or send e-mail to friends or family members. With their help, make a list of topics they frequently write about.

October, 1993

Dear Marjorie:

Why do I only ever write to you when I'm totally ticked off about something? I guess because you're probably the only one who'll understand. God, I wish you were back in the office.

(*Surprisingly, that's true. I mean Marjorie could drive me bananas at times, one of those people who had to tell you the entire story line from a movie she'd seen the night before, including the punch line, but basically good-hearted.*)

Leonora is getting me down totally. I cannot stand that woman and she doesn't seem to know. It's funny really because I like most people. I've always made a big detour around the "clashers," you know the ones I mean: the ones who reach for something just as you do, or speak just as you're speaking. I've been moving around Leonora like that, but she doesn't seem to get the message.

I swear people are like cats. One circuit of a room and a cat can always scent out a hostile lap. People are just the same, or at least some people. They sense when you don't like them and they hang around trying to show you that they really are nice. As far as I'm concerned, they can stand on their heads, punch me, hug me, nothing changes. I know right from the beginning if I'm going to like a person.

(*Actually, now that I think about it, I didn't really like Marjorie from the beginning. I mean Marjorie could never answer a simple question with a "Yes" or "No." She had to go into every last detail of what happened. Like you'd ask, "Did anyone see my pen?" and Marjorie would launch into a complicated story about how the phone had rung suddenly and she couldn't find hers anywhere and how the guy on the end of the line had been impatient and she'd just had to borrow mine. I didn't care a darn. I mean, just give it back and cut the crap, but not Marjorie.*)

I tell you, Marjorie, it's impossible to avoid Leonora, she sits three desks away from me in the newsroom. She's one of those types who's gone back to basics. Remember Carswell in the Life Section who wrote about quilts and baskets? Like Carswell, only worse. Two years ago Leonora stopped wearing make-up, threw her mascara and blusher in the wastebasket and decided to go "au naturel." Now she shops at Evening Star. You know the kind of stuff, all Indian cotton and creases, dangly earrings made of tin? I swear to God she wears the same three outfits year in year out. She has this peasant blouse she pulls up to her neck in the winter, and in the summer she's a kind of Anna Magnani peasant, all off the shoulder. Her hair's frizzy, a bush in fact, and not just on her head but under her arms too, it's revolting.

People like her break me up. Sits on my desk morning, noon, and night and gives me all this stuff about her philosophy of life. She's a vegetarian . . . "meat kills" all that crap, meanwhile she's smoking

herself to death. You should hear what she goes on about. "You're sick if you let yourself be." You just want to come into the office with a cold, half dying and listen to her going on about having control of your life, not giving in to germs, etc.

I can hear you now, Marjorie, telling me to calm down, not let her get to me, but I'd like you to try it. The thing about her that kills me is that she's a real sham, especially when it comes to men. She's a blinker, Marjorie. Remember how we always used to have a laugh about the eyelash batters like Sue Anne? Believe me, Sue Anne is an amateur compared to this one. Not only that, she lisps when she's talking to men, like she's about six years of age again. They love it, dumb jerks. It's enough to make you puke just to watch it in action.

"You're jealous," I can hear you say, Marjorie, but I swear I'm not. Visualize this! You remember how Bill Merton, the editor of the Business Section always used to come in with his socks full of holes? Last week Leonora came in with a darning needle and wool and there she is sitting with her hand stuck up that creep's sweaty socks.

(*Mind you, not that Marjorie wasn't a sucker when it came to men, too. There's this great independent career woman, terrific writer, who could turn marshmallow in front of the right man. Not that it did her much good. For some reason men didn't take to Marjorie. She came on far too strong. "Take me, I'm yours," kind of thing, scared the heck out of them.*

Actually, I don't think Bill Merton's a creep. I've liked him from the first day I stepped into the newsroom, but there's no point letting Marjorie know that. She kind of uses things like this when you least expect it, preferably when someone else is around. I know there are a lot of ways of getting Bill's attention. For instance, taking his socks home and darning them or even doing them on the spot like Leonora did, but I just can't bring myself to do such a thing. I mean I wouldn't lower myself. You have to have some pride. If you don't have pride, you're dead. I don't know why all the guys I meet want to be mothered. It drives me crazy, but what's worse is that there's always someone like Leonora around to oblige. I mean you can't win. Another thing is, I can never lie to a man. I have to tell the truth, but truth is something they don't want to hear. At least Bill doesn't. You see, I've been out with him, so I know. He took me home to cook dinner for his two young sons, if you can call that "going out." He's been divorced for about three years. His wife ran away with a waiter . . . a maître d' actually, but Bill always calls him "the waiter." After meeting the sons, I don't blame her for running away. Anyway, the only way I could even think about living with this guy is if his sons left home and that isn't likely to happen. They're monsters. The first thing they asked was, "Are you Dad's new broad?" Bill thought it was cute. I told him it was rude. He hasn't asked me out since. Leonora's been to his place . . . cooked them all meatless lasagna. I've tasted Leonora's meatless lasagna. It's more than those brats deserve. Anyway, all I can do now is wait around for the sons to grow up. By then he'll be into younger women.)

The thing is, I feel guilty as hell about Leonora. Last year, when I ended up in

hospital with the flu, guess who was the first one to visit me? Leonora. She turned up at the hospital with a pot of chrysanthemums. I've always hated chrysanths. They have that sort of strong, earthy smell, nothing you can classify as a perfume, just a smell of hot soil. It was typical in a way she should have chosen the one flower I hate.

I still remember I was burning up in that hospital bed, felt like dying, and there she was sitting on the bed, right on the sheets so that my toes were squashed flat, going on about the power of the mind and how sickness was a subconscious desire. When you're half-dead it's just what you want to hear: that you have no control over your life. In a way, though, I guess she was right. If I had control, she wouldn't be part of my life.

But how do you put someone like that off? Especially when they're always doing you good turns. She brings me homemade yogurt all the time, plain yogurt. I hate plain yogurt. I like the kind with all the gooey fruit at the bottom that you can mix in and pretend you're not eating yogurt. I've even told her I hate yogurt. Well, I suppose I didn't exactly tell her . . . what I said was, I like the kind with fruit, but I don't think she heard me.

Something else she does that drives me bananas: she's always trying to make you feel like your values are all wrong. Last week, I remember, I was all excited I found this fabulous old basket, perfect to put my plants in, something to make the apartment look quaint.

"You're always buying things," she accused me. "I've given up all that kind of stockpiling." Well whoopdeedo! I mean what does she want, a medal? "My work is the only thing important to me." She stared up at the ceiling all dreamily. "I want to be able to pick up and move, maybe to Crete or Piraeus and not have to worry about possessions."

She didn't bother saying how she planned to live when she got there. For sure not on this performance poetry she writes. I didn't tell you about that, it's all sibilant *s*'s and hisses. It's ghastly.

"I don't want to have anything tying me down, nothing to worry about. I mean I could just walk out of my apartment tomorrow and carry one knapsack on my back and I wouldn't have a thing to worry about."

Marjorie, I wanted to yell, "Go! Go! Good riddance." And what did I do? I smiled, for Pete's sake, I smiled. I couldn't think of one cutting thing to say. I suppose that's why I'm dumping on you now.

Sorry, pal, but at least I've got it off my chest. I wish you weren't so far away.

Remember the good times?

(*Well, we did have some good times, Marjorie and me. I mean once you forgot about all the annoying things, she wasn't bad company.*)

Anyway, toodleoo for now. Write soon! Love, Sylvia

April, 1994

Dear Marjorie:

I don't know if you remember my mentioning Leonora to you? I think I wrote a few nasty things about her last year. Anyway, I feel really rotten about that because guess what? She's got cancer and only has a few months to live. It's horrible. It's like with all that travelling-light stuff she gave us she knew she was going somewhere, but it sure as hell wasn't Crete.

She's been in hospital for a couple of months now and I visit her several times a week. She can't stand the hospital food, so I try and cook her up something, without meat of course, although I don't know what harm it would do her now.

I feel so sick and sad every time I look at her. She's sort of fading away on the pillows. What's worse than anything for her is that this is something she finally can't control. Oh, she talks a lot about how she's getting better and the challenge of it all, but you can see just looking in her eyes she knows she's dying.

The most awful thing of all was that she told me the other day how much she'd always admired me, especially for my honesty. Can you beat that? I feel like the lowest kind of maggot. I started crying, and then I knew I didn't hate her at all. I suppose I have been a bit jealous of her because she didn't mind showing herself as she was. I mean she had the confidence for that. Something else struck me about her too, that I wasn't right about people not liking her. Everyone likes her, not just the men, but the women too. Or maybe they are just pretending because she's dying. I've noticed that before. I guess it's got something to do with people not being able to stand their own guilt.

Well, anyway, the thing about Leonora is that she was generous. You see, already I'm talking about her as if she were dead. But if you had to visit her three times a week, Marjorie, you'd see she is dead. It wasn't really a case of darning Bill's socks because she wanted him. In fact, she told me the other day that she felt sorry for him because he had such a shaky personality. Can you beat that?

Life is too damned unfair sometimes. I almost wish it wasn't Leonora who was dying, that it was me, because I feel I deserve to die for writing all those things about her. Please burn the letter if you still have it.

I swear I would give anything to have her back, sitting on my desk blowing smoke in my eyes, I would see her completely differently. Instead, the female who's taken over her job is a real cold fish. We always keep a pot of coffee on the go in the office. I swear she drinks it all herself. Every time I want a cup of coffee, there's none left. It's maddening. She also wears far too much perfume. It stinks up the entire room. She must think the perfume will convince people how sweet she is, but it doesn't work. I can tell nobody likes her.

September 30th, 1994

I didn't get the letter finished the other day because Leonora died. Her funeral was today. It was awful, everybody crying and I cried hardest of all. I swear, Marjorie, I felt like dying too. How can you go on when you realize that you can be so wrong about a person? What's even worse is that Leonora left me her notebook with all her latest poems, which means that she never really knew I hated her poetry. Here I am, the one who thinks it's so great to be honest, and a dying woman leaves *me*, the one who hates her poetry the worst, her latest poems!

October 8th, 1994

I'm having trouble finishing this letter. There are so many interruptions. I can't stand seeing this woman Myrna at Leonora's desk. She's one of these *filers*. Everyone's desk in the newsroom is a pigpen. Not Myrna's. She has pigeon holes, cardboard files, boxes with labels, baskets within baskets. If you want something, she can put her hand on it in a minute. She doesn't smoke either. In fact she's started a movement to ban smoking in the newsroom. I was the first one she tried to sign up. She takes her lunch everyday at the same time as me. She always wants to sit in the coffee shop with me. I don't know how to tell her I'd rather be on my own.

I swear to God, Marjorie, people are exactly like cats!

Write soon!

Love, Sylvia

After Reading

1. Describe the **tone** of the different letters in this piece of writing. For each descriptor, give examples of the language that creates the tone.

2. For each of the following, find the meaning and word origin: *au naturel*, *maître d'*, and *sibilant*.

3. Analyze the effect of the italicized thoughts on our understanding of Sylvia, the letter writer.

4. Referring to the list you made on the board before you read the story, and including other ideas you can think of now, explain how Sylvia is like a cat.

5. a) Rereading the story closely, find evidence of the pattern Sylvia's friendship with other women tends to follow.

   b) Keeping this pattern in mind, write a letter Sylvia might have written to Marjorie in April 1995 in which she talks about her changing relationship with Myrna. Try to imitate the language and tone of Sylvia's **style**.

   c) With a partner, exchange your work. Make written suggestions to your partner about ideas that should be reordered, added, deleted, and substituted. Revise your work. Be prepared to read your letter aloud and discuss the similarities and differences between your and your classmates' letters.

6. Write a letter to a friend in which you complain about something that is bothering you.

   or

   Write a letter from Marjorie responding to Sylvia's line: "How can you go on when you realize you can be so wrong about a person?"

Food for Thought

Before Reading

Explain to a partner how you prepare a meal that you know how to cook.

How to Cook Chinese Rice

ANDY QUAN

It's not necessary to have a rice cooker or a wok to cook perfect, delicious white rice every time. Here's how. First, if you want your rice to turn out like it does in Chinese restaurants, you have to use Chinese rice. This is the long grain stuff; the short, fat, sticky rice is Japanese. Don't buy Uncle Ben's processed rice, or rice with faces of white people on the boxes. Second, how many people are you going to serve? Use one-half of a Chinese rice bowl (or about ½ cup) per person. Now, rinse the rice in cold water until all of the starch comes off and the water is relatively clear. If you don't do this, then your rice will be starchy, dry perhaps. It will fall apart in single grains. This is how white people usually cook their rice. Next, put the rice in a pot that has a tight-fitting lid, cover it with just about an inch of water, 2.5 cm, or up to the first joint of a normal-sized index finger. Have confidence; cooking, like all other meaningful activities, requires a state of mind where you believe in yourself. Repeat after me: "I can cook rice." Cook at maximum or near- to medium-high; the water will still be bubbling away at a good rate. Wait until the water has boiled down to the same level as the rice. Then, put your lid on the pot and turn the heat down to absolute minimum so the hot steam can cook the rice. Steam for about ten to fifteen minutes. Hopefully, you'll be able to tell when it's cooked. All the steam will escape. Ready? Serve it any way you want, and thank my mother for the recipe.

A Bowl of Red

JOE FIORITO

Chili is the perfect NAFTA food. It was invented in the USA with Mexican ingredients and it throws enough heat to keep a Canadian warm in the winter. It's also cheap, which is an important consideration now that so few of us have jobs.

But no one makes chili any more. You hardly ever see it on a restaurant menu, and the only time you see it on TV is during the first ten seconds of some antacid commercial. I hate that. Spicy food doesn't cause heartburn, bad cooking does.

If you want chili, you have to make it at home. There are two schools of thought on how to proceed. The main one you're familiar with. Brown some meat, add some onions and green peppers, some tomatoes, beans, cumin and chili powder. This is the usual way.

There is another way, recommended by chili-Jesuits who make their chili with meat and chilis, and nothing else. The meat is beef, browned on its own fat. The seasoning is a mix of dried and powdered chilis. There are no tomatoes added. Beans, if you want 'em, are on the side. I've made it both ways. I like it both ways.

I do have some advice.

Don't use hamburger. Don't pay for someone else to cut your meat. Don't pay for fat and water. Buy the toughest-looking lump of beef you can find. It'll be cheaper than hamburger and it will taste better. Cut it up for yourself; cubes if you prefer, or strips, which is how I like it. You think that kind of meat's too tough? Come on. Chili melts the hardest hearts, slow cooking softens the toughest beef.

Also, if you're going to use beans, use real beans. Canned ones are mushy, they cost ten times what dry beans cost and they don't taste as good. Be a cow-person and try pinto beans. Or be trendy and use black beans. You can even mix things up—use a combination of red kidney beans and white cannellini beans. Just remember to soak them overnight, and to cook them before you add them to your pot of chili.

Secret ingredients? Some people add beer or mustard to a pot of chili. Chili's not a subtle dish, with a dash of this, a splash of that, and a tiny bit of something else. Some people even add celery salt, although I've no idea why.

However (you knew there'd be a however!), if you see any of those dried ancho chilis, the ones that are dusty and black and look like chunks of bakelite plastic after a nuclear meltdown, buy them. Take one and crumble it up. Pour boiling water over it and let it steep for a bit while you're browning the meat. Throw the ancho chili and a cup of the soaking liquid into the pot. However you make your chili, adding an ancho will improve it. Anchos are ineffably smoky, with a taste as complex as good chocolate.

Serve your chili plain, or with some raw chopped onion or a little grated cheddar on top. No sour cream. That would be effete.

I like a bowl of chili once a month, but for some reason the smell of it makes me sad. The last time I made some, we went out while the pot simmered and when we came back the house was warm and filled with the smell of chili and meat and beans. I thought my heart was breaking. And I've no idea why. I'm not sure I want to know. But I will say this. When you make chili, make a big pot. You want leftovers. Chili, like a broken heart, improves with age.

Starvin' Guy Chicken Pie

JANET AND GRETA PODLESKI

Our version of the hungry man dinner is a chicken pot pie that's so jammed with hearty goodness, you might have to solicit the help of a few family members to stuff it into the oven! Topped off with an innovative biscuit crust, this one's sure to please the whole clan!

1 cup chopped onions
1 clove garlic, minced
1 cup low-sodium, reduced-fat chicken broth
1½ cups peeled, cubed potatoes
1½ cups chopped carrots
1 cup sliced green beans (cut into 1-inch pieces)
1 can (10 ounces) reduced-fat Cream of Mushroom Soup (Campbell's Healthy Request), undiluted
1½ tablespoons all-purpose flour
2 cups chopped cooked chicken breast (about ¾ of a pound)
2 tablespoons chopped fresh parsley
½ teaspoon *each* dried basil and ground thyme
¼ teaspoon black pepper

Biscuit Crust
1 cup all-purpose flour
2 teaspoons baking powder
½ teaspoon ground sage
¼ teaspoon salt
2 tablespoons butter or margarine
⅓ cup skim milk

Spray a large saucepan with non-stick spray. Add onions and garlic. Cook over medium heat until tender, about 5 minutes. Add broth, potatoes, carrots, and beans. Bring to a boil. Reduce heat to medium-low. Partially cover and simmer for 12 minutes. The potatoes should be slightly undercooked. Remove from heat.

In a small bowl, stir together mushroom soup and flour. Add to vegetables, along with chicken, parsley, basil, thyme, and pepper. Stir well. Pour into a medium casserole dish.

To prepare crust, combine flour, baking powder, sage, and salt in a large bowl. Using a pastry blender, cut in butter or margarine until mixture resembles coarse crumbs. Stir in milk. Form a ball with the dough. Add a bit more flour if dough is too sticky. Roll out on a floured surface to fit top of casserole. Place dough over chicken mixture. Prick several times with a fork. Bake at 400° for 25 minutes, until crust is golden brown. Let cool for 5 minutes before serving.

Makes 4 servings.
PER SERVING: 355 calories, 11.2 g fat, 34.4 g carbohydrate, 29.6 g protein, 918 mg sodium, 85 mg cholesterol
CALORIES FROM FAT: 28.2%

After Reading

1. Identify three **humorous** comments in Andy Quan's recipe for Chinese rice. Compare your choices with a partner and discuss why you think Quan included them in his recipe.

2. Compare Joe Fiorito's recipe for chili with one in a conventional cookbook. Write a paragraph explaining which version you prefer and why.

3. Starvin' Guy Chicken Pie is a more conventional recipe. Describe the characteristics of a typical recipe.

4. Rewrite a recipe for your favourite meal in the style of Andy Quan's or Joe Fiorito's recipe.

5. Make a list of five verbs that are found in a typical recipe. Find synonyms for these words in a thesaurus. Discuss with a partner which synonyms could or could not be used in a recipe.

6. Bring in your favourite family recipe and create a class cookbook. Sell copies of your cookbook to contribute to a school fund-raising campaign.

UNIT 2
Literature

Once Upon a Time

NADINE GORDIMER

". . . YOU HAVE BEEN WARNED . . ."

Before Reading

Using a dictionary, look up and record the meaning of the word *apartheid*. Discuss as a class what you know about apartheid in South Africa.

Someone has written to ask me to contribute to an anthology of stories for children. I reply that I don't write children's stories; and he writes back that at a recent congress/book fair/seminar, a certain novelist said every writer ought to write at least one story for children. I think of sending him a postcard saying I don't accept that I "ought" to write anything.

And then last night I woke up—or rather was wakened without knowing what had roused me.

A voice in the echo chamber of the sub-conscious?

A sound.

A creaking of the kind made by the weight carried by one foot after another along a wooden floor. I listened. I felt the apertures of my ears distend with concentra-tion. Again: the creaking. I was waiting for it; waiting to hear if it indicated that feet were moving from room to room, coming up the passage—to my door. I have no burglar bars, no gun under my pillow, but I have the same fears as people who do take these pre-cautions, and my windowpanes are thin as rime, could shatter like a wineglass. A woman was murdered (how do they put it) in broad daylight in a house two blocks away, last year, and the fierce dogs who guarded an old widower and his collection of antique clocks were strangled before he was knifed by a casual laborer he had dismissed without pay.

I was staring at the door, making it out in my mind rather than seeing it, in the dark. I lay quite still—a victim already— but the arrhythmia of my heart was fleeing, knocking this way and that against its body cage. How finely tuned the senses are, just out of rest, sleep! I could never listen intently as that in the distractions of the day; I was reading every faintest sound, identifying and classifying its possible threat.

But I learned that I was to be neither threatened nor spared. There was no human weight pressing on the boards, the creaking was a buckling, an epicenter of stress. I was in it. The house that surrounds me when I sleep is built on undermined ground; far beneath my bed, the floor, the house's foundations, the stopes and passages of gold mines have hollowed the rock, and when some face trembles, detaches, and falls, three thousand feet below, the whole house shifts slightly, bringing uneasy strain to the balance and counterbalance of brick, cement, wood, and glass that hold it as a structure around me. The misbeats of my heart tailed off like the last muffled flourishes on one of the wooden xylophones made by the Chopi and Tsonga migrant miners who might have been down there, under me in the earth at that moment. The stope where the fall was could have been disused, dripping water from its ruptured veins; or men might now be interred there in the most profound of tombs.

I couldn't find a position in which my mind would let go of my body—release me to sleep again. So I began to tell myself a story; a bedtime story.

In a house, in a suburb, in a city, there were a man and his wife who loved each other very much and were living happily ever after. They had a little boy, and they loved him very much. They had a cat and a dog that the little boy loved very much.

They had a car and a caravan trailer for holidays, and a swimming pool which was fenced so that the little boy and his playmates would not fall in and drown. They had a housemaid who was absolutely trustworthy and an itinerant gardener who was highly recommended by the neighbors. For when they began to live happily ever after, they were warned by that wise old witch, the husband's mother, not to take on anyone off the street. They were inscribed in a medical benefit society, their pet dog was licensed, they were insured against fire, flood damage, and theft, and they subscribed to the local Neighborhood Watch, which supplied them with a plaque for their gates lettered YOU HAVE BEEN WARNED over the silhouette of a would-be intruder. He was masked; it could not be said if he was black or white, and therefore proved the owner was no racist.

It was not possible to insure the house, the swimming pool, or the car against riot damage. There were riots, but these were outside the city, where people of another color were quartered. These people were not allowed into the suburb except as reliable housemaids and gardeners, so there was nothing to fear, the husband told the wife. Yet she was afraid that someday such people might come up the street and tear off the plaque YOU HAVE BEEN WARNED and open the gates and stream in. . . . Nonsense, my dear, said the husband, there are police and soldiers and tear gas and guns to keep them away. But to please her—for he loved her very much and buses were being burned, cars stoned, and schoolchildren shot by the police in those quarters out of sight and hearing of

55

the suburb—he had electronically controlled gates fitted. Anyone who pulled off the sign YOU HAVE BEEN WARNED and tried to open the gates would have to announce his intentions by pressing a button and speaking into a receiver relayed to the house. The little boy was fascinated by the device and used it as a walkie-talkie in cops-and-robbers play with his small friends.

The riots were suppressed, but there were many burglaries in these suburbs and somebody's trusted housemaid was tied up and shut in a cupboard by thieves while she was in charge of her employers' house. The trusted housemaid of the man and wife and little boy was so upset by this misfortune befalling a friend—left, as she herself often was, with responsibility for the possessions of the man and his wife and the little boy—that she implored her employers to have burglar bars attached to the doors and windows of the house, and an alarm system installed. The wife said, She is right. Let us take heed of her advice. So from every window and door in the house where they were living happily ever after they now saw the trees and sky through bars, and when the little boy's pet cat tried to climb in by the fanlight to keep him company in his little bed at night, as it customarily had done, it set the alarm keening through the house.

The alarm was often answered—it seemed—by other burglar alarms, in other houses, that had been triggered by pet cats or nibbling mice. The alarms called to one another across the gardens in shrills and bleats and wails that everyone soon became accustomed to, so that the din aroused the inhabitants of the suburb no more than the croak of frogs and musical grating of cicadas' legs. Under cover of the electronic harpies' discourse, intruders sawed the iron bars and broke into homes, taking away hi-fi equipment, television sets, cassette players, cameras and radios, jewelry and clothing, and sometimes were hungry enough to devour everything in the refrigerator or paused audaciously to drink the whisky in the cabinets or patio bars. Insurance companies paid no compensation for single malt, a loss made keener by the proper owner's knowledge that the thieves wouldn't even have been able to appreciate what it was they were drinking.

Then the time came when many of the people who were not trusted housemaids and gardeners hung about the suburb because they were unemployed. Some importuned for a job: weeding or painting a roof; anything, *baas*,[1] madam. But the man and his wife remembered the warning about taking on anyone off the street. Some drank liquor and fouled the street with discarded bottles. Some begged, waiting for the man and his wife to drive the car out of the electronically operated gates. They sat about with their feet in the gutters, under the jacaranda trees that made a green tunnel of the street—for it was a beautiful suburb, spoiled only by their presence—and sometimes they fell asleep lying right before the gates in the midday

_____

[1]*baas*: master

56

sun. The wife could never see anyone go hungry. She sent the trusted housemaid out with bread and tea, but the trusted housemaid said these were loafers and *tsotsis*,[2] who would come and tie her up and shut her up in a cupboard. The husband said, She's right. Take heed of her advice. You only encourage them with your bread and tea. They are looking for a chance. . . . And he brought the little boy's tricycle from the garden into the house every night, because if the house was surely secure, once locked and with the alarm set, someone might still be able to climb over the wall or the electronically closed gates into the garden.

You are right, said the wife, then the wall should be higher. And the wise old witch, the husband's mother, paid for the extra bricks as her Christmas present to her son and his wife—the little boy got a Spaceman outfit and a book of fairy tales.

But every week there were more reports of intrusion: in broad daylight and the dead of night, in the early hours of the morning, and even in the lovely summer twilight—a certain family was at dinner while the bedrooms were being ransacked upstairs. The man and his wife, talking of the latest armed robbery in the suburb, were distracted by the sight of the little boy's pet cat effortlessly arriving over the seven-foot wall, descending first with a rapid bracing of extended forepaws down on the sheer vertical surface, and then a graceful launch, landing with swishing tail within the property. The whitewashed wall was marked with the cat's comings and goings; and on the street side of the wall there were larger red-earth smudges that could have been made by the kind of broken running shoes, seen on the feet of unemployed loiterers, that had no innocent destination.

When the man and wife and little boy took the pet dog for a walk round the neighborhood streets, they no longer paused to admire this show of roses or that perfect lawn; these were hidden behind an array of different varieties of security fences, walls, and devices. The man, wife, little boy, and dog passed a remarkable choice: There was the low-cost option of pieces of broken glass embedded in cement along the top of walls, there were iron grilles ending in lance-points, there were attempts at reconciling the aesthetics of prison architecture with the Spanish Villa style (spikes painted pink) and with the plaster urns of neoclassical façades (twelve-inch pikes finned with zigzags of lightning and painted pure white). Some walls had a small board affixed, giving the name and telephone number of the firm responsible for the installation of the devices. While the little boy and pet dog raced ahead, the husband and wife found themselves comparing the possible effectiveness of each style against its appearance; and after several weeks when they paused before this barricade or that without needing to speak, both came out with the conclusion that only one was worth considering. It was the ugliest but the most honest in its suggestion of the pure concentration-camp style, no frills, all

---

[2]*tsotsis*: hoodlums

evident efficacy. Placed the length of walls, it consisted of a continuous coil of stiff and shining metal serrated into jagged blades, so that there would be no way of climbing over it and no way through its tunnel without getting entangled in its fangs. There would be no way out, only a struggle getting bloodier and bloodier, a deeper and sharper hooking and tearing of flesh. The wife shuddered to look at it. You're right, said the husband, anyone would think twice. . . . And they took heed of the advice on the small board fixed to the wall: Consult DRAGON'S TEETH, The People for Total Security.

Next day a gang of workmen came and stretched the razor-bladed coils all round the walls of the house where the husband and wife and little boy and pet dog and cat were living happily ever after. The sunlight flashed and slashed off the serrations; the cornice of razor thorns encircled the home, shining. The husband said, Never mind. It will weather. The wife said, You're wrong. They guarantee it's rust-proof. And she waited until the little boy had run off to play before she said, I hope the cat will take heed. . . . The husband said, Don't worry, my dear, cats always look before they leap. And it was

true that from that day on the cat slept in the little boy's bed and kept to the garden, never risking a try at breaching security.

One evening, the mother read the little boy to sleep with a fairy tale from the book the wise old witch had given him at Christmas. Next day he pretended to be the Prince who braves the terrible thicket of thorns to enter the palace and kiss the Sleeping Beauty back to life. He dragged a ladder to the wall. The shining coiled tunnel was just wide enough for his body to creep in, and with the first fixing of its razor-teeth in his knees and hands and head he screamed and struggled deeper into the tangle. The trusted housemaid and itinerant gardener, whose "day" it was, came running, the first to see and to scream with him, and the itinerant gardener tore his hands trying to get at the little boy. Then the man and his wife burst wildly into the garden and for some reason (the cat, probably) the alarm set up wailing against the screams while the bleeding mass of the little boy was hacked out of the security coil with saws, wire-cutters, choppers, and they carried it— the man, the wife, the hysterical trusted housemaid, and the weeping gardener— into the house.

After Reading

1. In your notebook, identify parts of the first paragraph of the story (after the introduction) that remind you of a typical **fairy tale** and parts that don't.

2. The author gives very few details about the individual members of the family in this story. Explain reasons for this in terms of the characteristics of the **short story**. (See the Glossary, page 302, for a description of the characteristics of short stories.)

3. Even though we see and hear about violence almost every day, the violent ending of this story still seems to have an impact on most readers. Explain why this might be the case.

4. Most fairy tales end with the **characters** "living happily ever after". The author of this story *starts* with a mother, a father, and a son "living happily ever after". Explain how the use of this phrase is **ironic**.

5. Describe the **irony** present in one of the following details of the story:
   - the boy playing cops and robbers with the walkie-talkie at the gate
   - the intruders sawing bars and eating food in the house they are robbing under the cover of the noise of electronic alarms
   - the growing problem of unemployment and the unwillingness to give a job or anything else to the unemployed
   - the mutilation of the boy as he plays at being the Prince coming to kiss Sleeping Beauty back to life.

6. State the **moral** and **theme** of this story and write two or three paragraphs giving evidence for your choice.

7. Nadine Gordimer is a South African and wrote this story before the end of apartheid in that country. Find references that indicate that apartheid has influenced the way this story has been written.

8. Gated communities are appearing in many parts of the world. Write a series of paragraphs proposing an alternative solution to fears about the safety of families and property in today's society.

Bearhug

MICHAEL ONDAATJE

Before Reading

1. Look at the title of the poem. Using a **graphic organizer**, write down all the things you associate with this word.

2. Distinguish between **open-ended questions** and questions that can be answered with one word. Explain which should be used in an **interview**.

Griffin calls to come and kiss him goodnight
I yell ok. Finish something I'm doing,
then something else, walk slowly round
the corner to my son's room.
5   He is standing arms outstretched
waiting for a bearhug. Grinning.

Why do I give my emotion an animal's name,
give it that dark squeeze of death?
This is the hug which collects
10   all his small bones and his warm neck against me.
The thin tough body under the pyjamas
locks to me like a magnet of blood.

How long was he standing there
like that, before I came?

An Interview With Michael Ondaatje

TANIA CHARZEWSKI

Handwriting (McClelland & Stewart, 1998) is Michael Ondaajte's first collection of new poems since his highly acclaimed *Secular Love* was published in 1984. *Handwriting*, Ondaatje's tenth book of poetry, is a collection of exquisitely crafted poems about love, history, and landscape set in the poet's first home—Sri Lanka. Though many came to know Michael Ondaatje through his brilliant novel *The English Patient*, he actually began his writing career as a poet with *The Dainty Monsters* (1969). He has since published nine other books of poetry, including *The Collected Works of Billy the Kid*, which won the Governor General's Award in 1970, and *There's a Trick with a Knife I'm Learning to Do*, which won the same prize in 1980. These and other books were followed by a selection of his best-loved poetry, *The Cinnamon Peeler*, in 1992. Michael Ondaatje spoke to Tania Charzewski recently in Toronto:

TC: You first appeared on the literary scene as a poet, and have won two Governor General's Awards for poetry (and one for your novel, *The English Patient*), but you have published mostly prose over the last ten years. Have you been working on the poems in *Handwriting* for a while?
MO: During the writing of *In the Skin of a Lion* I had to stop writing poetry—the book was getting too complicated to hold onto *and* write poems. And I didn't write poems during the writing of *The English Patient*, but as soon as I finished that book I knew I wanted to. And needed to. To get back to something I was missing. The large canvas of a novel—the time spent shaping and structuring it—is in some ways very far from composing lyrics, and I wanted to do that. But I did find it difficult to go back to poetry and so really this book is the result of work from 1993 to the present, though I have been writing other stuff during this time as well. But I would go back again and again writing and rewriting and tightening the poems and reconsidering them. They were the toughest poems to write and I am sure they are very different from my earlier ones.

TC: Critics describe your novels as intensely poetic. How different is the act of writing poetry from the act of writing prose?
MO: It is completely different. A poem is closer to what it feels like talking to one person; something overheard; a novel, even though it might seem private and personal, means you are speaking in some ways from a stage. There is a context for the soliloquy. In fact I don't feel the novels are poetic in terms of language but in form. I think that is what I brought to the novel from poetry. A poem is much quicker and more subterranean, I suppose, though I do like to bring that aspect to the novels I have worked on.

TC: *Handwriting* covers an amazing tapestry of Sri Lankan history. You must have had to do a great deal of research.
MO: I've been back there a lot in the last few years. And there has also been much shuffling around in libraries.

TC: In *Running in the Family*, a partly fictionalized memoir of your childhood and family in Ceylon (Sri Lanka), you describe what you are doing as "traveling back to the family to touch them into words." In a sense, do you see yourself doing this with the broader sweep of history in this book?

MO: I have wanted to write about Sri Lanka for some time without "family" being the subject. In some way I am not interested in "family," in a literary way, any longer, though I stay with my family whenever I am there. I was interested in the history of Sri Lanka and interested as you said in a larger sense of it, not just immediate history as seen by politicians and journalists.

TC: You once said that your books are sometimes inspired by one "resonant image," such as the desert plane crash in *The English Patient*. Were there one or two images that led you to write the poems in *Handwriting*, or is it a completely different creative impulse when writing a book of poems?

MO: I suppose each new poem begins with a resonant image or phrase that you explore and perhaps change. With this book there was the recurring image of burial and "unburial."

TC: You once said "a poem which focuses on some small moment or tiny reversal of emotion is more dramatic to me than many long works of action." Did you feel that the medium of poetry was the best way for you to embrace a thousand or more years of history?

MO: In some ways, yes! You can write or catch history in a very different way by approaching it with poetry. You are sensually within the event, the language can suggest the various possibilities and confusions. If I want a good portrait of what it means to be someone living in Canada today I would read Dionne Brand's poetry sooner than a more "official" or journalistic voice. The form of poetry took me to places and issues and emotions I had never thought about before. I began with nothing. There wasn't a set plan or thesis to work out.

TC: One of the extraordinary things in these poems is the juxtaposition of a culture's loss of civilization and art with an individual's personal sense of grief and loss. Do you see one as a metaphor for the other?

MO: Yes, I think that is very central to the book in retrospect. Though history also has a great sense of renewal if you look at it long enough. So there is that frail hope.

After Reading

1. Point out the shift in the **narrator**'s **tone** from the beginning to the end of the poem, making sure to quote the words or images used to create the shift.

2. a) Complete the following **topic sentence**: If we learn something from the poem "Bearhug", it is . . .

   b) Starting with your completed topic sentence, create an outline for developing the rest of the paragraph using the following headings to organize your outline: Main Point, Proofs, Conclusion. (See The Reference Shelf, pages 262–267.)

3. Describe the differences between writing **poetry** and writing a novel according to Michael Ondaatje.

4. a) Discuss with the class Ondaatje's opinion that poetry can capture emotions and drama just as well as longer **fiction**.

   b) Examine the different emotions the poet has captured within his poem and explain how he has suggested those emotions. (Hint: Go back to the graphic organizer you made before you read "Bearhug" and see if some of the ideas you thought about then are present in the poem.)

5. a) Several questions asked by the interviewer are not **open-ended questions**. Explain why she is still able to get good answers from Michael Ondaatje.

   b) Rephrase her questions so that she would be assured of getting full and interesting answers.

6. a) With a small group, research a famous person you would like to know more about. Use as many different types of sources as you can.

   b) Design and make an oral presentation on that person, including the following:
      - a role-played interview focusing on the person's values, beliefs, and views on life, with answers based on your research
      - biographical information including visuals
      - an interview segment where classmates ask questions of the person

Charles

SHIRLEY JACKSON

"Today Charles hit the teacher."

The day my son Laurie started kindergarten he renounced corduroy overalls with bibs and began wearing blue jeans with a belt. I watched him go off the first morning with the older girl next door, seeing clearly that an era of my life was ended, my sweet-voiced nursery-school tot replaced by a long-trousered, swaggering character who forgot to stop at the corner and wave goodbye to me.

He came home the same way, the front door slamming open, his hat on the floor, and the voice suddenly become raucous shouting, "Isn't anybody *here*?"

At lunch he spoke insolently to his father, spilled his baby sister's milk, and remarked that his teacher said we were not to take the name of the Lord in vain.

"How *was* school today?" I asked, elaborately casual.

"All right," he said.

"Did you learn anything?" his father asked.

Laurie regarded his father coldly. "I didn't learn nothing," he said.

"Anything," I said. "Didn't learn anything."

"The teacher spanked a boy, though," Laurie said, addressing his bread and butter. "For being fresh," he added, with his mouth full.

"What did he do?" I asked. "Who was it?"

Laurie thought. "It was Charles," he said. "He was fresh. The teacher spanked him and made him stand in a corner. He was awfully fresh."

"What did he do?" I asked again, but Laurie slid off his chair, took a cookie, and left, while his father was still saying, "See here, young man."

The next day Laurie remarked at lunch, as soon as he sat down, "Well, Charles was bad again today." He grinned enormously and said, "Today Charles hit the teacher."

"Good heavens," I said, mindful of the Lord's name. "I suppose he got spanked again?"

"He sure did," Laurie said. "Look up," he said to his father.

"What?" his father said, looking up.

"Look down," Laurie said. "Look at my thumb. Gee, you're dumb." He began to laugh insanely.

"Why did Charles hit the teacher?" I asked quickly.

"Because she tried to make him color with red crayons," Laurie said. "Charles wanted to color with green crayons so he hit the teacher and she spanked him and said nobody play with Charles but everybody did."

The third day—it was Wednesday of the first week—Charles bounced a see-saw on the head of a little girl and made her bleed, and the teacher made him stay inside all during recess. Thursday Charles had to stand in a corner during story-time because he kept pounding his feet on the floor. Friday Charles was deprived of blackboard privileges because he threw chalk.

On Saturday I remarked to my husband, "Do you think kindergarten is too unsettling for Laurie? All this toughness and bad grammar, and this Charles boy sounds like such a bad influence."

"It'll be all right," my husband said reassuringly. "Bound to be people like Charles in the world. Might as well meet them now as later."

On Monday Laurie came home late, full of news. "Charles," he shouted as he came up the hill; I was waiting anxiously on the front steps. "Charles," Laurie yelled all the way up the hill, "Charles was bad again."

"Come right in," I said, as soon as he came close enough. "Lunch is waiting."

"You know what Charles did?" he demanded, following me through the door. "Charles yelled so in school they sent a boy in from first grade to tell the teacher she had to make Charles keep quiet, and so Charles had to stay after school. And so all the children stayed to watch him."

"What did he do?" I asked.

"He just sat there," Laurie said, climbing into his chair at the table. "Hi, Pop, y'old dust mop."

"Charles had to stay after school today," I told my husband. "Everyone stayed with him."

"What does this Charles look like?" my husband asked Laurie. "What's his other name?"

"He's bigger than me," Laurie said. "And he doesn't have any rubbers and he doesn't ever wear a jacket."

Monday night was the first Parent-Teachers meeting, and only the fact that the baby had a cold kept me from going; I wanted passionately to meet Charles's mother. On Tuesday Laurie remarked suddenly, "Our teacher had a friend come to see her in school today."

"Charles's mother?" my husband and I asked simultaneously.

"Naaah," Laurie said scornfully. "It was a man who came and made us do exercises; we had to touch our toes. Look." He climbed down from his chair and squatted down and touched his toes. "Like this," he said. He got solemnly back into his chair and said, picking up his fork, "Charles didn't even *do* exercises."

"That's fine," I said heartily. "Didn't Charles want to do the exercises?"

"Naaah," Laurie said. "Charles was so fresh to the teacher's friend he wasn't *let* do exercises."

"Fresh again," I said.

"He kicked the teacher's friend," Laurie said. "The teacher's friend told Charles to touch his toes like I just did and Charles kicked him."

"What are they going to do about Charles, do you suppose?" Laurie's father asked him.

Laurie shrugged elaborately. "Throw him out of school, I guess," he said.

Wednesday and Thursday were routine: Charles yelled during story hour and hit a boy in the stomach and made him cry. On Friday Charles stayed after school again and so did all the other children.

With the third week of kindergarten Charles was an institution in our family; the baby was being a Charles when he filled his wagon full of mud and pulled it through the kitchen; even my husband, when he caught his elbow in the telephone cord and pulled telephone, ashtray, and a bowl of flowers off the table, said, after the first minute, "Looks like Charles."

During the third and fourth weeks it looked like a reformation in Charles; Laurie reported grimly at lunch on Thursday of the third week, "Charles was so good today the teacher gave him an apple."

"What?" I said, and my husband added warily, "You mean Charles?"

"Charles," Laurie said. "He gave the crayons around and he picked up the books afterward and the teacher said he was her helper."

"What happened?" I asked incredulously.

"He was her helper, that's all," Laurie said, and shrugged.

"Can this be true, about Charles?" I asked my husband that night. "Can something like this happen?"

"Wait and see," my husband said cynically. "When you've got a Charles to deal with, this may mean he's only plotting."

He seemed to be wrong. For over a week Charles was the teacher's helper; each day he handed things out and he picked things up; no one had to stay after school.

"The PTA meeting's next week again," I told my husband one evening. "I'm going to find Charles's mother there."

"Ask her what happened to Charles," my husband said. "I'd like to know."

"I'd like to know myself," I said.

On Friday of that week things were back to normal. "You know what Charles did today?" Laurie demanded at the lunch table, in a voice slightly awed. "He told a little girl to say a word and she said it and the teacher washed her mouth out with soap and Charles laughed."

"What word?" his father asked unwisely, and Laurie said, "I'll have to whisper it to you, it's so bad." He got down off his chair and went around to his father. His father bent his head down and Laurie whispered joyfully. His father's eyes widened.

"Did Charles tell the little girl to say *that*?" he asked respectfully.

"She said it *twice*," Laurie said. "Charles told her to say it *twice*."

"What happened to Charles?" my husband asked.

"Nothing," Laurie said. "He was passing out the crayons."

Monday morning Charles abandoned the little girl and said the evil word himself three of four times, getting his mouth washed out with soap each time. He also threw chalk.

My husband came to the door with me that evening as I set out for the PTA meeting. "Invite her over for a cup of tea after the meeting," he said. "I want to get a look at her."

"If only she's there," I said prayerfully.

"She'll be there," my husband said. "I don't see how they could hold a PTA meeting without Charles's mother."

At the meeting I sat restlessly, scanning each comfortable matronly face, trying to determine which one hid the secret of Charles. None of them looked to me haggard enough. No one stood up in the meeting and apologized for the way her son had been acting. No one mentioned Charles.

After the meeting I identified and sought out Laurie's kindergarten teacher. She had a plate with a cup of tea and a piece of marshmallow cake; I had a plate with a cup of tea and a piece of marshmallow cake. We maneuvered up to one another cautiously, and smiled.

"I've been so anxious to meet you," I said. "I'm Laurie's mother."

"We're all so interested in Laurie," she said.

"Well, he certainly likes kindergarten," I said. "He talks about it all the time."

"We had a little trouble adjusting, the first week or so," she said primly, "but now he's a fine little helper. With occasional lapses, of course."

"Laurie usually adjusts very quickly," I said. "I suppose this time it's Charles's influence."

"Charles?"

"Yes," I said, laughing, "you must have your hands full in that kindergarten, with Charles."

"Charles?" she said. "We don't have any Charles in the kindergarten."

After Reading

1. Make a chart showing the similarities between some of the "fresh" remarks and inappropriate behaviour of Laurie at home and of Charles at school as reported by Laurie.

2. Write your explanation for Laurie's stories about the non-existent Charles.

3. In a small group, write and perform a **script** based on the talk Laurie and his mother have the morning after parents' night.

4. Shirley Jackson's **short stories** are noted for her use of **surprise endings**. With a partner, reread the story carefully to discover any clues or **foreshadowing** the author presented to prepare the reader for the ending.

5. Identify the grammatical error in Laurie's remark, "I didn't learn nothing".

6. Write a **memoir** about a memorable teacher or student or event in your kindergarten class.

Stones

SANDRA BIRDSELL

". . . her laughter was like rubbing two stones together."

Before Reading

1. Read the first line of the story. From it, predict what this story may be about.

2. Read the rest of the first paragraph. Describe your first impressions of the **narrator**.

Mother made a new apron the day after she and Father quarrelled and he slammed the door and went walking. She didn't come away from the kitchen window for a long time, and I tiptoed around the house feeling nervous because she hadn't noticed that it was past my bedtime.

She was wearing the apron when she met the doctor's wife, Mrs. Hallman, out by the clothes-line, only you couldn't see it for the pouch of clothespegs tied around her thick waist. Mrs. Hallman stood tall and slim, her red toenails sticking out the end of her white sandals and she smelled like the sweet william that grew in a patch beside the back porch. I hung around like a sticky fly in August and listened while they talked. Mother played with the pegs in the pouch and made little squares in the dirt with her foot while Mrs. Hallman said how pleased she was to be living in the country instead of the city, so much nicer for the children, didn't she think? Then she asked which one I was and Mother told her. Lureen the second of five and one was coming.

Mrs. Hallman said, "Oh how nice," her Jane Russell lips forming a raspberry circle and I wished suddenly that Mother would take off the pouch so the ricrac on the apron would show. Mrs. Hallman patted her flat stomach and told Mother that it sure was good to be slim again and that was *it* for her. Then she laughed and her voice went high and tinkly like a wind chime. Mother laughed too, and her laughter was like rubbing two stones together.

At supper Mother said to Father that the kids were terrible. And how could she invite Mrs. Hallman in? He hadn't built the cage he'd promised now for a month and Rudy let Jeepers loose again in the kitchen and Sharon wouldn't come down from the kitchen table. She'd offered Mrs. Hallman some tomatoes, but they're allergic to tomatoes, and it was too bad, but she couldn't play bridge with Mrs. Hallman because she had better things to do with her time.

When Mrs. Hallman came for coffee, Mother would send me to the cellar for a jar of jelly and spread a clean tablecloth. Then she would sit drawing circles with her finger, smiling and nodding while Mrs. Hallman rattled her charm bracelet and talked about Toronto and Minneapolis and "my husband the doctor." I would sit listening to her wind chime laughter, unable to move when told to go out and play with the others.

When Mrs. Hallman left, Mother would bang pots and pans on the stove or put on Father's fishing hat and chop weeds in the garden, making chunks of earth fly up around her feet.

The oldest daughter, Emily, and I became friends. She played store with real groceries and let me watch. She had bubble gum and pop whenever she wanted and sometimes gave me sips. She had her own bicycle and she wouldn't let me ride it. I gave up my perch in the maple tree where I'd spent the summer building a tree-house and began moping about the kitchen complaining of having nothing to do. When I asked Mother why we didn't have one measly bike, she slammed the oven door hard and said stoves were more important than bicycles and if we ever got anything new around this house it would be a stove that works right.

Then Rudy tried fly-casting at the telephone wires and caught a fishhook in his finger. Mother sent me to the Hallmans' and the doctor said he'd come over and then stayed to have a slice of fresh bread, his eyes never leaving the cupboard where Mother had piled her batches of bread and buns. And when he asked if it was really true, did she really make that delicious bread, she smiled at him the way she smiles at Father when he pulls the little curl on the back of her neck and says she's keeping her girlish figure.

The doctor stood in the door with two loaves of our bread under his arm and asked if they could have the recipe. He said some more and Mother laughed high and tinkly like the wind chimes and said she'd always wanted to play bridge, she'd just never had anyone offer to teach her and yes, she'd be glad to give him the recipe.

She sent me the next day with the recipe which I put under a stone for a moment while I helped Rudy untangle Father's fishing reel, which was tied to a kite. We couldn't fix it, so we buried the reel in the garden and when I got back, I stood and watched the wind flip the paper under the stone. Then I saw Emily's bicycle lying in her driveway and I lifted the stone and let the recipe blow away. I told Mother the doctor's wife said she didn't have time to bake bread.

When Father came home for supper, Mother was banging pots on the stove and said that she wouldn't bother with bridge after all, she had too much to do. Father said there was no rest for the wicked and Mother laughed, and her laughter was like rubbing two stones together.

After Reading

1. In two or three well-written sentences, retell the story.

2. a) Compare the descriptions of the two women's laughter in paragraph three. Explain how the **similes** capture the personalities of each of these characters.

   b) With a partner, consider why the mother's laughter sounds like wind chimes when she is talking to the doctor. Discuss your answer with the class.

3. In your notebook, record how your feelings about the **narrator** change from the first paragraph of the story to the end.

4. The narrator sees her family as the "have-nots" and the Hallmans as the "haves". List the **symbols** in the story that represent these two expressions.

5. With the class, determine why the narrator "loses" the recipe and then lies to her mother about it at the end of the story. Choose one idea from the class discussion to create a **thesis** and write a series of linked paragraphs developing your thesis. Have one of your classmates edit your work.

6. With a partner, prepare an **interior monologue** in which the mother discloses her thoughts about the Hallmans and about her own family.

7. From the story, describe the **setting** (both time and place). Evaluate the importance of this setting to the story's events, **characters**, and **theme**.

8. Choose some of the words and phrases used to describe Mrs. Hallman. Describe the **tone** created by the author's **diction**.

9. Imagine you are making a film of this story. With a partner, reread the second paragraph and create a **storyboard** of this scene, capturing the **atmosphere** and the two distinct characters in your camera movements and shots. Write appropriate **dialogue**. (See The Reference Shelf, pages 286–289.)

Silent Words

An Excerpt

RUBY SLIPPERJACK

"There were no words to describe the beauty of this place."

Before Reading

This story is set in northwestern Ontario. Find Collins and Armstrong, two towns mentioned in the story, on a map.

Silent Words is the story of a young Aboriginal boy from northwestern Ontario who is searching for his mother, after running away from his father. On his search, he encounters many people who teach him about Aboriginal traditions, and about himself.

I woke up early the next morning. Ol' Jim was still sleeping, which was a surprise. I had to go to the bush. I must have had too much water to drink last night. I sat up and pulled my socks and running shoes on and quickly ducked outside. There was a heavy mist all around us. It must have been raining. I heard the mallards already quacking by the pond. They sure get up early, if they even go to sleep at all.

. . .

"There was a lake with trees all around it, and it was floating above the treetops across there. Why did it look like that?" I asked.

Ol' Jim shrugged and said, "It's called a mirage. With the mist in the air and the sun coming up on the horizon, it creates a reflection. When the mist starts to dry up, the picture begins to fade."

Oh, that made sense. I smiled and glanced at the tent and Ol' Jim nodded. That told me I should get busy taking the stuff down to the lake. We had to be on our way again. While I ran to get more wood, Ol' Jim quickly took down the tent, and I folded and tied it up into a bundle. Slowly the stuff accumulated inside the

canoe, and all too soon the duck was ready, the bannock was golden brown, and the tea was brewing in the pot.

We sat in front of the fire and took our time eating. The sun had rapidly dried up the mist, and it looked like another very hot day. The water was calm here in the bay. If we were going to paddle along the big long lake, I hoped the wind wasn't going to blow too hard.

When we had finished cleaning up the campsite and loading up our stuff, we slowly paddled to where Ol' Jim had dropped his line of hooks. I watched him carefully winding up the rope and tugging at it as he placed the hooks in a row inside the canoe. Suddenly his arm was pulled sharply into the water. He heaved and pulled and the canoe rocked to the side. I grabbed on tightly as Ol' Jim groaned, and soon a huge strange-looking fish emerged. It was long, dark, and slick. It had no scales, only some flat circles of bone along its back and sides. The nose was pointed and rubbery with a huge sucker mouth underneath the head and thick white whiskers. I watched Ol' Jim giggling excitedly as he hit the four-foot-long fish over the head with the blunt side of the axe. The fish trembled and Ol' Jim hauled it into the canoe. When he pulled the rest of the rope up I was very thankful to see there weren't any more of those monsters to share the canoe with us.

"Sturgeon!" said Ol' Jim. "What a delicious treat we will have. That is the best-tasting fish you will ever eat!"

I was not too sure as I glanced at the peculiar creature lying at the bottom of the canoe. Well, we would have enough for lunch and supper anyway. The fog in the low bushes of the swamps to our right was disappearing quickly now as the sun shone its way through the haze. Seagulls were already squawking and creating a big racket somewhere to the north of us. We paddled by the sharp point of Best Island, and I looked along the beach I had gone tearing down the evening before. There were no words to describe the beauty of this place.

I breathed in the fresh air and listened to the swishing of the water against the canoe, the birds chirping along the shore, the ducks quacking in the bay, the croaking frogs, the buzzing flies from the bushes, the seagulls squawking up above, the occasional splash of fish on the water . . . the place seemed to thrive in a certain natural rhythm. It reminded me of the time I had listened to Henry's stomach.

We paddled along the shoreline. Ol' Jim said, under his breath, "He was laid to rest there, the Medicine Man." We were passing by some majestic sand cliffs. There were trees standing upright by their roots, the trunks about five feet off the sandy ground. Strange. Ol' Jim's voice came

again, "The mass burial ground over there is all but forgotten now."

I turned, but didn't catch where he had indicated it was. We paddled on for about a half-hour when I noticed a pile of round rocks jutting out in a pyramid in the middle of the lake.

Ol' Jim must have seen that I had noticed the rocks because before I could think of a question, I heard him say, "Don't point at the rocks. They are not to be pointed at."

"Why?" I asked.

"A big wind will come and swamp us. We will drown here in the middle of the lake," he said.

"But how did they get there? Can we paddle there to see?" I craned my neck to get a better look.

"No. They are sacred rocks. We would stop to offer tobacco if we had to pass by them. But right now we have no business going there."

I watched the pile of rocks as we glided farther and farther away. There were long stretches of sand beaches everywhere.

After a couple of hours of following the shoreline Ol' Jim steered to a small island at the mouth of a river. We stopped and he built a fire by the shore. He cut up the tail part of the sturgeon and threw it into the teapot, which he had filled with water. This, he set to simmer while he arranged the rope with the three-inch-long hooks again. Next, he used the fish guts to bait the hooks and placed them in order inside the canoe. The teapot began to boil and he added some of the salvaged clean flour to it, and we ended up with a tasty sturgeon dumpling stew!

Ol' Jim slit the rest of the sturgeon into a flat piece with crisscross cuts. The fish was held flat by the roasting stick, which was slit down the middle, and was sandwiched in between and held flat by two smaller crossed sticks. This he propped over the hot ashes. I watched the flesh turn pink, then brown. I ran to explore the area and soon found another of the old leather ropes tied around a tree, quite high up. People must have lived here too, long ago.

I scrambled around between huge boulders and munched on some dry blueberries before I made my way to the shoreline again. I saw minnows flashing in the shallow water by the bay. Then I heard Ol' Jim chanting and singing. It sounded eerie, and I could feel the hair on the back of my neck stand up. I sat on a boulder in the shade and listened for a long time until all was quiet. Then I decided to head back.

When I was close to the campfire site, I heard Ol' Jim talking to himself again. He was by the lake, rummaging around in his packsack. I threw some sticks into the fire and sat down. We ate the roasted sturgeon in silence.

We spent a lot of time on the island, and it was already evening when we approached the mouth of the river. I could hear the roar of the rapids. Here, Ol' Jim carefully strung the big hooks on the rope right across the channel. I watched the rope sink to the bottom. He sank both of his lead-end ropes, tied around rocks, to the bottom of the lake. He did, however, make sure that he could reach the end rope by the shore with his paddle.

We pitched the tent by the canoe-landing clearing at the portage. I didn't like it here very much. As far as I was concerned, the river was far too noisy to hear anything. A bear could walk up and sniff my behind before I even heard it! This was also the first time Ol' Jim had to cut the poles for the tent himself. That told me that people don't normally sleep on this portage, so why were we? I didn't voice my concerns however. He seemed to know what he was doing, and who was I to question why he did things?

We built a fire and made a pot of tea. We ate a bit more of the roasted sturgeon. There was so much noise, I didn't bother trying to talk. When it came time to go to bed I just curled up in my sleeping bag and went to sleep.

Sometime during the dark hours, a loud hooting echoed in my eardrums and shot up my spine, sending shivers through me. It took a while before I recognized the sound—an owl. I must say that was the loudest and closest-sounding owl I had ever heard. I listened to the obnoxious creature as it forced every other creature within hearing distance to stay awake and listen to it. A few minutes later, I realized that I was not listening to one owl but two—one to the east of us and the other answering from the west. Ol' Jim and I were cornered. What did he care, anyway? He snored softly through the whole owl conversation without a pause. I listened until I discovered that I could actually force my ears to shut out Mr. and Mrs. Owl by concentrating on the continual, uninterrupted sound of the rapids—the water rushing and pouring, swirling around the rocks. I had to go to the bathroom, but no way was I going to go out there all by myself in the dark!

Early the next morning, Ol' Jim shook me awake. "Come on, get your shoes on and let's go check the hooks."

I jumped up and pulled on my socks and shoes while Ol' Jim got a good fire going. I hated to leave the comforting smell of fire smoke and the warmth as we headed out into the cool early morning mist. As soon as the sound of the rapids faded, the quiet returned and my ears got a well-deserved rest. I turned and smiled at my quiet companion.

I could hear a loon calling, sad and lonesome all by himself somewhere out on the lake. Suddenly another loon answered and soon they were carrying on like two old friends catching up on news.

I looked at Ol' Jim and asked seriously, "Why do people say 'the lonely call of a loon,' or 'the eerie hoot of an owl' when I have never heard these things by themselves? There are always two or a whole bunch of them!"

Ol' Jim chuckled and said, "Well, when you don't understand the language, all the voices sound the same, don't they?"

Along the shoreline, I noticed a long awkward stick move at the top and realized that it was the head of a very long-legged bird. One leg bent at the knee and poised there for a minute before he moved the other leg.

"Blue heron," said Ol' Jim behind me, as he paddled past the creature amidst the reeds.

Soon we reached the spot where the rope was, and Ol' Jim fished in the lead rope with his paddle while I made an effort to have the canoe stay facing one direction. Ol' Jim was pulling us along the length of the canoe when something caused the whole front end to swerve left and right.

Then, suddenly, another huge sturgeon came into view. I dodged to the side quickly and immediately Ol' Jim's voice rang out, "Take it easy now, it's a very big one!"

With plenty of water swishing and splashing, Ol' Jim finally managed to bonk it on the head with an axe and haul it into the canoe. I saw the dark moustaches on the fish. The one yesterday had white moustaches. I could see a huge sucker mouth on the underside of his head. Again, I was relieved when Ol' Jim threw in the rest of his hooks and there were no more monsters of this kind attached to them.

When we returned to camp, Ol' Jim had to make two roasting sticks. The flattened top part of the fish was on one stick and the flattened tail part was on the other. That was a lot of fish to eat! The supporting crossed sticks were pushed over the flesh to keep it flat while it was propped to smoke and slowly cook over the hot ashes. If Ol' Jim can keep it from getting rotten, we will be eating it for about three days.

While he was busy cooking the sturgeon, I hauled the rest of the things over the portage. The path wasn't too long and it was rather pleasant, except for the noise of the rapids. After the third trip of taking my time, I sat beside Ol' Jim and waited. Finally he took the roasting stick aside and cut off a piece onto a sheet of birchbark for me. I decided I liked sturgeon roasted better than boiled. It had just enough fat, the flesh was firm, and no bones! Then we sat around with our cups of tea. I didn't feel the need to be in such a big hurry any more. I was jam-packed full.

Ol' Jim said his son was just on the next lake. We should get there by evening. Somehow, I didn't want this trip to end so soon. I wanted to travel with Ol' Jim like this forever.

I asked, "How long do you usually stay there? Are you coming back by canoe again?"

Ol' Jim squinted against the campfire smoke and said, "Well now, I usually stay there until freeze-up, then I fly on the aeroplane with my son back to Collins. The aeroplane comes to the camp every week to bring supplies and things. Now, that's not saying you have to stay there with me all that time. There's school, don't forget. You will have to go home to go to school. You can get on whenever the plane lands. It goes back to Armstrong. You can take the train from there. If you don't have any money, I will give you some. So don't worry about anything. Enjoy what you see around you right now. Things will work out."

Finally Ol' Jim wrapped the rest of the sturgeon in birchbark and put it inside the food box. He picked up the paddles and arranged them over his shoulders as he lifted the canoe. I busied myself with the food box and teapot and hurried along in front of him. On the other side, I watched the swirl of water as it flowed from the rapids into a pool with clumps of white foam floating around in it. The foam washed ashore by the portage as I waited

for Ol' Jim to put the canoe down. I could tell it was going to be a very hot day again.

After we loaded the canoe, we took our time paddling along with the current onto another portage. Everything was very quiet and peaceful here. I had a holding-your-breath-waiting-for-something-to-happen feeling. I liked this portage though. It had flat rocks and quiet-looking openings in the bush that I wished I had time to play in. We touched shore on a quiet bay with a gently sloping rock padded with soft mud. The flies weren't bad and it seemed like a very friendly place. I walked across the portage three times, deliberately carrying only a few things at a time.

As we sat eating a couple of pieces of sturgeon and bannock at the other end of the portage, I smelled a skunk. The ground was all sandy and it had low pine trees everywhere. Ol' Jim indicated that it was a good habitat for skunks and such. Well, I wasn't about to wait for a skunk to come and invite himself for lunch, so I was in a bit of a hurry again to get under way. We paddled slowly and softly along some long and lonely beaches, high sand-cliffs, and rocky shores.

I noticed a cloud of flies above the water as we paddled across the bay. I pointed at them and Ol' Jim nodded and stopped paddling. The canoe drifted forward. I stopped paddling too and watched the cloud of flies hovering above the surface of the water come closer and closer. Suddenly, with a swoosh, a huge black furry thing rose up above the water!

A shock went through me, and I was about to jump out of the canoe when I heard Ol' Jim's calm voice. "Steady, boy.

It's a moose coming up above the water. He dunks his whole body into the water sometimes when the flies are driving him crazy."

The moose came up about five yards away from our canoe. The canoe floated over the waves from the moose, then we just drifted slowly past him. He didn't seem to notice us at all because he just dunked his head back in again.

We saw some ducks and their babies. The young ones were almost the same size as their parents now, but they weren't as colourful. Baby seagulls were also flying around in their dirty grey feathers, pretending that they were just as pretty as their snow white parents. Then, right in front of the canoe, we had a couple of playful otters put on a display for us. Showing off and taking advantage of having an audience, they did some tricks and backflips and tried to outdo each other.

Toward afternoon, we came across some very high rock cliffs. We paused again in the now-familiar routine of leaving some tobacco on a shelf in the cliff. Here, Ol' Jim said, is where he would have put his fishnet in if it wasn't in pieces back there at the channel in Whitewater Lake. I smiled.

I turned to see him looking up at the towering rock, and he said, "There are drawings on the ones at the other end of the lake."

"Drawings? What kind of drawings?" I asked.

Suddenly he indicated that I should be quiet and look. I turned to see four large black animals by the water. Moose! Then I noticed another one between the cedar trees. He had his head stretched out toward the branches. The other four moose by the water saw us at that moment and, without a sound, they melted away into the bushes.

"Strange, very strange," said Ol' Jim behind me as he put his paddle into the water. We shot forward so fast the water gurgled at the front of the canoe. I swung my arms with new energy, trying to match the paddle dips behind me.

It was late when we came around a point, and Ol' Jim steered the canoe close to the shoreline all the way around the bay. Then I saw the smoke coming from a cabin by the lake in front of a small sand beach.

In the quiet evening, it looked so calm and inviting. I set my paddle across my lap and breathed a big sigh. We were here. I noticed the dock and several gas cans lined up along the shoreline. A boat and an unfinished cabin sat farther along the beach. We paddled along in silence.

After Reading

1. a) In your opinion, is the title *Silent Words* effective?

    b) Why do you think the writer chose a **first person narrative** for her story?

2. a) Describe two aspects of Canadian Aboriginal culture that are presented in the story.

    b) Describe two things the **narrator** learns from Ol' Jim during their travels.

3. Select and look up the meaning of five to ten words, such as *bannock*, *mirage*, and *obnoxious*, to add to your list of new or unfamiliar words.

4. Using the library and a photocopy machine, create an illustrated guide to the fish, birds, and animals mentioned in the story. Write a brief annotation to accompany each picture.

5. In your **journal**, write an account of a learning experience you had in nature.

6. Prepare a **brochure**, aimed at urban southern Ontarians, **advertising** a wilderness canoe trip in northern Ontario.

7. Prepare a short **research report** on a Canadian Aboriginal writer and his or her work.

The Nest

ROBERT ZACKS

"My mother was . . . actually wrong."

Before Reading

As a class, discuss the statement: "Parents know best".

Jimmy was fourteen. He was listening to his mother tell him, in her kindly, measured speech, why she didn't want him to go on the hike, and his clear grey eyes were clouded with sullen rebellion.

"All right, Mom," he said in the controlled voice he had learned from his parents. "If you say I can't go, then I can't, can I?"

Mrs. Swanson said gravely, "You make me sound like a dictator, Jimmy."

"Well, you are, kind of, aren't you?" said Jimmy coldly. "I have to do what you say."

His mother winced a little. She bit her lower lip and considered this.

"It isn't as simple as that," she said, pushing her mind with some difficulty toward coping with the point Jimmy had made. She smiled a little, however, in pleas-ure at such evidence of Jimmy's growing power to analyse a situation. "My decisions are made for your own good, Jimmy."

He misunderstood her smile. He thought she was relegating him to his position as a child. All his parents seemed to do these days was figure out how to hem him in. "Jimmy, you mustn't—"

The words, the restrictions, they wrapped around him like tentacles of an octopus, crushing in on his chest so he couldn't seem to breathe.

He was on his feet, yelling, the controlled, polite speech lost in his bursting anguish for freedom. "Everything is for my own good. Everything! But you aren't telling me the truth. You know why you don't want me to go on the hike? Because of Paul. You just don't like him."

He sucked in his breath, almost sobbing, shocked at himself and yet glad. Mrs. Swanson had an unhappy look. The Swansons were a happy family; but these days a strange restlessness had come into it.

"No," she admitted. "I don't think Paul is good for you. I don't like your associating with him."

Jimmy said, all his heart and soul in his words, "I like Paul. He's my best friend."

"His father is a drunkard," said Mrs. Swanson quietly. "And Paul came out of reform school, didn't he? He stole from a candy store—"

"He's *nice*!" cried Jimmy, pain in his voice. "And he isn't a crook. He made a mistake. He told me what happened. He was showing off. And now nobody will be friends—"

"But he's formed a gang already, hasn't he? I've heard about it."

"It's just a club, that's all," said Jimmy. "And—and I'm a member. The club is running the hike."

"We won't discuss it further." Mrs. Swanson's voice was suddenly like steel. She stood up. She hesitated, pitying him, and tried to soften it with logic. "Remember, Jimmy, every time we've disagreed, it turned out I knew what I was talking about."

But he didn't listen further. Jimmy turned and blindly ran off the porch across the lawn toward the meeting place at Briggs' Drugstore.

After three blocks he slowed down, panting, his face set with fury. The habit of thinking, encouraged by his parents at every opportunity, began to function.

"'I know what's best for you. I know what's best for you.' That's all I ever hear!" muttered Jimmy.

To his reluctant mind sprang memories. The time he insisted he could swim to the raft. Mr. Swanson had curtly said no, he couldn't risk it. Jimmy had raged, with his father quietly letting him run down. Then his father had told him to go ahead, but that he'd swim next to him.

Jimmy's throat strangled suddenly at the memory: the water was constricting his windpipe dreadfully, his eyes were bulging, his legs and arms numb with exhaustion from the too-long swim. And then the wonderful, strong, blessed arms of his father turning him on his back, pulling him back to shore—

It was confusing. Jimmy shook his head in bewilderment. Suddenly he felt uncertain, the rebellion drained out of him.

Paul was waiting for him at the drugstore with a stillness upon his face as he leaned against the glass front. He was about fourteen, with dark hair and bright dark eyes. He wore dungarees. Jimmy saw, when he came closer, traces of tears on Paul's cheeks.

"Well," said Paul fiercely, "let's go."

Jimmy started. "Where's everybody?"

"They changed their minds," said Paul, hate in his voice.

The two boys looked at each other, and Jimmy understood. It made fury grow in him, it made him want to hit somebody. All those parents had stopped the gang from going with Paul because he was once in a reform school.

81

Paul said, his voice odd, "Maybe you can't go either?"

Jimmy looked deep into Paul's eyes. His heart beat fast with friendship and loyalty. "Don't be a jerk. Come on," he said cheerfully.

Paul's face changed. The hate seeped away, leaving sweetness and humbleness. He flung an arm over Jimmy's shoulder happily.

"Your—your mother doesn't care if you go, huh?" he said.

Jimmy swallowed. Paul needed this so badly. So very badly. Paul had no mother at all. And his father just didn't like looking at the world without Paul's mother, and was always drunk.

"Nah," said Jimmy. "She—she even said I should bring you to supper, afterwards. What shall I tell her, huh?"

Paul turned ashen, then flushed a deep scarlet. "Sure," he muttered. "Be glad to."

"I got to call her," said Jimmy numbly. "Just a minute."

Jimmy went into the drugstore and called his mother. He told her in a choking voice he was going on the hike, just he and Paul, and he didn't care how mad she got. "Nobody else came," he shouted into the telephone, "because all the mothers—" He was unable to go on for a moment. Then he finished. "I'm bringing him to supper afterwards, Mom. I said you asked him."

He hung up before she could answer.

They had a wonderful day. Wonderful. It was May, and the leaves on the trees were chartreuse and new. They went six miles out of town. They watched chipmunks skitter. They lay on their backs and stared at fleecy white clouds changing shape. Paul's face showed his contentment. His eyes were dreamy.

But Jimmy, in one cloud, saw the stern face of his mother.

But Mrs. Swanson's face, when she greeted Paul, wasn't stern at all. She looked uncertain as she studied his wistful, shy smile. Jimmy knew, of course, that his parents would wait until later to lecture him. They never made a scene before other people.

Throughout supper, Mr. Swanson was very friendly to their guest. But Jimmy could see that at the same time his father was carefully studying Paul. And Paul, never knowing, thinking they'd wanted him, had invited him, glowed and showed the side of his personality that Jimmy liked.

After they'd washed the dishes (at Paul's suggestion), Mr. Swanson nodded to Paul. "Come on, Paul," he said. "I'll show you my tool shop."

As Paul eagerly followed him down the basement steps, Mrs. Swanson touched Jimmy's shoulder. Jimmy's heart thudded as he reluctantly lingered behind. He turned and glared in defiance.

"I don't care," he whispered. "Nobody else came. I couldn't—"

"Jimmy," she said softly, and bent and kissed him. "I'm proud of you, Jimmy. You did the right thing at the right time."

"But you said—" faltered Jimmy. "I mean—"

Her eyes were very bright. "I was wrong," she said steadily. "This time I was wrong. You were right. He's a nice boy, I think."

She turned away, patting his cheek as she did so.

At first, joy filled Jimmy. Joy and pride. *I'm the one who's right,* he thought, dazed. *My mother was wrong. Actually wrong. She admitted it.*

And then came a queer and a frightening sense of loss, as well as of gain. It was like being alone, high up on a precipice where the footing was slippery with moss. Jimmy felt he had to be careful of each step. He had always been sure, even in his anger, of being able to depend on the wisdom of his father and mother. They'd always been right.

But not any more. Now they *might* be wrong. And Jimmy would have to decide.

After Reading

1. State the significance of the title of the story. Suggest an alternative that you feel works as well as the author's title.

2. Explain why the author includes Jimmy's recollection of swimming to the raft after his father had refused him permission to try.

3. Describe in your own words the feelings Jimmy experienced in the last two paragraphs of the story.

4. Create a **storyboard** for a **montage of shots** that captures the events of the hike Jimmy and Paul go on in the story. Select a song for the soundtrack accompanying this segment in a film version of the story.

5. In your **journal**, write an account of a time your parents or guardians supported you in a difficult decision you had to make.

6. With a partner, write a short **anecdote** based on humorous **dialogue** you heard recently at home, in the classroom, or around the school. Use the dialogue in this story as a model for correctly punctuating the **direct speech** in your anecdote.

7. With a small group, rewrite this story into a play. Be prepared to present your play to the class.

The Jade Peony

An Excerpt

WAYSON CHOY

"I must say goodbye to this world properly or wander in this foreign devil's land forever."

Before Reading

1. On the basis of the title, the author's name, and the above quotation from the story, predict what this story will be about.

2. With your classmates or a partner, talk about something you own that has sentimental meaning.

When Grandmama died at 83, our whole household held its breath. She had promised us a sign of her leaving, final proof that her present life had ended well. My parents knew that without any clear sign, our own family fortunes could be altered, threatened. My stepmother looked endlessly into the small cluttered room the ancient lady had occupied. Nothing was touched; nothing changed. My father, thinking that a sign should appear in Grandmama's garden, looked at the frost-killed shoots and cringed: *no, that could not be it.*

My two older teenage brothers and my sister, Liang, age 14, were embarrassed by my parents' behaviour. What would all the white people in Vancouver think of us? We were Canadians now, *Chinese-Canadians*, a hyphenated reality that my parents could never accept. So it seemed, for different reasons, we all held our breath waiting for *something*.

I was eight when she died. For days she had resisted going into the hospital . . . a cold, just a cold . . . and instead gave constant instruction to my stepmother and sister on the boiling of *ginseng*[1] roots

---

[1] A natural herb said to possess many theraputic properties

mixed with bitter extract. At night, between racking coughs and deadly silences, Grandmama had her back and chest rubbed with heated camphor oil and sipped a bluish decoction of an herb called Peacock's Tail. When all these failed to abate her fever, she began to arrange the details of her will. This she did with my father, confessing finally, "I am too stubborn. The only cure for old age is to die."

My father wept to hear this. I stood beside her bed; she turned to me. Her round face looked darker, and the gentleness of her eyes, the thin, arching eyebrows, seemed weary. I brushed the few strands of gray, brittle hair from her face; she managed to smile at me. Being the youngest, I had spent nearly all my time with her and could not imagine that we would ever be parted. Yet when she spoke, and her voice hesitated, cracked, the sombre shadows of her room chilled me.

Her wrinkled brow grew wet with fever, and her small body seemed even more diminutive.

"I-I am going to the hospital, Grandson." Her hand reached out for mine. "You know, Little Son, whatever happens I will never leave you." Her palm felt plush and warm, the slender, old fingers boney and firm, so magically strong was her grip that I could not imagine how she could ever part from me. Ever.

Her hands *were* magical. My most vivid memories are of her hands: long, elegant fingers, with impeccable nails, a skein of fine, barely-seen veins, and wrinkled skin like light pine. Those hands were quick when she taught me, at six, simple tricks of juggling, learnt when she was a village girl in Southern Canton; a troupe of actors had stayed on her father's farm. One of them, "tall and pale as the whiteness of petals," fell in love with her, promising to return. In her last years, his image came back like a third being in our two lives. He had been magician, acrobat, juggler, and some of the things he taught her she had absorbed and passed on to me through her stories and games. But above all, without realizing it then, her hands conveyed to me the quality of their love.

Most marvellous for me was the quick-witted skill her hands revealed in making windchimes for our birthdays: windchimes in the likeness of her lost friend's only present to her, made of bits of string and scraps, in the centre of which once hung a precious jade peony. This wondrous gift to her broke apart years ago, in China, but Grandmama kept the jade pendant in a tiny red silk envelope, and kept it always in her pocket, until her death.

These were not ordinary, carelessly made chimes, such as those you now find in our Chinatown stores, whose rattling noises drive you mad. But making her special ones caused dissension in our family, and some shame. Each one that she made was created from a treasure trove of glass fragments and castaway costume jewellery, in the same way that her first windchime had been made. The problem for the rest of the family was in the fact that Grandmama looked for these treasures wandering the back alleys of Keefer[2] and

---

[2]Main streets in Vancouver's Chinatown

Pender Streets, peering into our neighbours' garbage cans, chasing away hungry, nervous cats and shouting curses at them.

"All our friends are laughing at us!" Older Brother Jung said at last to my father, when Grandmama was away having tea at Mrs. Lim's.

"We are not poor," Oldest Brother Kiam declared, "yet she and Sek-Lung poke through those awful things as if"—he shoved me in frustration and I stumbled against my sister—"they were beggars!"

"She will make Little Brother crazy!" Sister Liang said. Without warning, she punched me sharply in the back; I jumped. "You see, look how *nervous* he is!"

I lifted my foot slightly, enough to swing it back and kick Liang in the shin. She yelled and pulled back her fist to punch me again. Jung made a menacing move towards me.

"Stop this, all of you!" My father shook his head in exasperation. How could he dare tell the Grand Old One, his aging mother, that what was somehow appropriate in a poor village in China, was an abomination here. How could he prevent me, his youngest, from accompanying her? If she went walking into those alleyways alone she could well be attacked by hoodlums. "She is not a beggar looking for food. She is searching for—for. . . ."

My stepmother attempted to speak, then fell silent. She, too, seemed perplexed and somewhat ashamed. They all loved Grandmama, but she was *inconvenient*, unsettling.

As for our neighbours, most understood Grandmama to be harmlessly crazy, others that she did indeed make lovely toys

but for what purpose? Why? they asked and the stories she told me, of the juggler who smiled at her, flashed in my head.

Finally, by their cutting remarks, the family did exert enough pressure so that Grandmama and I no longer openly announced our expeditions. Instead, she took me with her on "shopping trips," ostensibly for clothes or groceries, while in fact we spent most of our time exploring stranger and more distant neighbourhoods, searching for splendid junk: jangling pieces of a vase, cranberry glass fragments embossed with leaves, discarded glass beads from Woolworth necklaces. . . . We would sneak them all home in brown rice sacks, folded into small parcels, and put them under her bed. During the day when the family was away at school or work, we brought them out and washed every item in a large black pot of boiling lye and water, dried them quickly, carefully, and returned them, sparkling, under her bed.

Our greatest excitement occurred when a fire gutted the large Chinese Presbyterian Church, three blocks from our house. Over the still-smoking ruins the next day, Grandmama and I rushed precariously over the blackened beams to pick out the stained glass that glittered in the sunlight. Small figure bent over, wrapped against the autumn cold in a dark blue quilted coat, happily gathering each piece like gold, she became my spiritual playmate: "There's a good one! *There!*"

Hours later, soot-covered and smelling of smoke, we came home with a Safeway carton full of delicate fragments, still early enough to steal them all into the house and put the small box under her bed.

"These are special pieces," she said, giving the box a last push, "because they come from a sacred place." She slowly got up and I saw, for the first time, her hand begin to shake. But then, in her joy, she embraced me. Both of our hearts were racing, as if we were two dreamers. I buried my face in her blue quilt, and for a moment, the whole world seemed silent.

"My juggler," she said, "he never came back to me from Honan[3] . . . perhaps the famine. . . ." Her voice began to quake. "But I shall have my sacred windchime . . . I shall have it again."

One evening, when the family was gathered in their usual places in the parlour, Grandmama gave me her secret nod: a light wink of her eye and a flaring of her nostrils. There was *trouble* in the air. Supper had gone badly, school examinations were due, father had failed to meet an editorial deadline at the *Vancouver Chinese Times*. A huge sigh came from Sister Liang.

"But it is useless this Chinese they teach you!" she lamented, turning to Stepmother for support. Silence. Liang frowned, dejected, and went back to her Chinese book, bending the covers back.

"Father," Oldest Brother Kiam began, waving his bamboo brush in the air, "you must realize that this Mandarin only confuses us. We are Cantonese speakers. . . ."

"And you do not complain about Latin, French or German in your English school?" father rattled his newspaper, a signal that his patience was ending.

"But, Father, those languages are *scientific*," Kiam jabbed his brush in the air. "We are now in a scientific, logical world."

Father was silent. We could all hear Grandmama's rocker.

"What about Sek-Lung?" Older Brother Jung pointed angrily at me. "He was sick last year, but this year he should have at least started Chinese school,[4] instead of picking over garbage cans!"

---

[3]Province located in southern China

[4]In order to maintain their heritage, concerned Chinese community members established many after-school language classes to teach the Toi-san dialect and later Cantonese and Mandarin dialects.

"He starts next year," Father said, in a hard tone that immediately warned everyone to be silent. Liang slammed her book.

Grandmama went on rocking quietly in her chair. She complimented my mother on her knitting, made a remark about the "strong beauty" of Kiam's brush-strokes which, in spite of himself, immensely pleased him. All this babbling noise was her family torn and confused in a strange land: everything here was so very foreign and scientific.

The truth was, I was sorry not to have started school the year before. In my inno-cence I had imagined going to school meant certain privileges worthy of all my brothers and sister's complaints. The fact that my lung infection in my fifth and sixth years, mistakenly diagnosed as TB, earned me some reprieve, only made me long for school the more. Each member of the family took turns on Sunday, teaching me or annoying me. But it was the count-less hours I spent with Grandmama that were my real education. Tapping me on my head she would say, "Come, Sek-Lung, we have our work" and we would walk up the stairs to her small crowded room. There, in the midst of her antique shawls, the old ancestral calligraphy and multi-coloured embroidered hangings, beneath the mysterious shelves of sweet herbs and bitter potions, we would continue doing what we had started that morning: the elaborate windchime for her death.

"I can't last forever," she declared, when she let me in the secret of this one. "It will sing and dance and glitter." Her long fingers stretched into the air, pan-tomiming the waving motion of her ghost chimes. "My spirit will hear its sounds and see its light and return to this house and say goodbye to you."

Deftly she reached into the Safeway carton she had placed on a chair beside me. She picked out a fish-shape amber piece, and with a long needle-like tool and a steel ruler, she scored it. Pressing the blade of a cleaver against the line, with the fingers of her other hand she lifted up the glass until it cleanly snapped into the exact shape she required. Her hand began to tremble, the tips of her fingers to shiver, like rippling water.

"You see that, Little One?" She held her hand up. "That is my body fighting with Death. He is in this room now."

My eyes darted in panic, but Grandmama remained calm, undisturbed, and went on with her work. Then I remembered the glue and uncorked the jar for her. Soon the graceful ritual move-ments of her hand returned to her, and I became lost in the magic of her task: dab-bled a cabalistic mixture of glue on one end and skilfully dropped the braided end of a silk thread into it. This part always amazed me: the braiding would slowly, *very* slowly, *unknot*, fanning out like a prized fishtail. In a few seconds the clear, homemade glue began to harden as I blew lightly over it welding to itself each sepa-rate strand.

Each jam-sized pot of glue was pre-cious; each large cork had been wrapped with a fragment of pink silk. I remember this part vividly, because each cork was treated to a special rite. First we went shop-ping in the best silk stores in Chinatown for the perfect square of silk she required. It had to be a deep pink, a shade of colour blushing towards red. And the tone had to match—as closely as possible—her precious jade carving, the small peony of white and light-red jade, her most lucky possession. In the centre of this semi-translucent carving, no more than an inch wide, was a pool of pink light, its veins whirling out into petals of the flower.

"This colour is the colour of my spirit," she said, holding it up to the window so I could see the delicate pastel against the broad strokes of sunlight. She dropped her voice, and I held my breath at the wonder of the colour. "This was given to me by the young actor who taught me how to juggle. He had four of them, and each one had a centre of the rare colour, the colour of Good Fortune." The pendant seemed to pause as she turned it: "Oh, Sek-Lung! He had white hair and white skin *to his toes! It's true*, I saw him bathing." She laughed and blushed, her eyes softened at the memory. The silk had to match the pink heart of the pendant: the colour was magical for her, to hold the unravelling strand of her memory. . . .

It was just six months before she died that we really began to work on her last windchime. Three thin bamboo sticks were steamed and bent into circlets: 30 exact lengths of silk thread, the strongest kind, were cut and braided at both ends and glued to stained glass. Her hands worked on their own command, each

hand racing with a life of its own: cutting, snapping, braiding, knotting. . . . Sometimes she breathed heavily and her small body growing thinner, sagged against me. *Death*, I thought, *He is in this room*, and I would work harder alongside her. For months Grandmama and I did this every other evening, a half dozen pieces each time. The shaking in her hand grew worse, but we said nothing. Finally, after discarding hundreds, she told me she had the necessary 30 pieces. But this time, because it was a sacred chime, I would not be permitted to help her tie it up or have the joy of raising it. "Once tied," she said, holding me against my disappointment, "not even I can raise it. Not a sound must it make until I have died."

"What will happen?"

"Your father will then take the centre braided strand and raise it.[5] He will hang it against my bedroom window so that my ghost may see it and hear it, and return. I must say goodbye to this world properly or wander in this foreign devil's land forever."

"You can take the streetcar!" I blurted, suddenly shocked that she actually meant to leave me. I thought I could hear the clear-chromatic chimes, see the shimmering colours on the wall: I fell against her and cried, and there in my crying I knew that she would die. I can still remember the touch of her hand on my head and the smell of her thick woollen sweater pressed against my face. "I will always be with you, Little Sek-Lung, but in a different way . . . you'll see."

---

[5] Traditionally, the family of the deceased must raise a beacon so that the loved one may visit one last time before departing this world. The beacon may be a windchime or something familiar to the spirit.

Months went by, and nothing happened. Then one late September evening, when I had just come home from Chinese School, Grandmama was preparing supper when she looked out our kitchen window and saw a cat—a long, lean white cat—jump into our garbage pail and knock it over. She ran out to chase it away, shouting curses at it. She did not have her thick sweater on and when she came back into the house, a chill gripped her. She leaned against the door. "That was not a cat," she said, and the odd tone of her voice caused my father to look with alarm at her. "I cannot take back my curses. It is too late." She took hold of my father's arm: "It was all white and had pink eyes like sacred fire."

My father stared at this, and they both looked pale. My brothers and sister, clearing the table, froze in their gestures.

"The fog has confused you," Stepmother said. "It was just a cat."

But Grandmama shook her head, for she knew it was a sign. "I will not live forever," she said. "I am prepared."

The next morning she was confined to her bed with a severe cold. Sitting by her, playing with some of my toys, I asked her about the cat. "Why did father jump at the cat with the pink eyes? He didn't see it, you did."

"But he and your mother know what it means."

"What?"

"My friend, the juggler, the magician, was as pale as white jade, and he had pink eyes." I thought she would begin to tell me one of her stories, a tale of enchantment or of a wondrous adventure, but she only paused to swallow; her eyes glittered, lost in memory. She took my hand, gently opening and closing her fingers over it. "Sek-Lung," she sighed, "*he* has come back to me."[6] Then Grandmama sank back into her pillow and the embroidered flowers lifted to frame her wrinkled face. I saw her hand over my own and my own began to tremble. I fell fitfully asleep by her side. When I woke up it was dark and her bed was empty. She had been taken to the hospital and I was not permitted to visit.

A few days after that she died of the complications of pneumonia. Immediately after her death my father came home and said nothing to us but walked up the stairs to her room, pulled aside the drawn lace curtains of her window and lifted the windchimes to the sky.

I began to cry and quickly put my hand in my pocket for a handkerchief. Instead, caught between my fingers, was the small, round firmness of the jade peony. In my mind's eye, I saw Grandmama smile and heard, softly, the pink centre beat like a beautiful, cramped heart.

---

[6]Certain sects of Buddhists believe the soul is transmigrated into another form in order to return to the world to work off Karma or the consequences of desire. To rid one's self of the Karmic wheel, enlightenment must be attained.

After Reading

1. Select two incidents from the story that reveal the tensions created between the generations due to the family's emigration from China to Canada.

2. State the **theme** of this story and write two paragraphs giving evidence for your choice.

3. Identify two or three significant **character** traits of Sek-Lung, the young **narrator** of the story, and give evidence from the text that supports your choices.

4. Make a list of words that are new or unfamiliar to you as used in the story and check their meanings in a dictionary. Add them to your new or unfamiliar words list.

5. Write a paragraph explaining the **symbolic** meaning the jade peony has for the grandmother. Write a second paragraph explaining the meaning it has for the narrator at the end of the story.

6. Explain the differences between how the family thinks its Canadian neighbours and friends view the behaviour of the grandmother and how they actually do view her.

7. Many Canadians think of themselves as hyphenated Canadians (e.g., French-Canadian or Chinese-Canadian), as the narrator does in the second paragraph of this story. Prepare a brief **report** to the class describing the impact of these terms on Canadian society.

8. Keefer and Pender Streets are in Vancouver. Honan is a province in southern China. Look up both in an atlas and, based on that information and the story, prepare a short report on the physical and psychological distance between the two places.

9. Using found objects, construct a wind chime like the ones described in the story.

As I Grew Older

LANGSTON HUGHES

Before Reading

1. a) Make a list of goals or dreams you had as a young child. How many
        of them came true?

    b) Make a list of dreams you have now. What are you doing to work
        toward these dreams?

It was a long time ago.
I have almost forgotten my dream.
But it was there then,
In front of me,
5   Bright like a sun—
My dream.

And then the wall rose,
Rose slowly,
Slowly,
10   Between me and my dream.
Rose slowly, slowly,
Dimming,
Hiding,
The light of my dream.
15   Rose until it touched the sky—
The wall.

Shadow.
I am black.

I lie down in the shadow.
20 No longer the light of my dream before me,
Above me.
Only the thick wall.
Only the shadow.

My hands!
25 My dark hands!
Break through the wall!
Find my dream!
Help me to shatter this darkness,
To smash this night,
30 To break this shadow
Into a thousand lights of sun,
Into a thousand whirling dreams
Of sun!

After Reading

1. In two sentences, retell the events of the poem.

2. a) The poet wrote the first two **stanzas** in the past tense and then shifted into the present tense. Considering the **theme** of the poem, explain why this shift is effective.

   b) The poem has many **sentence fragments** and exclamations. Defend the writer's use of sentence fragments. (See The Reference Shelf, page 242.)

3. Using both print and visuals, make a poster that represents the poem's **theme**.

4. In a group of two or three, create a choral reading of the poem. Be prepared to explain the effects you were trying to achieve through your reading. As you listen to other groups perform, take note of the **mood** they have tried to capture.

5. Briefly research Langston Hughes' life. Prepare a report discussing how your understanding of the poem changes with this background information.

Priscilla and the Wimps

RICHARD PECK

*". . . she could have put together a gang that would
turn Klutter's Kobras into garter snakes."*

Before Reading

1. In a **journal** entry, write about a time someone intimidated you or
   about a time you intimidated someone else.

2. Discuss this statement with the class: "Schools should be a safe
   place for all students and should not tolerate any type of violence
   or intimidation".

Listen, there was a time when you couldn't
even go to the *rest room* around this school
without a pass. And I'm not talking about
those little pink tickets made out by some
teacher. I'm talking about a pass that
could cost anywhere up to a buck, sold by
Monk Klutter.

Not that Mighty Monk ever touched
money, not in public. The gang he ran,
which ran the school for him, was his collection agency. They were Klutter's Kobras,
a name spelled out in nail-heads on six
well-known black plastic windbreakers.

Monk's threads were more . . . subtle.
A pile-lined suede battle jacket with lizard-
skin flaps over tailored Levis and a pair of
ostrich-skin boots, brassed-toed and suitable for kicking people around. One of his
Kobras did nothing all day but walk a half
step behind Monk, carrying a fitted bag
with Monk's gym shoes, a roll of rest-room
passes, a cashbox, and a switchblade that
Monk gave himself manicures with at
lunch over at the Kobras' table.

Speaking of lunch, there were a few
cases of advanced malnutrition among the
newer kids. The ones who were a little
slow in handing over a cut of their lunch
money and were therefore barred from the
cafeteria. Monk ran a tight ship.

I admit it. I'm five foot five, and when the Kobras slithered by, with or without Monk, I shrank. And I admit this, too: I paid up on a regular basis. And I might add: so would you.

This school was old Monk's Garden of Eden. Unfortunately for him, there was a serpent in it. The reason Monk didn't recognize trouble when it was staring him in the face is that the serpent in the Kobras' Eden was a girl.

Practically every guy in school could show you his scars. Fang marks from Kobras, you might say. And they were all highly visible in the shower room: lumps, lacerations, blue bruises, you name it. But girls usually got off with a warning.

Except there was this one girl named Priscilla Roseberry. Picture a girl named Priscilla Roseberry, and you'll be light years off. Priscilla was, hands down, the largest student in our particular institution of learning. I'm not talking fat. I'm talking big. Even beautiful, in a bionic way. Priscilla wasn't inclined toward organized crime. Otherwise, she could have put together a gang that would turn Klutter's Kobras into garter snakes.

Priscilla was basically a loner except she had one friend. A little guy named Melvin Detweiler. You talk about The Odd Couple. Melvin's one of the smallest guys above midget status ever seen. A really nice guy, but, you know—little. They even had lockers next to each other, in the same bank as mine. I don't know what they had going. I'm not saying this was a romance. After all, people deserve their privacy.

Priscilla was sort of above everything, if you'll pardon a pun. And very calm, as only the very big can be. If there was anybody who didn't notice Klutter's Kobras, it was Priscilla.

Until one winter day after school when we were all grabbing our coats out of our lockers. And hurrying, since Klutter's Kobras made sweeps of the halls for after-school shakedowns.

Anyway, up to Melvin's locker swaggers one of the Kobras. Never mind his name. Gang members don't need names. They've got group identity. He reaches down and grabs little Melvin by the neck and slams his head against his locker door. The sound of skull against steel rippled all the way down the locker row, speeding the crowds on their way.

"Okay, let's see your pass," snarls the Kobra.

"A pass for what this time?" Melvin asks, probably still dazed.

"Let's call it a pass for very short people," says the Kobra, "a dwarf tax." He wheezes a little Kobra chuckle at his own wittiness. And already he's reaching for Melvin's wallet with the hand that isn't circling Melvin's windpipe. All this time, of course, Melvin and the Kobra are standing in Priscilla's big shadow.

She's taking her time shoving her books into her locker and pulling on a very large-size coat. Then, quicker than the eye, she brings the side of her enormous hand down in a chop that breaks the Kobra's hold on Melvin's throat. You could hear a pin drop in the hallway. Nobody'd ever laid a finger on a Kobra, let alone a hand the size of Priscilla's.

Then Priscilla, who hardly ever says anything to anybody except to Melvin, says to the Kobra, "Who's your leader, wimp?"

This practically blows the Kobra away. First he's chopped by a girl, and now she's acting like she doesn't know Monk Klutter, the Head Honcho of the World. He's so amazed, he tells her. "Monk Klutter."

"Never heard of him," Priscilla mentions. "Send him to see me." The Kobra just backs away from her like the whole situation is too big for him, which it is.

Pretty soon Monk himself slides up. He jerks his head once, and his Kobras slither off down the hall. He's going to handle this interesting case personally. "Who is it around here doesn't know Monk Klutter?"

He's standing inches from Priscilla, but since he'd have to look up at her, he doesn't. "Never heard of him," says Priscilla.

Monk's not happy with this answer, but by now he's spotted Melvin, who's grown smaller in spite of himself. Monk breaks his own rule by reaching for Melvin with his own hands. "Kid," he said, "you're going to have to educate your girl friend."

His hands never quite make it to Melvin. In a move of pure poetry Priscilla has Monk in a hammerlock. His neck's popping like gunfire, and his head's bowed under the immense weight of her forearm. His suede jacket's peeling back, showing pile.

Priscilla's behind him in another easy motion. And with a single mighty thrust

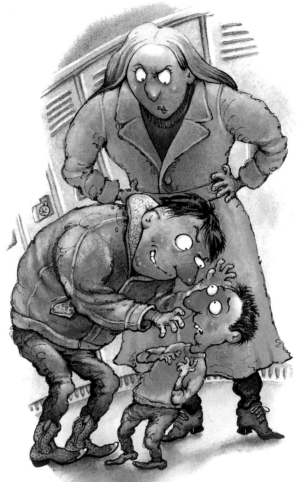

forward, frog-marches Monk into her own locker. It's incredible. His ostrich-skin boots click once in the air. And suddenly he's gone, neatly wedged into the locker, a perfect fit. Priscilla bangs the door shut, twirls the lock, and strolls out of school. Melvin goes with her, of course, trotting along below her shoulder. The last stragglers leave quietly.

Well, this is where fate, an even bigger force than Priscilla, steps in. It snows all that night, a blizzard. The whole town ices up. And school closes for a week.

After Reading

1. This story is a classic example of a **surprise ending**. With a partner, write a **report** on how the author has prepared the reader for the ending and whether the ending is effective.

2. Despite the serious subject matter, the story still manages to have a pleasant comic **tone**. Explain how the choice of names for the characters and the use of **alliteration** help to keep the tone light. Suggest other ways in which the author maintains the comic tone of the story.

3. In paragraph six of the story, the school is described as "Monk's Garden of Eden". This is an **allusion** to the story of Adam and Eve in the book of Genesis in the Bible. Research the role of the serpent in the Biblical story and decide whether the allusion adds meaning to the story.

4. Write a **monologue** that expresses the thoughts of Monk during the first few minutes he is in the locker.

5. Look up the word *fate* in a dictionary. Evaluate its use in the last paragraph of the story.

6. As a class, **role play** the trial of Priscilla Roseberry for the murder of Mighty Monk Klutter. Assign roles to members of the class to play Priscilla, the defense and prosecuting attorneys, and witnesses. Class members who do not have one of these roles can be members of the jury.

7. The **plot** of this story and of "On the Sidewalk, Bleeding" are based on membership in teenage gangs. After reading both stories, prepare a short **research report** on teenage gangs. Have a class discussion about the appeal and dangers of membership in a gang.

8. This story is **fiction**. If the incidents were real, the ending could have been tragic. Write an **essay** on the steps students can take to keep their schools safe.

On the Sidewalk, Bleeding

EVAN HUNTER

"He was not a Royal. He was simply Andy . . ."

Before Reading

In your **journal**, describe aspects of your personal appearance (e.g., hair, clothing, hats, make-up, jewellery) that help create your identity.

The boy lay bleeding in the rain. He was sixteen years old, and he wore a bright purple silk jacket, and the lettering across the back of the jacket read THE ROYALS. The boy's name was Andy, and the name was delicately scripted in black thread on the front of the jacket, just over the heart. *Andy*.

He had been stabbed ten minutes ago. The knife had entered just below his rib cage and had been drawn across his body violently, tearing a wide gap in his flesh. He lay on the sidewalk with the March rain drilling his jacket and drilling his body and washing away the blood that poured from his open wound. He had known excruciating pain when the knife had torn across his body, and then suddenly comparative relief when the blade pulled away. He had heard the voice saying, "That's for you, Royal!" and then the sound of footsteps hurrying into the rain, and then he had fallen to the sidewalk, clutching his stomach, trying to stop the flow of blood.

He tried to yell for help, but he had no voice. He did not know why his voice had deserted him, or why the rain had become so suddenly fierce, or why there was an open hole in his body from which his life ran redly, steadily. It was 11:30 p.m., but he did not know the time.

There was another thing he did not know.

He did not know he was dying. He lay on the sidewalk, bleeding, and he thought only: *That was a fierce rumble. They got me good that time*, but he did not

98

know he was dying. He would have been frightened had he known. In his ignorance, he lay bleeding and wishing he could cry out for help, but there was no voice in his throat. There was only the bubbling of blood from between his lips whenever he opened his mouth to speak. He lay silent in his pain, waiting, waiting for someone to find him.

He could hear the sound of automobile tires hushed on the muzzle of rain-swept streets, far away at the other end of the long alley. He lay with his face pressed to the sidewalk, and he could see the splash of neon far away at the other end of the alley, tinting the pavement red and green, slickly brilliant in the rain.

He wondered if Laura would be angry.

He had left the jump to get a package of cigarettes. He had told her he would be back in a few minutes, and then he had gone downstairs and found the candy store closed. He knew that Alfredo's on the next block would be open until at least two, and he had started through the alley, and that was when he'd been ambushed. He could hear the faint sound of music now, coming from a long, long way off, and he wondered if Laura was dancing, wondered if she had missed him yet. Maybe she thought he wasn't coming back. Maybe she thought he'd cut out for good. Maybe she'd already left the jump and gone home. He thought of her face, the brown eyes and the jet-black hair, and thinking of her he forgot his pain a little, forgot that blood was rushing from his body. Someday he would marry Laura. Someday he would marry her, and they would have a lot of kids, and then they would get out of the neighborhood. They would move to a clean project in the Bronx, or maybe they would move to Staten Island. When they were married, when they had kids. . . .

He heard footsteps at the other end of the alley, and he lifted his cheek from the sidewalk and looked into the darkness and tried to cry out, but again there was only a soft hissing bubble of blood on his mouth.

The man came down the alley. He had not seen Andy yet. He walked, and then stopped to lean against the brick of the building, and then walked again. He saw Andy then and came toward him, and he stood over him for a long time, the minutes ticking, ticking, watching him and not speaking.

Then he said, "What'sa matter, buddy?"

Andy could not speak, and he could barely move. He lifted his face slightly and looked up at the man, and in the rain-swept alley he smelled the sickening odor of alcohol and realized the man was drunk. He did not feel any particular panic. He did not know he was dying, and so he felt only mild disappointment that the man who had found him was drunk.

The man was smiling.

"Did you fall down, buddy?" he asked. "You mus' be as drunk as I am." He grinned, seemed to remember why he had entered the alley in the first place, and said, "Don' go away. I'll be ri' back."

The man lurched away. Andy heard his footsteps, and then the sound of the man colliding with a garbage can, and some mild swearing, and then the sound of the man urinating, lost in the steady wash of the rain. He waited for the man to come back.

It was 11:39.

When the man returned, he squatted alongside Andy. He studied him with drunken dignity.

"You gonna catch cold here," he said. "What'sa matter? You like layin' in the wet?"

Andy could not answer. The man tried to focus his eyes on Andy's face. The rain spattered around them.

"You like a drink?"

Andy shook his head.

"I gotta bottle. Here," the man said. He pulled a pint bottle from his inside jacket pocket. He uncapped it and extended it to Andy. Andy tried to move, but pain wrenched him back flat against the sidewalk.

"Take it," the man said. He kept watching Andy. "Take it." When Andy did not move, he said, "Nev' mind, I'll have one m'self." He tilted the bottle to his lips, and then wiped the back of his hand across his mouth. "You too young to be drinkin', anyway. Should be 'shamed of yourself, drunk an' layin' in a alley, all wet. Shame on you. I gotta good minda calla cop."

Andy nodded. Yes, he tried to say. Yes, call a cop. Please. Call one.

"Oh, you don't like that, huh?" the drunk said. "You don' wanna cop to fin' you all drunk an' wet in a alley, huh? Okay, buddy. This time you get off easy." He got to his feet. "This time you lucky," he said. He waved broadly at Andy, and then almost lost his footing. "S'long, buddy," he said.

Wait, Andy thought. *Wait, please, I'm bleeding.*

"S'long," the drunk said again. "I see you aroun'," and then he staggered off up the alley.

Andy lay and thought: *Laura, Laura. Are you dancing?*

The couple came into the alley suddenly. They ran into the alley, together, running from the rain, the boy holding the girl's elbow, the girl spreading a newspaper over her head to protect her hair. Andy lay crumpled against the pavement, and he watched them run into the alley laughing, and then duck into the doorway not ten feet from him.

"Man, what rain!" the boy said. "You could drown out there."

"I have to get home," the girl said. "It's late, Freddie. I have to get home."

"We got time," Freddie said. "Your people won't raise a fuss if you're a little late. Not with this kind of weather."

"It's dark," the girl said, and she giggled.

"Yeah," the boy answered, his voice very low.

"Freddie . . . ?"

"Um?"

"You're . . . you're standing very close to me."

"Um."

There was a long silence. Then the girl said, "Oh," only that single word, and Andy knew she'd been kissed, and he suddenly hungered for Laura's mouth. It was then that he wondered if he would ever kiss Laura again. It was then that he wondered if he was dying.

No, he thought, I can't be dying, not from a little street rumble, not from just getting cut. Guys get cut all the time in rumbles. I can't be dying. No, that's stupid. That don't make any sense at all.

"You shouldn't," the girl said.

"Why not?"

"I don't know."

"Do you like it?"

"Yes."

"So?"

"I don't know."

"I love you, Angela," the boy said.

"I love you, too, Freddie," the girl said, and Andy listened and thought: *I love you, Laura. Laura, I think maybe I'm dying. Laura, this is stupid but I think maybe I'm dying. Laura, I think I'm dying!*

He tried to speak. He tried to move. He tried to crawl toward the doorway where he could see the two figures in embrace. He tried to make a noise, a sound, and a grunt came from his lips, and then he tried again, and another grunt came, a low animal grunt of pain.

"What was that?" the girl said, suddenly alarmed, breaking away from the boy.

"I don't know," he answered.

"Go look, Freddie."

"No. Wait."

Andy moved his lips again. Again the sound came from him.

"Freddie!"

"What?"

"I'm scared."

"I'll go see," the boy said.

He stepped into the alley. He walked over to where Andy lay on the ground. He stood over him, watching him.

"You all right?" he asked.

"What is it?" Angela said from the doorway.

"Somebody's hurt," Freddie said.

"Let's get out of here," Angela said.

"No. Wait a minute." He knelt down beside Andy. "You cut?" he asked.

Andy nodded. The boy kept looking at him. He saw the lettering on the jacket then. THE ROYALS. He turned to Angela.

"He's a Royal," he said.

"Let's . . . what . . . what do you want to do, Freddie?"

"I don't know. I don't want to get mixed up in this. He's a Royal. We help him and the Guardians'll be down our necks. I don't want to get mixed up in this, Angela."

"Is he . . . is he hurt bad?"

"Yeah, it looks that way."

"What shall we do?"

"I don't know."

"We can't leave him here in the rain." Angela hesitated. "Can we?"

"If we get a cop, the Guardians'll find out who," Freddie said. "I don't know, Angela. I don't know."

Angela hesitated a long time before answering. Then she said, "I have to get home, Freddie. My people will begin to worry."

"Yeah," Freddie said. He looked at Andy again. "You all right?" he asked. Andy lifted his face from the sidewalk, and his eyes said: *Please, please help me,* and maybe Freddie read what his eyes were saying, and maybe he didn't.

Behind him, Angela said, "Freddie, let's get out of here! Please!" There was urgency in her voice, urgency bordering on the edge of panic. Freddie stood up. He looked at Andy again, and then mumbled,

"I'm sorry," and then he took Angela's arm and together they ran toward the neon splash at the other end of the alley.

Why, they're afraid of the Guardians, Andy thought in amazement. But why should they be? I wasn't afraid of the Guardians. I never turkeyed out of a rumble with the Guardians. I got heart. But I'm bleeding.

The rain was soothing somehow. It was a cold rain, but his body was hot all over, and the rain helped to cool him. He had always liked rain. He could remember sitting in Laura's house one time, the rain running down the windows, and just looking out over the street, watching the people running from the rain. That was when he'd first joined the Royals. He could remember how happy he was the Royals had taken him. The Royals and the Guardians, two of the biggest. He was a Royal. There had been meaning to the title.

Now, in the alley, with the cold raining washing his hot body, he wondered about the meaning. If he died, he was Andy. He was not a Royal. He was simply Andy, and he was dead. And he wondered suddenly if the Guardians who had ambushed him and knifed him had ever once realized he was Andy? Had they known that he was Andy, or had they simply known that he was a Royal wearing a purple silk jacket? Had they stabbed *him*, Andy, or had they only stabbed the jacket and the title, and what good was the title if you were dying?

I'm Andy, he screamed wordlessly. *I'm Andy, I'm Andy!*

An old lady stopped at the other end of the alley. The garbage cans were stacked there, beating noisily in the rain. The old lady carried an umbrella with broken ribs, carried it with all the dignity of a queen. She stepped into the mouth of the alley, a shopping bag over one arm. She lifted the lids of the garbage cans delicately, and she did not hear Andy grunt because she was a little deaf and because the rain was beating a steady relentless tattoo on the cans. She had been searching and foraging for the better part of the night. She collected her string and her newspapers, and an old hat with a feather on it from one of the garbage cans, and a broken footstool from another of the cans. And then she delicately replaced the lids and lifted her umbrella high and walked out of the alley mouth with queenly dignity. She had worked swiftly and soundlessly, and now she was gone.

The alley looked very long now. He could see people passing at the other end of it, and he wondered who the people were, and he wondered if he would ever get to know them, wondered who it was on the Guardians who had stabbed him, who had plunged the knife into his body.

"That's for you, Royal!" the voice had said, and then the footsteps, his arms being released by the others, the fall to the pavement. "That's for you, Royal!" Even in his pain, even as he collapsed, there had been some sort of pride in knowing he was a Royal. Now there was no pride at all. With the rain beginning to chill him, with the blood pouring steadily between his fingers, he knew only a sort of dizziness, and within the giddy dizziness, he could only think: *I want to be Andy*.

It was not very much to ask of the world.

He watched the world passing at the other end of the alley. The world didn't know he was Andy. The world didn't know he was alive. He wanted to say, "Hey, I'm alive! Hey, look at me! I'm alive! Don't you know I'm alive? Don't you know I exist?"

He felt weak and very tired. He felt alone and wet and feverish and chilled, and he knew he was going to die now, and the knowledge made him suddenly sad. He was not frightened. For some reason, he was not frightened. He was only filled with an overwhelming sadness that his life would be over at sixteen. He felt all at once as if he had never done anything, never seen anything, never been anywhere. There were so many things to do and he wondered why he'd never thought of them before, wondered why the rumbles and the jumps and the purple jacket had always seemed so important to him before, and now they seemed like such small things in a world he was missing, a world that was rushing past at the other end of the alley.

I don't want to die, he thought. *I haven't lived yet.*

It seemed very important to him that he take off the purple jacket. He was very close to dying, and when they found him, he did not want them to say, "Oh, it's a Royal." With great effort, he rolled over onto his back. He felt the pain tearing at his stomach when he moved, a pain he did not think was possible. But he wanted to take off the jacket. If he never did another thing, he wanted to take off the jacket. The jacket had only one meaning now, and that was a very simple meaning.

If he had not been wearing the jacket, he would not have been stabbed. The knife had not been plunged in hatred of Andy. The knife hated only the purple jacket. The jacket was a stupid meaningless thing that was robbing him of his life. He wanted the jacket off his back. With an enormous loathing, he wanted the jacket off his back.

He lay struggling with the shiny wet material. His arms were heavy, and pain ripped fire across his body whenever he moved. But he squirmed and fought and twisted until one arm was free and then the other, and then he rolled away from the jacket and lay quite still, breathing heavily, listening to the sound of his breathing and the sound of the rain and thinking: *Rain is sweet, I'm Andy.*

She found him in the alleyway a minute past midnight. She left the dance to look for him, and when she found him she knelt beside him and said, "Andy, it's me, Laura."

He did not answer her. She backed away from him, tears springing into her eyes, and then she ran from the alley hysterically and did not stop running until she found the cop.

And now, standing with the cop, she looked down at him, and the cop rose and said, "He's dead," and all the crying was out of her now. She stood in the rain and said nothing, looking at the dead boy on the pavement, and looking at the purple jacket that rested a foot away from his body.

The cop picked up the jacket and turned it over in his hands.

"A Royal, huh?" he said.

The rain seemed to beat more steadily now, more fiercely.

She looked at the cop and, very quietly, she said, "His name is Andy."

The cop slung the jacket over his arm. He took out his black pad, and he flipped it open to a blank page.

"A Royal," he said.

Then he began writing.

After Reading

1. With a partner, prepare a brief **report** for the class on one of the following:
    *   the importance of the **setting** (time, place, weather) to the story
    *   the significance of the four **characters** who come into the alley as Andy lies dying, but do not help him
    *   **suspense** in the story
    *   the **symbolic** meaning of Andy's jacket in the story

2. Although she seems to have a small part in the story, references to Laura provide the reader with important information. Explain Laura's importance to our understanding of
    *   Andy
    *   the police officer
    *   the **theme** of the story

3. Identify three significant character traits of Andy and give evidence from the text that supports your choices.

4. This story contains many effective descriptive sentences. Select one and explain how it contributes to the story.

5. State the **theme** of this story and write a few paragraphs giving evidence for your choice.

6. Write a **script** to present to the class dramatizing the events of this story. You will need seven actors and one member to act as director and sound effects person.

7. Write a **newspaper report** of the incident in this story. Give it a suitable headline.

Mistaken

VIKRAM SETH

Before Reading

Think about a time you thought you knew someone and waved or said hello before realizing he or she was a perfect stranger. How did you feel?

I smiled at you because I thought that you
Were someone else; you smiled back; and there grew
Between two strangers in a library
Something that seemed like love; but you loved me
5   (If that's the word) because you thought that I
Was other than I was. And by and by
We found we'd been mistaken all the while
From that first glance, that first mistaken smile.

After Reading

1. At first, this looks like a **free verse** poem. Record the elements that prevent it from being free verse.

2. Describe the **tone** the poet is trying to create in this poem. Write out the words or phrases that capture that tone.

3. With a partner, examine the line divisions. For each, explain what effect is created by breaking the line in that particular place. Consider meaning, **rhythm**, feeling, and emphasis when answering.

4. Defend the poet's use of the three semicolons and the one set of parentheses in his poem.

5. Make a list of **topics** for this poem, and beside each topic create a statement of **theme**. Choose the best theme statement and defend it in a well-written paragraph.

How We Met

KRISTIN RUSHOWY

"It was the first time I'd actually met a guy."

Before Reading

How would you feel if your family told you that they had already selected your marriage partner?

Raeesa and Zein Dawood's marriage was arranged by their parents. They met when Raeesa was 15 and living in Karachi, Pakistan, and Zein was a student at York University. Raeesa, now 23, came to Canada in 1994 after marrying Zein. She's in her final year of a commerce degree at University of Toronto. Zein, 31, was also born in Karachi but his family moved to Canada when he was 6. He attended Upper Canada College and graduated from York in 1993 with a degree in administrative studies. He's now a manager at his family's yarn manufacturing company. The Dawoods have a three-year-old son, Aamir, and live in King City with Zein's parents.

Raeesa: We didn't know each other, but our families come from the same community in Karachi. His extended family still lives there, and his parents visit a lot. Basically, his grandparents and parents wanted a girl from there. His brother also married a girl from Pakistan.

His family had heard a little bit about me and my parents had heard about him. There are many intermarriages between our families, going way back; we share many aunts and uncles.

After his brother got married, there was a lot of talk about Zein, that he was very smart and doing his degree at York University, and how other women wanted him for their daughters. Zein was in Pakistan in December of 1990 for a cousin's wedding, I was about 15 years old then. His family wanted to see me.

My parents took a while thinking about it because I wanted to study abroad. They wanted me to decide if I wanted to get married or not because I was still quite young. But my parents really liked his family, they thought it was a very good opportunity for me.

Zein was actually leaving the night we first met each other—he was still in university and had to get back for some courses. His whole family came to see me at my place. We all talked, and then Zein and I spent time by ourselves.

He was so shy, but so nice. I was nervous, but not as nervous as he. He was biting his nails.

It was the first time I'd actually met a guy. My parents had three or four proposals for me before that, but they had never had me meet anyone. It shows they thought of him so exceptionally well they allowed him to meet me. I was the first person he met. I could see that he liked me the minute he saw me.

We talked about trivial things. I asked him what his favourite colour was and he just said yellow. To this day I've never seen him own anything yellow. He asked me about what I liked to do, what my hobbies were, whether I could cook. I told him, "No, I don't know how to cook."

My mother thought Zein was very kind and very gentle and shy. It was nice for her, she didn't want anyone very Westernized for me, she could see in his attitude that he had been brought up according to our culture. My parents were looking for someone from a very good family, an educated family. They knew I wanted someone who was intelligent and

broad-minded so I could study, do what I wanted.

Our parents brought us together, but it was up to us. I had a lot of time to think about it. We had a long engagement, my parents wanted it that way so we could get to know each other and he would have time to visit. We started calling, and when he came to visit in the summers we would spend every day together, whether with the family or without. I came to Canada for a month and we had a nice engagement party.

When I first met him, I knew that I would be marrying his family, not just him. Even if you don't live with your in-laws, you're in contact with them all the time. I met my mother-in-law at the same time I met Zein, and right away I knew that I liked her, we just kind of bonded immediately. It was fantastic. I mean, half the battle's won.

Generally, in our community, it's up to the boy's parents to propose and then the girl's parents say yes or no. It was quite obvious by the time they left my place that they wanted me. The next day, the first thing in the morning, his grandmother called my mother. My mother said she'd have to think about it.

Then my parents decided after four or five days to say yes. I was their baby, and even though I have an elder sister who got married eight years before me, my mother was a little bit apprehensive, especially because Zein lived in Canada.

Zein was on a ski trip when we got engaged. He obviously knew he was getting engaged because he called me when he got home. Then he came to visit me in

June. Up to then, I wasn't sure if I'd done the right thing. But when I saw him again, it dawned on me.

It was more his nature, his character. Even though he's older than me, he was never condescending or tried to treat me like a kid. He treats me with respect.

To tell you the truth, we didn't have much in common in the beginning. I'm a very artsy person, I like going to museums and reading a lot of books and I'm interested in history. He's more into computers and sports. But we want to make each other happy, so I've become a computer nut and a big Maple Leafs fan, and he hangs around in museums.

I travelled a lot when I was growing up, I knew so much about Western lifestyle. I adjusted very quickly to Canada. In fact, I find sometimes Zein's more traditional than I am because he knows what he knows from when he was a kid, stuff that's 20 years old now.

It's not just me and him, our families have come together. I'm committed to his family and I'm sure he's committed to mine. Our marriage is something to be proud of for them.

Zein: I'd heard Raeesa was extremely intelligent, and that she was the prettiest woman in Pakistan. It was really my mother who set this up, she was always going back to Pakistan and talking with my grandmother to see who was the best person for me. Then we were in Pakistan and she said there was someone she'd found for me, and would I be interested in meeting her?

She hadn't met Raeesa, but we'd seen Raeesa at a wedding a few days before—by chance our paths crossed—and had gotten information about her.

That first time we met, Raeesa played the piano for me and showed me her paintings. She's very talented. We talked about what she was doing, where she wanted to go in the future with her studies. I wasn't nervous about meeting her father and brother, but when we were first alone, I was nervous. I didn't know what to ask her or what to do. You're meeting someone who could be your future wife.

But she put me at ease, made me feel comfortable. I felt as if I was home. I went home and my parents and I discussed it. I told them to go ahead with it. I went back to Canada on a Friday, and on the Monday got a call saying I was engaged.

I was thinking about it after, "Is she the right person?" You can't really judge a person in a half an hour. I didn't know then it was going to work out as well as it has. We were in constant contact after getting engaged, calling and writing to each other. I told all my friends and showed them her picture. They couldn't believe I got that lucky and were asking my mom to get them engaged too.

I wanted an arranged marriage because it works. My older brother had an arranged marriage and it worked. My cousins did, too. There was never any pressure not to have an arranged marriage because that's the way I wanted it, although my other friends from university were dating and getting engaged here.

After Reading

1. Based on the information in this article, write the **dialogue** that might have taken place at the first meeting of Raeesa and Zein Dawood.

2. Create a list of the qualities of a successful marriage that are identified in the description of the Dawood's relationship. Compare your list with a partner and discuss whether the basis for a marriage that is not arranged would be any different.

3. Pakistan is not the only country that encourages arranged marriages. Prepare a short **research report** on other cultures in which arranged marriages are common.

4. Write a **journal** entry in which you explain the pros and cons of an arranged marriage as a means of selecting a spouse for you.

5. **Interview** a parent or another adult and write your own "How We Met" article.

A Marriage Proposal

ANTON CHEKHOV

"What a way to enter matrimonial bliss!"

Before Reading

Make a list titled What I Look for in a Perfect Marriage Partner. As a class, find qualities you all agree with.

Note: In Russia, a person is sometimes referred to as the son or daughter of his or her father. Hence, Ivan Lomov, the son of Vassil Lomov, is called Ivan Vassilevitch (son of Vassil). Stepan Chubukov, the son of Stepan Chubukov Sr., is referred to as Stepan Stepanovitch (son of Stepan). Natalia Chubukov, the daughter of Stepan Chubukov, is referred to as Natalia Stepanovna (daughter of Stepan).

CHARACTERS

Chubukov—*a wealthy, middle-aged gentleman who owns an estate in nineteenth-century Russia*

Natalia—*his daughter, an unmarried woman ready to take a husband*

Lomov—*a neighbour gentleman, a neurotic bachelor of thirty-five*

(Chubukov's *mansion—the living room. Lomov enters, formally dressed in evening jacket, white gloves, top hat. He is nervous from the start.*)

Chubukov: (*Rising*) Well, look who's here! Ivan Vassilevitch! (*Shakes his hand warmly*) What a surprise, old man! How are you?

Lomov: Oh, not too bad. And you?

Chubukov: Oh, we manage, we manage. Do sit down, please. You know, you've been neglecting your neighbours, my dear fellow. It's been ages. Say, why the formal dress? Tails, gloves, and so forth. Where's the funeral, my boy? Where are you headed?

Lomov: Oh, nowhere. I mean, here; just to see you, my dear Stepan Stepanovitch.

Chubukov: Then why the full dress, old boy? It's not New Year's, and so forth.

111

Lomov: Well, you see, it's like this. I have come here, my dear Stepan Stepanovitch, to bother you with a request. More than once, or twice, or more than that, it has been my privilege to apply to you for assistance in things, and you've always, well, responded. I mean, well, you have. Yes. Excuse me, I'm getting all mixed up. May I have a glass of water, my dear Stepan Stepanovitch? (*Drinks*)

Chubukov: (*Aside*) Wants to borrow some money. Not a chance! (*Aloud*) What can I do for you my dear friend?

Lomov: Well, You see, my dear Stepanitch . . . Excuse me, I mean Stepan my Dearovitch . . . No, I mean, I get all confused, as you can see. To make a long story short, you're the only one who can help me. Of course, I don't deserve it, and there's no reason why I should expect you to, and all that.

Chubukov: Stop beating around the bush! Out with it!

Lomov: In just a minute. I mean, now, right now. The truth is, I have come to ask the hand . . . I mean, your daughter, Natalia Stepanovna, I, I want to marry her!

Chubukov: (*Overjoyed*) Great heavens! Ivan Vassilevitch! Say it again!

Lomov: I have come humbly to ask for the hand . . .

Chubukov: (*Interrupting*) You're a prince! I'm overwhelmed, delighted, and so forth. Yes, indeed, and all that! (*Hugs and kisses* Lomov) This is just what I've been hoping for. It's my fondest dream come true. (*Sheds a tear*) And, you know, I've always looked upon you, my boy, as if you were my own son. May God grant to both of you His Mercy and His Love, and so forth. Oh, I have been wishing for this . . . But why am I being so idiotic? It's just that I'm off my rocker with joy, my boy! Completely off my rocker! Oh, with all my soul I'm . . . I'll go get Natalia, and so forth.

Lomov: (*Deeply moved*) Dear Stepan Stepanovitch, do you think she'll agree?

Chubukov: Why, of course, old friend. Great heavens! As if she wouldn't! Why she's crazy for you! Good God! Like a lovesick cat, and so forth. Be right back. (*Leaves*)

Lomov: God, it's cold. I'm gooseflesh all over, as if I had to take a test. But the main thing is, to make up my mind, and keep it that way. I mean, if I take time out to think, or if I hesitate, or talk about it, or have ideals, or wait for real love, well, I'll just never get married! Brrrr, it's cold! Natalia Stepanovna is an excellent housekeeper. She's not too bad looking. She's had a good education. What more could I ask? Nothing. I'm so nervous, my ears are buzzing. (*Drinks*) Besides, I've just got to get married. I'm thirty-five already. It's sort of a critical age. I've got to settle down and lead a regular life. I mean, I'm always getting palpitations, and I'm nervous, and I get upset so easy. Look, my lips are quivering, and my eyebrow's twitching. The worst thing is the night. Sleeping. I get into bed, doze off, and, suddenly, something inside me jumps. First my head snaps, and then my shoulder blade, and I roll out of bed like a lunatic and try to walk it off. Then I try to go back to sleep, but, as soon as I do, something jumps again! Twenty times a night, sometimes . . .

(Natalia Stepanovna *enters*)

Natalia: Oh, it's only you. All Papa said was: "Go inside, there's a merchant come to collect his goods." How do you do, Ivan Vassilevitch?

Lomov: How do you do, dear Natalia Stepanovna?

Natalia: Excuse my apron, and not being dressed. We're shelling peas. You haven't been around lately. Oh, do sit down. (*They do*) Would you like some lunch?

Lomov: No thanks, I had some.

Natalia: Well, then smoke if you want. (*He doesn't*) The weather's nice today . . . but yesterday, it was so wet the workmen couldn't get a thing done. Have you got much hay in? I felt so greedy I had a whole field done, but now I'm not sure I was right. With the rain it could rot, couldn't it? I should have waited. But why are you so dressed up? Is there a dance or something? Of course, I must say you look splendid, but . . . Well, tell me, why are you so dressed up?

Lomov: (*Excited*) Well, you see, my dear Natalia Stepanovna, the truth is, I made up my mind to ask you to . . . well, to, listen to me. Of course, it'll probably surprise you and even maybe make you angry, but . . . (*Aside*) God it's cold in here!

Natalia: Why, what do you mean? (*A pause*) Well?

Lomov: I'll try to get it over with. I mean, you know, my dear Natalia Stepanovna that I've known, since childhood, even, known, and had the privilege of knowing, your family. My late aunt, and her husband, who, as you know, left me my estate, they always had the greatest respect for your father, and your late mother. The Lomovs and the Chubukovs have always been very friendly, you might even say affectionate. And, of course, you know, our land borders on each other's. My Oxen Meadows touch your birch grove . . .

Natalia: I hate to interrupt you, my dear Ivan Vassilevitch, but you said: "my Oxen Meadows." Do you really think they're yours?

Lomov: Why of course they're mine.

Natalia: What do you mean? The Oxen Meadows are ours, not yours!

Lomov: Oh, no, my dear Natalia Stepanovna, they're mine.

Natalia: Well, this is the first I've heard about it! Where did you get that idea?

Lomov: Where? Why, I mean the Oxen Meadows that are wedged between your birches and the marsh.

Natalia: Yes, of course, they're ours.

Lomov: Oh, no, you're wrong, my dear Natalia Stepanovna, they're mine.

Natalia: Now, come, Ivan Vassilevitch! How long have they been yours?

Lomov: How long? Why, as long as I can remember!

Natalia: Well, really, you can't expect me to believe that!

Lomov: But, you can see for yourself in the deed, my dear Natalia Stepanovna. Of course, there was once a dispute about them, but everyone knows they're mine now. There's nothing to argue about. There was a time when my aunt's grandmother let your father's grandfather's peasants use the land, but they were supposed to bake bricks for her in return. Naturally, after a few years they began to act as if they owned it, but the real truth is . . .

Natalia: That has nothing to do with the case! Both my grandfather and my great-grandfather said that their land went as far as the marsh, which means that the Meadows are ours! There's nothing whatever to argue about. It's foolish.

Lomov: But I can show you the deed, Natalia Stepanovna.

Natalia: You're just making fun of me . . . Great Heavens! Here we have the land for hundreds of years, and suddenly you try to tell us it isn't ours. What's wrong with you, Ivan Vassilevitch? Those meadows aren't even fifteen acres, and they're not worth three hundred rubles, but I just can't stand unfairness! I just can't stand unfairness!

Lomov: But, you must listen to me. Your father's grandfather's peasants, as I've already tried to tell you, they were supposed to bake bricks for my aunt's grandmother. And my aunt's grandmother, why, she wanted to be nice to them . . .

Natalia: It's just nonsense, this whole business about aunts and grandfathers and grandmothers. The Meadows are ours! That's all there is to it!

Lomov: They're mine!

Natalia: Ours! You can go on talking for two days, and you can put on fifteen evening coats and twenty pairs of gloves, but I tell you they're ours, ours, ours!

Lomov: Natalia Stepanovna, I don't want the Meadows! I'm just acting on principle. If you want, I'll give them to you.

Natalia: I'll give them to *you*! Because they're ours! And that's all there is to it! And if I may say so, your behaviour, my dear Ivan Vassilevitch, is very strange. Until now, we've always considered you a good neighbour, even a friend. After all,

last year we lent you our threshing machine, even though it meant putting off our own threshing until November. And here you are treating us like a pack of gypsies. Giving me my own land, indeed! Really! Why that's not being a good neighbour. It's sheer impudence, that's what it is . . .

Lomov: Oh, so you think I'm just a land-grabber? My dear lady, I've never grabbed anybody's land in my whole life, and no-one's going to accuse me of doing it now! (*Quickly walks over to the pitcher and drinks some more water*) The Oxen Meadows are mine!

Natalia: That's a lie. They're ours!

Lomov: Mine!

Natalia: A lie! I'll prove it. I'll send my mowers out there today!

Lomov: What?

Natalia: My mowers will mow it today!

Lomov: I'll kick them out!

Natalia: You just dare!

Lomov: (*Clutching his heart*) The Oxen Meadows are mine! Do you understand? Mine!

Natalia: Please don't shout! You can shout all you want in your own house, but here I must ask you to control yourself.

Lomov: If my heart wasn't palpitating the way it is, if my insides weren't jumping like mad, I wouldn't talk to you so calmly. (*Yelling*) The Oxen Meadows are mine!

Natalia: Ours!

Lomov: Mine!

Natalia: Ours!

Lomov: Mine!

(*Enter* Chubukov)

Chubukov: What's going on? Why all the shouting?

Natalia: Papa, will you please inform this gentleman who owns the Oxen Meadows, he or we?

Chubukov: (*To* Lomov) Why, they're ours, old fellow.

Lomov: But how can they be yours, my dear Stepan Stepanovitch? Be fair. Perhaps my aunt's grandmother did let your grandfather's peasants work the land, and maybe they did get so used to it that they acted as if it was their own, but . . .

Chubukov: Oh, no, no . . . my dear boy. You forget something. The reason the peasants didn't pay your aunt's grandmother, and so forth, was that the land was disputed, even then. Since then it's been settled. Why, everyone knows it's ours.

Lomov: I can prove it's mine.

Chubukov: You can't prove a thing, old boy.

Lomov: Yes I can!

Chubukov: My dear lad, why yell like that? Yelling doesn't prove a thing. Look, I'm not after anything of yours, just as I don't intend to give up anything of mine. Why should I? Besides, if you're going to keep arguing about it, I'd just as soon give the land to the peasants, so there!

Lomov: There's nothing! Where do you get the right to give away someone else's property?

Chubukov: I certainly ought to know if I have the right or not. And you had better realize it, because, my dear young man, I am not used to being spoken to in that tone of voice, and so forth. Besides which, my dear young man, I am twice as old as you are, and I ask you to speak to me without getting yourself into such a tizzy, and so forth!

Lomov: Do you think I'm a fool? First you call my property yours, and then you expect me to keep calm and polite! Good neighbours don't act like that, my dear Stepan Stepanovitch. You're no neighbour, you're a land grabber!

Chubukov: What was that? What did you say?

Natalia: Papa, send the mowers out to the meadows at once!

Chubukov: What did you say, sir?

Natalia: The Oxen Meadows are ours, and we'll never give them up, never, never, never, never!

Lomov: We'll see about that. I'll go to court. I'll show you!

Chubukov: Go to court? Well, go to court, and so forth! I know you, just waiting for a chance to go to court, and so forth. You pettifogging shyster, you! All of your family is like that. The whole bunch of them!

Lomov: You leave my family out of this! The Lomovs have always been honourable, upstanding people, and not a one of them was ever tried for embezzlement, like your grandfather was.

Chubukov: The Lomovs are a pack of lunatics, the whole bunch of them!

Natalia: The whole bunch!

Chubukov: Your grandfather was a drunkard, and what about your other aunt, the one who ran away with the architect? And so forth.

Natalia: And so forth!

Lomov: Your mother was a hunch back! (*Clutches at his heart*) Oh, I've got a stitch in my side . . . My head's whirling . . . Help! Water!

Chubukov: Your father was a rum-soaked gambler.

Natalia: And your aunt was queen of the scandalmongers!

Lomov: My left foot's paralyzed. You're a plotter . . . Oh, my heart. It's an open secret that in the last elections you brib . . . I'm seeing stars! Where's my hat?

Natalia: It's a low-mean, spiteful . . .

Chubukov: And you're a two-faced, malicious schemer!

Lomov: Here's my hat . . . Oh, my heart . . . Where's the door? How do I get out of here? . . . Oh, I think I'm going to die . . . My foot's numb. (*Goes*)

Chubukov: (*Following him*) And don't you ever set foot in my house again!

Natalia: Go to court, indeed! We'll see about that!

(Lomov *staggers out*)

Chubukov: The devil with him!
(*Gets a drink, walks back and forth excited*)
Natalia: What a rascal! How can you trust your neighbours after an incident like that?
Chubukov: The villain! The scarecrow!
Natalia: He's a monster! First he tries to steal our land, and then he has the nerve to yell at you.
Chubukov: Yes, and that turnip, that stupid rooster, has the gall to make a proposal. Some proposal!
Natalia: What proposal?
Chubukov: Why, he came to propose to you.
Natalia: To propose? To me? Why didn't you tell me before?
Chubukov: So he gets all dressed up in his formal clothes. That stuffed sausage, that dried up cabbage!
Natalia: To propose to me? Ohhhh!
(*Falls into a chair and starts wailing*)
Bring him back! Back! Go get him! Bring him back! Ohhhh!
Chubukov: Bring who back?
Natalia: Hurry up, hurry up! I'm sick. Get him! (*Complete hysterics*)
Chubukov: What for? (*To her*) What's the matter with you? (*Clutches his head*) Oh, what a fool I am! I'll shoot myself! I'll hang myself! I ruined her chances!
Natalia: I'm dying. Get him!
Chubukov: All right, all right, right away! Only don't yell!
(*He runs out*)
Natalia: What are they doing to me? Get him! Bring him back! Bring him back!
(*A pause. Chubukov runs in*)
Chubukov: He's coming, and so forth, the snake. Oof! You talk to him. I'm not in the mood.

Natalia: (*Wailing*) Bring him back! Bring him back!
Chubukov: (*Yelling*) I told you, he's coming! Oh Lord, what agony to be the father of a grown-up daughter. I'll cut my throat some day, I swear I will. (*To her*) We cursed him, we insulted him, abused him, kicked him out, and now . . . because you, you . . .
Natalia: Me? It was all your fault?
Chubukov: My fault? What do you mean my fau . . .?
(*Lomov appears in the doorway*)
Talk to him yourself!
(*Goes out. Lomov enters, exhausted*)
Lomov: What palpitations! My heart! And my foot's absolutely asleep. Something keeps giving me a stitch in the side . . .
Natalia: You must forgive us, Ivan Vassilevitch. We all got too excited. I remember now. The Oxen Meadows are yours.
Lomov: My heart's beating something awful. My Meadows. My eyebrows, they're both twitching!
Natalia: Yes, the Meadows are all yours, yes, yours. Do sit down. (*They sit*) We were wrong, of course.
Lomov: I argued on principle. My land isn't worth so much to me, but the principle . . .
Natalia: Oh, yes, of course, the principle, that's what counts. But let's change the subject.
Lomov: Besides, I have evidence. You see, my aunt's grandmother let your father's grandfather's peasants use the land . . .
Natalia: Yes, yes, yes, but forget all that. (*Aside*) I wish I knew how to get him going. (*Aloud*) Are you going to start hunting soon?

Lomov: After the harvest I'll try for grouse. But oh, my dear Natalia Stepanovna, have you heard about the bad luck I've had? You know my dog, Guess? He's gone lame.

Natalia: What a pity. Why?

Lomov: I don't know. He must have twisted his leg, or got in a fight, or something. (*Sighs*) My best dog, to say nothing of the cost. I paid Mironov 125 rubles for him.

Natalia: That was too high, Ivan Vassilevitch.

Lomov: I think it was quite cheap. He's a first class dog.

Natalia: Why Papa only paid eighty-five rubles for Squeezer, and he's much better than Guess.

Lomov: Squeezer better than Guess! What an idea! (*Laughs*) Squeezer better than Guess!

Natalia: Of course he's better. He may still be too young but on points and pedigree, he's a better dog even than any Volchanetsky owns.

Lomov: Excuse me, Natalia Stepanovna, but you're forgetting he's overshot, and overshot dogs are bad hunters.

Natalia: Oh, so he's overshot, is he? Well this is the first time I've heard about it.

Lomov: Believe me, his lower jaw is shorter than his upper.

Natalia: You've measured them?

Lomov: Yes. He's all right for pointing, but if you want him to retrieve . . .

Natalia: In the first place, our Squeezer is a thoroughbred, the son of Harness and Chisel, while your mutt doesn't even have a pedigree. He's as old and worn out as a pedlar's horse.

Lomov: He may be old, but I wouldn't take five Squeezers for him. How can you argue? Guess is a dog, Squeezer's a laugh. Anyone you can name has a dog like Squeezer hanging around somewhere. They're under every bush. If he only cost twenty-five rubles you got cheated.

Natalia: The devil is in you today, Ivan Vassilevitch! You want to contradict everything. First you pretend the Oxen Meadows are yours, and now you say Guess is better than Squeezer. People should say what they really mean, and you know Squeezer is a hundred times better than Guess. Why say he isn't?

Lomov: So, you think I'm a fool or a blind man, Natalia Stepanovna! Once and for all, Squeezer is overshot!

Natalia: He is not!

Lomov: He is so!

Natalia: He is not!

Lomov: Why shout, my dear lady?

Natalia: Why talk such nonsense? It's terrible. Your Guess is old enough to be buried, and you compare him with Squeezer!

Lomov: I'm sorry, I can't go on. My heart . . . it's palpitating!

Natalia: I've always noticed that the hunters who argue most don't know a thing.

Lomov: Please! Be quiet a moment. My heart's falling apart . . . (*Shouts*) Shut up!

Natalia: I'm not going to shut up until you admit that Squeezer's a hundred times better than Guess.

Lomov: A hundred times worse! His head . . . My eyes . . . shoulder . . .

Natalia: Guess is half-dead already!

Lomov: (*Weeping*) Shut up! My heart's exploding!

Natalia: I won't shut up!

(Chubukov *comes in*)

Chubukov: What's the trouble now?

Natalia: Papa, will you please tell us which is the better dog, his Guess or our Squeezer?

Lomov: Stepan Stepanovitch, I implore you to tell me just one thing. Is your Squeezer overshot or not? Yes or no?

Chubukov: Well what if he is? He's still the best dog in the neighbourhood, and so forth.

Lomov: Oh, but isn't my dog, Guess, better? Really?

Chubukov: Don't get yourself so fraught up, old man. Of course, your dog has his good points—thoroughbred, firm on his feet, well sprung ribs, and so forth. But, my dear fellow, you've got to admit he has two defects; he's old and he's short in the muzzle.

Lomov: Short in the muzzle? Oh, my heart! Let's look at the facts! On the Marusinsky hunt my dog ran neck and neck with the Count's, while Squeezer was a mile behind them . . .

Chubukov: That's because the Count's groom hit him with a whip.

Lomov: And he was right, too! We were fox hunting; what was your dog chasing sheep for?

Chubukov: That's a lie! Look, I'm going to lose my temper . . . (*Controlling himself*) my dear friend, so let's stop arguing, for that reason alone. You're only arguing because we're all jealous of somebody else's dog. Who can help it? As soon as you realize some dog is better than yours, in this case our dog, you start in with this and that, and the next thing you know—pure jealousy! I remember the whole business.

Lomov: I remember too!

Chubukov: (*Mimicking*) "I remember too!" What do you remember?

Lomov: My heart . . . my foot's asleep . . . I can't . . .

Natalia: (*Mimicking*) "My heart . . . my foot's asleep." What kind of a hunter are you? You should be hunting cockroaches in the kitchen, not foxes. "My heart!"

Chubukov: Yes, what kind of a hunter are you anyway? You should be sitting at home with your palpitations, not tracking down animals. You don't hunt anyhow. You just go out to argue with people and interfere with their dogs, and so forth. For God's sake, let's change the subject before I lose my temper. Anyway, you're just not a hunter.

Lomov: But you, you're a hunter? Ha! You only go hunting to get in good with the Count, and to plot, and intrigue, and scheme . . . Oh, my heart! You're a schemer, that's what!

Chubukov: What's that? Me a schemer? (*Shouting*) Shut up!

Lomov: A schemer!

Chubukov: You infant! You puppy!

Lomov: You old rat! You hawk!

Chubukov: You shut up, or I'll shoot you down like a partridge! You idiot!

Lomov: Everyone knows that—oh, my heart—that your wife used to beat you . . . Oh, my feet . . . my head . . . I'm seeing stars . . . I'm going to faint!

(*He drops into an armchair*)

Quick, a doctor! (*Faints*)

Chubukov: (*Going on, oblivious*) Baby! Weakling! Idiot! I'm getting sick. (*Drinks water*) Me! I'm sick!

Natalia: What kind of a hunter are you? You can't even sit on a horse! (*To her* *father*) Papa, what's the matter with him? Look papa! (*Screaming*) Ivan Vassilevitch! He's dead.

Chubukov: I'm choking, I can't breathe . . . Give me air.

Natalia: He's dead! (*Pulling* Lomov's *sleeve*) Ivan Vassilevitch! Ivan Vassilevitch! What have you done to me? He's dead! (*She falls into an armchair. Screaming hysterically*) A doctor! A doctor! A doctor!

Chubukov: Ohhhh . . . What's the matter? What happened?

Natalia: (*Wailing*) He's dead! He's dead!

Chubukov: Who's dead? (*Looks at* Lomov) My God, he is! Quick! Water! A doctor! (*Puts glass to* Lomov's *lips*) Here, drink this! Can't drink it—he must be dead, and so forth . . . Oh what a miserable life! Why don't I shoot myself! I should have cut my throat long ago! What am I waiting for? Give me a knife! Give me a pistol! (Lomov *stirs*) Look, he's coming to. Here, drink some water. That's it.

Lomov: I'm seeing stars . . . misty . . . Where am I?

Chubukov: Just you hurry up and get married, and then the devil with you! She accepted.

(*Puts* Lomov's *hand in* Natalia's) She accepts and so forth! I give you my blessing, and so forth! Only leave me in peace!

Lomov: (*Getting up*) Huh? What? Who?

Chubukov: She accepts! Well! Kiss her, damn you!

Natalia: He's alive! Yes, yes, I accept.

Chubukov: Kiss each other!

Lomov: Huh? Kiss? Kiss who? (*They kiss*) That's nice. I mean, excuse me, what happened? Oh, now I get it . . . my heart . . . those stars . . . I'm very happy, Natalia Stepanovna. (*Kisses her hand*) My foot's asleep.

Natalia: I . . . I'm happy too.

Chubukov: What a load off my shoulders! Whew!

Natalia: Well, now maybe you'll admit that Squeezer is better than Guess?

Lomov: Worse!

Natalia: Better!

Chubukov: What a way to enter matrimonial bliss! Let's have some champagne!

Lomov: He's worse!

Natalia: Better! Better, better, better, better!

Chubukov: (*Trying to shout her down*) Champagne! Bring some champagne! Champagne! Champagne!

After Reading

1. a) Comedy often depends on **stereotyped characters**. Describe the "types" of the three characters in *A Marriage Proposal* and tell how these types increase the **humour** of the play.

   b) Think of some comedies on television today. With your classmates, make a list of shows, their stereotyped characters, and the types they play.

2. Lomov has a short **soliloquy** in which he tells the **audience** how he feels about Natalia and marriage. **Summarize** this speech. Evaluate his reasons for getting married and predict the type of marriage he and Natalia will have.

3. a) Divide your notebook page in half. On one side, write down the negative feelings Chubukov has about his daughter's marriage. On the other side, write down all the positive feelings he has about his daughter's marriage. Quote from the text wherever possible.

   b) With a partner, write and perform the toast Chubukov might propose at the wedding reception and Lomov's reply to the toast. Be sure to capture the unique speech patterns of both characters. If you have equipment available, videotape your performance.

4. a) Describe the major **conflict** in the play and the way the playwright almost, but not quite, resolved it by the end of the play.

   b) Write a **review** of *A Marriage Proposal*. Include comments on characterization, **dialogue**, and the effectiveness of the ending. Create a catchy title for your review once you've completed it.

5. Make a list of props that are essential to this play. Beside each one, explain what it will add to the visual impact of the play.

6. Create a **pamphlet** titled How *Not* to Propose Marriage, in which you give advice based on the experiences of Lomov and Natalia. Focus on the lettering and the **layout** as well as the content, making your pamphlet eye-catching and attractive.

Ice Bangles

An Excerpt

NAZNEEN SADIQ

"She had fulfilled her promise of being something other than a dark complexioned woman."

Before Reading

1. Create a list of traditions in your family. These traditions could be daily, weekly, or only for special occasions.

2. With your class, discuss why special events or occasions we think of as so exciting and magical in childhood change as we grow to be adults. On the board, make a list of events that have changed since childhood.

They danced in a semi-circle on the wooden dais. The plates of henna paste studded with burning candles dipped and twirled with them. It was a family tradition to choose the most beautiful women for the dance. A way of saying to the in-laws, "Look how wonderful we are". Naila danced with her sisters and cousins in a city in northern Pakistan, the hypnotic tattoo of the long wooden drum quickening her steps to keep up with the others, the melody, almost forgotten, resurfacing, coiling around her like the scent of roses and jasmine.

As she spun around, the carousel of colours and faces swam before her: her two-year-old Canadian daughter squirming in the arms of an older family member. The smiling faces of her aunts and uncles packed into the enormous marquee. Her brother, the bridegroom, seated in the centre flashing her a look which said "What a carnival". His bride-to-be, a saffron-shrouded figure seated on a cushioned stool. Bent and motionless, with coral-tinted toes peeping out of her gilt sandals, she observed the festivities through a saffron coloured veil. The clusters of women with embroidered silks and wedding jewelry. Her father immaculately clad in a three-piece English wool suit ushering people in. Stouffville, Ontario, became a memory put on hold, unreal and thousands of miles away.

"Your brother getting married, please attend," had been the words of the telegram which had arrived in Canada three weeks ago. It was followed a week later by another cable which read "Bring clothes and jewelry". That cable was from her mother, a subtle reminder that she was not to arrive as a Canadian, whatever that was, but a daughter of the house. She had dashed off to Georg Jensen on Bloor Street and bought a tulip-shaped silver candleholder as a wedding gift. This was her way of expressing her independence from the system she had left. The sleek and unadorned sensuous lines of the piece were a contrast to the embossed and heavily cut silver the family would give to her brother and his wife.

When she landed in Islamabad, the capital of Pakistan, holding her daughter and the Canadian wedding present, she was pressed into the melee of the wedding. She was taken off to meet her brother's fiancee, a slight petite woman with masses of black hair and the dark complexion of a southerner. She did not come up to her family's standard of the lighter-complexioned beauties, but was connected to a powerful family. It wasn't really her father who mattered but her grandfather, a wiry autocratic man who controlled the largest government financial institution. She was informed by her mother that she had to go and pay her respects to him as well.

Preferably before she met the bride-to-be. She fought her mother on that score, and decided that she didn't care whose granddaughter she was. What mattered was that she was going to marry her brother.

Fatimeh sat in a large room with her trousseau littered around her, peering myopically through oversized spectacles. When Naila came up to greet her, she removed the glasses and tossed her head back defiantly. Her eyes widened imperiously, and the cloud of hair shifted like a silken armour around her. They observed each other warily, as strangers who had parts assigned to them without their permission.

Naila was embarrassed herself, because she knew that waiting outside the room were clusters of people who would want to know immediately if she approved of her sister-in-law. She also knew that this approval was based solely on the colour of the bride's skin. Standing before her was a woman free and strong enough to choose her own husband, but hopelessly tangled in a subtle web of discrimination which Pakistanis practised with shocking malice. The fair-skinned northerners had practised for centuries the same discrimination which their British masters had been accused of. Her mother, who had hoped secretly for a Kashmiri wife for her only son, had been cheated.

Fatimeh had a Master's degree from the University and studied French at the Alliance Française. She had exerted the strength of her personality and her slightly comic stance towards life to charm her brother. Despite this, she needed the weight of her grandfather's status, a necklace of dazzling value and a trousseau of three hundred accessorized outfits to compensate for her tawny skin. Naila's charming devil-may-care brother, who had spent two years in London rounding off his engineering degree with training in computers, had come home only to reject the fair-skinned candidates lined up for him. He had settled instead for the slightly over-aged and physically under-endowed Fatimeh.

She had already caught the scent of disparaging comments made by distant relatives who had hoped that her brother would marry one of their daughters.

"Welcome to the family," she said to Fatimeh, who gazed at her quite serenely.

"I'm so fed up with all these people in the house, do you have a cigarette?" said her brand new sister-in-law.

"Oh, of course." Naila laughed at this surprising request.

"Don't tell your brother, he doesn't know as yet."

"Of course not, I promise," she said hurriedly.

"I've heard so much about you," said Fatimeh, smoke streaming through her nostrils, looking like a fallen angel.

"So have I," she blurted back.

"Your fair brother marrying such a dark woman?" came the sardonic reply.

"Not at all." The protest leapt out of Naila.

"Wait till you see me dressed up," informed her sister-in-law, a rich womanly smile stretching across her flawless skin.

"I like you already," she replied.

"I was going to write to you," said Fatimeh.

"I would have loved hearing from you," she replied, relieved that the blunt exchange was over.

"I wanted a *Better Homes and Gardens* cookbook from Canada."

"I wish I'd known, I bought you a candle holder," she replied, and they both laughed, cookbook tying them, holding them together in an arc of laughter and a new friendship.

"Well, well, what do you think?" Her cousin's sharp eyes skewered her.

"I like her very much," she replied.

"May God shower his blessings on this marriage," intoned her cousin seeking refuge behind a show of piety.

The horse was a pure white Arabian and its groom tagged close to the procession. Her brother had mounted the horse just before the gates of the bride's house. He was dressed in a formal brocade tunic and tight silken trousers. The wedding turban completely veiled with flowers and tinsel hid his entire face. Seated behind him was a young cousin who was dressed as a replica of the groom. The little boy jabbed at the horse's flank with his turned-up brocade slippers, and the skittish Arabian would have dumped his cargo on the gravel-strewn drive, if the groom had not murmured warning commands to him.

Naila and her other two sisters held the reins on either side, and she thought of Kathleen in Stouffville and how she would have loved the extravagant spectacle of a Pakistani wedding, particularly one which had revived dying customs to satisfy Eastern showmanship. Her well-educated liberal parents had organized a pageant.

Her brother had parked his brand new Volkswagen, purchased during his stay in London, and mounted a horse.

Waiting in the gardens of the sprawling mansion ahead of them, two thousand wedding guests chatted and mingled. The bride would appear as soon as the bridegroom was seated under the canopied dais. Sitting with her brother on the dais and waiting for the bride, Naila thought of the solemn Anglican wedding she had attended in Toronto, but there was a common link. The expectant hush which awaited the first glimpse of the bride was the same.

Fatimeh was led up to the dais by a solid phalanx of her female relatives. She appeared in their jewelled and sequined midst as a glittering icon. She had to be supported because she was almost bent double from the collective weight of her jewelry and clothes. When she climbed the dais and sat next to her brother, she settled herself statuesquely, straightening her shoulders. A collar of oversized turquoise encircled her slender throat, and a filigree web studded with rubies and pearls spilled over her chest. She later found out that a third of her father's pension fund had been handed over to the jeweller who had made the ruby set.

Her sister-in-law's face, dusted with gold powder, was luminous and breathtaking. She had fulfilled her promise of being something other than a dark complexioned woman. Fatimeh shot an amused glance at her before she lowered her gilt-dusted eyelids to assume the pose of modesty. Her head bent, and the wedding veil covered her face, locking her into a private and unreachable space. Yet in the split-second moment of the glance directed at her, Fatimeh had revealed her own contempt for the traditions of her culture.

"Well, she certainly looks beautiful," whispered her elder sister, something reluctant and grudging lacing its way

125

through the compliment. She turned around to face her sister, who wore massive gold earrings and had her three daughters ringed around her feet like puppies. There was a gleam of infuriating superiority razor-sharp in her eyes. It was a quality Naila had never quite noticed before. She could picture her quietly confident sister-in-law wreaking havoc with the ill-placed smugness which emanated from her sister. There were undercurrents which leapt from the concealed grudging note of her sister's voice. She found them mildly offensive, and a surge of protectiveness for Fatimeh coursed through her.

Her mother came and cupped Fatimeh's face in both hands and kissed her forehead. The official stamp of approval spread like a ripple in the sea of people around the bridal dais, and the stampede towards the bridal couple began. Each guest would congratulate the bride and she would raise a hand with the thumb tucked in and "salaam" them. In return, a roll of currency would be pressed into her hand. Each amount was noted and gathered by a family member standing behind the couple. Fatimeh sat like a robot, the hand rising and falling with precision for over three hours. The pile of bank notes overflowed from beaded handbags. She turned around and whispered to her brother that they needed an oversized garbage bag. He rolled his eyes and gave her a droll smile. She thought about the band of kids who prowled through her neighbourhood in Stouffville at Halloween dragging pillowcases and garbage bags to collect candy.

Balancing a plate of food in hand and disentangling the hands of her daughter from the pleats of her sari, she found herself viewing everything around her with new eyes. She felt as though she had stumbled on the set of some theatrical production. Everything was larger than life. The silken clothes were too shiny, and the twenty-two carat gold jewelry was too yellow. The wedding buffet tables with mountains of pilaf and tureens of seasoned meats stretched in unending lines. The abundance was oppressive, but the faces around her remained comforting.

Peeping over the concrete walls of the enormous grounds were clusters of children, eyes peering through dishevelled hair bunched around gaunt faces. These were the children of the domestic servants, who wanted to see the goings-on of the privileged throng inside. She was conscious for the first time of social divisions and found them disturbing. Five years of living in Canada had awakened a social conscience which emerged with the embarrassment of adolescent acne.

She had been breathless with excitement before she had left Canada. Her elder sister's wedding years ago held memories of childish excesses: a surfeit of sweets, and handfuls of money which came her way for being the bride's little sister. Naila remembered prancing before her mother's dressing table in clothes stitched for the wedding.

She had wanted to touch a familiar part of her life again, and experience well-known emotions. Now she felt as though she was a voyeur, observing unknown, and feeling a detachment that was as alien as it was terrifying.

After Reading

1. Describe the **atmosphere** created in the first two paragraphs. Record the words that created that **tone**.

2. From the story, select the details that show that Naila feels a sense of rebellion against the traditions of her family and her culture.

3. a) When she first meets Naila, Fatimeh is described in the following way: "[her] cloud of hair shifted like a silken armour around her". Explain why this is an effective **simile** for the bride-to-be.

   b) Describe the **irony** created by the new sister-in-law's statement: "I'm so fed up with all these people in the house, do you have a cigarette?"

4. Make a list of the hints that the modern world has crept into this very traditional marriage celebration.

5. a) Point out places in the story in which the reader could be confused about which woman the pronoun *she* is referring to. Describe how the reader can overcome this confusion.

   b) Rewrite one of these paragraphs, solving the pronoun reference problem. (See The Reference Shelf, page 232.)

6. "She had fulfilled her promise of being something other than a dark complexioned woman." Using examples from the story, explain the importance of this observation to the story in a well-developed paragraph.

7. a) Examine the **character** of Naila, her brother, and Fatimeh, recording references to their backgrounds, how they act, how they react, what they say, what they think, and what is said about them. Write a **character description** for each one.

   b) In groups of four, create a radio talk show in which you **interview** the three characters about the events leading up to and including the wedding. Use your research and character descriptions to build the questions and answers. Perform your talk show for the class.

8. In a short **persuasive essay**, support or refute the following **thesis** statement: Naila's feelings at the end of the story were inevitable.

Twelfth Night

Excerpts From Act II, Scene 4

WILLIAM SHAKESPEARE

Before Reading

With a partner, discuss whether love means the same thing to men and to women.

Note: At the beginning of Twelfth Night, Viola is shipwrecked in the fictional city of Illyria. To gain employment as a messenger with the Duke of Illyria, she disguises herself as a young man, Cesario. The Duke loves the lady Olivia and frequently sends Viola (Cesario) to Olivia with messages of his love. In this scene, Viola and the Duke speak of love and Viola comes dangerously close to revealing her true identity and the fact that she has fallen in love with the Duke.

Duke Orsino's *palace.*
Enter Duke, Viola, Curio, *and others.*

Duke: Give me some music. Now, good-morrow, friends.
Now, good Cesario, but that piece of song,
That old and antique song we heard last night.
Methought it did relieve my passion much,
More than light airs and recollected terms
Of these most brisk and giddy-paced times.
Come, but one verse.
Curio: He is not here, so please your lordship, that should sing it.
Duke: Who was it?

Curio: Feste, the jester, my lord; a fool that the lady Olivia's father took much
delight in. He is about the house.

Duke: Seek him out, and play the tune the while.

[*Exit* Curio. *Music plays*.]

Come hither, boy. If ever thou shalt love,
In the sweet pangs of it remember me;
For such as I am all true lovers are,
Unstaid and skittish in all motions else,
Save in the constant image of the creature
That is beloved. How dost thou like this tune?

Viola: It gives a very echo to the seat
Where Love is throned.

Duke: Thou dost speak masterly.
My life upon't, young though thou art, thine eye
Hath stay'd upon some favour that it loves.
Hath it not, boy?

Viola: A little, by your favour.

Duke: What kind of woman is't?

Viola: Of your complexion.

Duke: She is not worth thee, then. What years, i' faith?

Viola: About your years, my lord.

Duke: Too old, by heaven. Let still the woman take
An elder than herself; so wears she to him,
So sways she level in her husband's heart.
For, boy, however we do praise ourselves,
Our fancies are more giddy and unfirm,
More longing, wavering, sooner lost and worn,
Than women's are.

Viola: I think it well, my lord.

Duke: Then let thy love be younger than thyself
Or thy affection cannot hold the bent;
For women are as roses, whose fair flower
Being once display'd, doth fall that very hour.

Viola: And so they are. Alas, that they are so;
To die, even when they to perfection grow!

        . . .

Duke: Let all the rest give place.

[Curio *and* Attendants *retire*.]

                        Once more, Cesario,
Get thee to yond same sovereign cruelty.

Tell her, my love, more noble than the world,
Prizes not quantity of dirty lands;
The parts that fortune hath bestow'd upon her,
Tell her, I hold as giddily as fortune;
But 'tis that miracle and queen of gems,
That nature pranks her in, attracts my soul.
Viola: But if she cannot love you, sir?
Duke: I cannot be so answer'd.
Viola: Sooth, but you must.
Say that some lady, as perhaps there is,
Hath for your love as great a pang of heart
As you have for Olivia. You cannot love her;
You tell her so; must she not then be answer'd?
Duke: There is no woman's sides
Can bide the beating of so strong a passion
As love doth give my heart; no woman's heart
So big, to hold so much. They lack retention.
Alas, their love may be called appetite,—
No motion of the liver, but the palate,—
That suffer surfeit, cloyment and revolt;
But mine is all as hungry as the sea,
And can digest as much. Make no compare
Between that love a woman can bear me
And that I owe Olivia.
Viola: Ay, but I know—
Duke: What dost thou know?
Viola: Too well what love women to men may owe.
In faith, they are as true of heart as we.
My father had a daughter loved a man,
As it might be, perhaps, were I a woman,
I should your lordship.
Duke: And what's her history?
Viola: A blank, my lord. She never told her love,
But let concealment, like a worm i' the bud,
Feed on her damask cheek. She pined in thought,
And with a green and yellow melancholy
She sat like patience on a monument,
Smiling at grief. Was not this love indeed?
We men may say more, swear more; but indeed
Our shows are more than will; for still we prove

130

Much in our vows, but little in our love.
Duke: But died thy sister of her love, my boy?
Viola: I am all the daughters of my father's house,
And all the brothers too; and yet I know not.
Sir, shall I to this lady?
Duke: Ay, that's the theme.
To her in haste; give her this jewel; say,
My love can give no place, bide no denay.
　　　[*Exeunt.*]

After Reading

1. As a class, discuss the following questions:
   - What does Viola say that suggests to the Duke that Cesario has fallen in love? At what point do you feel Viola comes closest to revealing her love for the Duke?
   - How does the Duke contrast the love that a man has for a woman with that of a woman for a man? How does Viola challenge his view? Do you agree more with the Duke's or with Viola's **point of view**?
   - What advice does the Duke give to Cesario regarding the selection of a mate?

2. Based on this short excerpt, write a **character description** of Viola, the Duke, and the lady Olivia. Use evidence from the text to justify your evaluation of the characters.

3. Prepare a short **research report** on why Shakespeare frequently had his heroines like Viola disguise themselves as men in his plays.

4. Create a diagram that illustrates how Shakespeare has created a perfect love triangle as part of his **plot**.

5. This excerpt contains several **similes**. Select one and explain how it helps the speaker convey an important idea.

6. Rewrite this excerpt as a **script** for a television soap opera.

7. Define the term *unrequited love*. Give evidence from this excerpt that, for the moment at least, both the Duke and Viola are experiencing unrequited love.

The Mistake

ISAAC ASIMOV

"I had to send him back to his own time. . . . The disgrace was more than he could take."

Before Reading

1. Imagine the advantages and disadvantages of bringing back a famous person from the past.

2. How does the title of the story engage the reader's interest?

"Oh, yes," said Dr. Phineas Welch, the famous scientist, "I can bring back the spirits of the dead."

Scott Robertson, the school's young English teacher, smiled and said, "Really, Dr. Welch?"

"I mean it," said the scientist. He looked to the right and to the left to be sure they were not being overheard. "And not just the spirits. I bring back bodies, too."

"I wouldn't have thought it was possible," said the English teacher.

"Why not? It's just a simple matter of temporal transference."

"Oh, you mean time travel," said the English teacher. "But that's quite—uh—unusual."

"Not if you know how."

"Well, tell me how, Dr. Welch."

"I can't tell you that," said the scientist. "But I have brought back quite a few men. Archimedes, Newton, Galileo. Poor fellows."

"Didn't they like it here?" asked the English teacher. "I should think they would have been fascinated by our modern science."

"Oh, they were," said the scientist. "They were. But not for long."

"What was wrong?"

"They couldn't get used to our way of life. They got terribly lonely and frightened. I had to send them back."

"That's too bad."

132

"Yes," said the scientist. "Great minds, but not flexible minds. Not universal. So I tried Shakespeare."

"WHAT?" yelled Robertson.

"Don't yell, my boy," said Welch. "It's bad manners."

"Did you say you brought back William Shakespeare?"

"I did. I needed someone with a universal mind. Someone who would understand people well enough to be able to live with them centuries after his own time. Shakespeare was the man. I've even got his signature. As a souvenir, you know."

"Do you have it with you?" asked the English teacher eagerly.

"Right here." The scientist fumbled in one vest pocket after another. "Ah, here it is."

He handed a little piece of cardboard to the English teacher. Printed on one side was: "L. Klein & Sons, Wholesale Hardware." On the other side, written in straggly script, was:

William Shakespeare

"Tell me," Robertson said. "What did he look like?"

"Not like his pictures. Bald and with an ugly mustache. Of course, I did my best to please him. I told him we thought highly of his plays and still performed them on stage. In fact, I said we thought they were the greatest examples of literature in the English language, maybe in any language."

"Good. Good!" said the English teacher.

"I said people had written volumes of commentaries about his plays. Naturally he wanted to see the books, so I got some for him from the library."

"And?" asked the English teacher.

"Oh, he was fascinated. Of course, he had trouble with the current idioms and references to events since 1600, but I helped out. Poor fellow. I don't think he ever expected to get so much attention for his works. He kept saying, 'God have mercy!'"

The scientist paused for a minute. "Then I told him that we even give college courses in Shakespeare."

"I teach a course like that," said the English teacher.

"I know," said Welch. "I enrolled him in your evening course called Introduction to Shakespeare. I never saw a man more eager than poor Bill to find out what people thought of him. He worked hard in the course, too."

"William Shakespeare was one of my students?" Robertson cried. He couldn't believe it. It was impossible. Or was it? He was beginning to recall a bald man with a strange way of talking. . . .

"I didn't enroll him under his real name, of course," said Dr. Welch. "Never mind what name he used. It was a mistake, that's all. A big mistake. Poor fellow."

"Why was it a mistake?" asked Robertson. "What happened?"

"I had to send him back to his own time," said Welch sadly. "The disgrace was more than he could take."

"What disgrace are you talking about?" asked the English teacher in a hoarse whisper.

Dr. Welch looked at him. "What disgrace? Why my dear man, you *flunked* him!"

After Reading

1. a) Look up the word *idiom* and write the definition in your own words.

   b) Examine the excerpt from *Twelfth Night* on pages 128 to 131 and comment on how **Elizabethan English** differs from **Standard Canadian English**.

   c) Explain why Shakespeare had "trouble with the current **idiom**".

2. a) Write two short **newspaper articles** about the disastrous Shakespeare experiment, one from the **perspective** of a national newspaper and the other from the **point of view** of a tabloid. Consider the differences in your **purpose**, **audience**, **tone**, word choice, and sentence structure when writing your drafts.

   b) Have a classmate read both articles and fill out a chart like the following, using four or five sentences from each article:

Sentence	First Four Words	Sentence Type	Verbs	No. of Words

   c) Examine your chart and make any necessary revisions to your two articles in your word choice and sentence order, structure, or length to make sure they fit your audience and purpose.

In Flanders Fields

COLONEL JOHN McCRAE

Before Reading

This is a famous Canadian poem. Those of you who have heard or read the poem before, discuss with the class what you already know about the poem and the poet.

In Flanders fields the poppies blow
Between the crosses, row on row,
That mark our place; and in the sky
The larks, still bravely singing, fly
5   Scarce heard amid the guns below.

We are the Dead. Short days ago
We lived, felt dawn, saw sunset glow,
Loved, and were loved, and now we lie
In Flanders fields.

10   Take up our quarrel with the foe:
To you from failing hands we throw
The torch; be yours to hold it high.
If ye break faith with us who die
We shall not sleep, though poppies grow
15   In Flanders fields.

After Reading

1. In your notebook, sketch the scene the writer has described in the first verse.

2. Explain how the poet suggests colours in the first verse and why this technique is just as effective as actually describing the colours to the readers.

3. Look up the definition of *enjambement* or *run-on lines* and describe the impact the author's use of this technique has in the way the poem is read.

4. Identify the **narrator** of the poem. Evaluate the effectiveness of this choice of narrator.

5. In a small group, prepare three or four **tableaux** that capture the **mood** or **tone** of this poem. Have one group member perform a **dramatic reading** of the poem while the rest of the group presents the tableaux. Consider adding music in the background to help set the **atmosphere**.

6. With a small group, research and prepare an oral presentation on one of the following topics:
   - the writing of "In Flanders Fields"
   - the Battle of Ypres
   - the role Canadians played in the First World War
   - a biography of Colonel John McCrae
   - conscription in the First World War
   - the role of women in the First World War
   - the role of Aboriginal Canadians in the First World War
   - another poet who wrote about the First World War

The Pen of My Aunt

JOSEPHINE TEY

"We Germans have come a long way from the geese."

Before Reading

Describe to a partner a time when you had to think, speak, or act quickly in order to get out of a difficult situation.

CHARACTERS:
Madame
Simone
Stranger
Corporal

SCENE:
A French country house during the Occupation by German forces in World War II. The lady of the house is seated in her drawing room.

Simone: (*Approaching*) Madame! Oh, madame! Madame, have you—
Madame: Simone.
Simone: Madame, Have you seen what—
Madame: Simone!
Simone: But madame—
Madame: Simone, this may be an age of

barbarism, but I will have none of it inside the walls of this house.
Simone: But madam, there is a—there is a—
Madame: (*Silencing her*) Simone. France may be an occupied country, a ruined nation, and a conquered race, but we will keep, if you please, the usages of civilization.
Simone: Yes, madame.
Madame: One thing we still possess, thank God; and that is good manners. The enemy never had it; and it is not something they can take from *us*.
Simone: No, madame.
Madame: Go out of the room again. Open the door—
Simone: Oh, *madame*! I wanted to tell you—

Madame: —Open the door, shut it behind you—quietly—take two paces into the room, and say what you came to say. (Simone *goes hastily out, shutting the door. She reappears, shuts the door behind her, takes two paces into the room, and waits.*) Yes, Simone?

Simone: I expect it is too late now; they will be here.

Madame: Who will?

Simone: The soldiers who were coming up the avenue.

Madame: After the last few months I should not have thought that soldiers coming up the avenue was a remarkable fact. It is no doubt a party with a billeting order.

Simone: (*Crossing to the window*) No, madame, it is two soldiers in one of their little cars, with a civilian between them.

Madame: Which civilian?

Simone: A stranger, madame.

Madame: A stranger? Are the soldiers from the Combatant branch?

Simone: No, they are those beasts of Administration. Look, they have stopped. They are getting out.

Madame: (*At the window*) Yes, it is a stranger. Do you know him, Simone?

Simone: I have never set eyes on him before, madame.

Madame: You would know if he belonged to the district?

Simone: Oh, madame, I know every man between here and St. Estèphe.

Madame: (*Dryly*) No doubt.

Simone: Oh, merciful God, they are coming up the steps.

Madame: My good Simone, that is what the steps were put there for.

Simone: But they will ring the bell and I shall have to—

Madame: And you will answer it and behave as if you had been trained by a butler and ten upper servants instead of being the charcoal-burner's daughter from over at Les Chênes. (*This is said encouragingly, not in unkindness.*) You will be very calm and correct—

Simone: Calm! Madame! With my inside turning over and over like a wheel at a fair!

Madame: A good servant does not have an inside, merely an exterior. (*Comforting*) Be assured, my child. You have your place here; that is more than those creatures on our doorstep have. Let that hearten you—

Simone: Madame! They are not going to ring. They are coming straight in.

Madame: (*Bitterly*) Yes. They have forgotten long ago what bells are for.

(*Door opens.*)

Stranger: (*In a bright, confident, casual tone*) Ah, there you are, my dear aunt. I am so glad. Come in, my friend, come in. My dear aunt, this gentleman wants you to identify me.

Madame: Identify you?

Corporal: We found this man wandering in the woods—

Stranger: The corporal found it inexplicable that anyone should wander in a wood.

Corporal: And he had no papers on him—

Stranger: And I rightly pointed out that if I carry all the papers one is supposed to these days, I am no good to God or man. If I put them in a hip pocket, I can't bend forward; if I put them in a front pocket, I can't bend at all.

Corporal: He said that he was your nephew, madame, but that did not seem

138

to us very likely, so we brought him there. (*There is the slightest pause; just one moment of silence.*)

Madame: But of course this is my nephew.

Corporal: He is?

Madame: Certainly.

Corporal: He lives here?

Madame: (*Assenting*) My nephew lives here.

Corporal: So! (*Recovering*) My apologies, madame. But you will admit that appearances were against the young gentleman.

Madame: Alas, Corporal, my nephew belongs to a generation who delight in flouting appearances. It is what they call "expressing their personality," I understand.

Corporal: (*With contempt*) No doubt, madame.

Madame: Convention is anathema to them, and there is no sin like conformity. Even a collar is an offence against their liberty, and a discipline not to be borne by free necks.

Corporal: Ah, yes, madame. A little more discipline among your nephew's generation, and we might not be occupying your country today.

Stranger: You think it was that collar of yours that conquered my country? You flatter yourself, Corporal. The only result of wearing a collar like that is varicose veins in the head.

Madame: (*Repressive*) Please! My dear boy. Let us not descend to personalities.

Stranger: The matter is not personal, my good aunt, but scientific. Wearing a collar like that retards the flow of fresh blood to the head, with the most disastrous

consequences to the gray matter of the brain. The hypothetical gray matter. In fact, I have a theory—

Corporal: Monsieur, your theories do not interest me.

Stranger: No? You do not find speculation interesting?

Corporal: In this world one judges by results.

Stranger: (*After a slight pause of reflection*) I see. The collared conqueror sits in the high places, while the collarless conquered lies about in the woods. And who comes best out of that, would you say? Tell me, Corporal, as man to man, do you never have a mad, secret desire to lie unbuttoned in a wood?

Corporal: I have only one desire, monsieur, and that is to see your papers.

Stranger: (*Taken off guard and filling in time*) My papers?

Madame: But is that necessary, Corporal? I have already told you that—

Corporal: I know that madame is a very good collaborator and in good standing—

Madame: In that case—

Corporal: But when we begin an affair we like to finish it. I have asked to see monsieur's papers, and the matter will not be finished until I have seen them.

Madame: You acknowledge that I am in "good standing," Corporal?

Corporal: So I have heard, madame.

Madame: Then I must consider it a discourtesy on your part to demand my nephew's credentials.

Corporal: It is no reflection on madame. It is a matter of routine, nothing more.

Stranger: (*Murmuring*) The great god Routine.

Madame: To ask for his papers was routine; to insist on their production is discourtesy. I shall say so to your Commanding Officer.

Corporal: Very good, Madam. In the meantime, I shall inspect your nephew's papers.

Madame: And what if I—

Stranger: (*Quietly*) You may as well give it up, my dear. You could as easily turn a steamroller. They have only one idea at a time. If the Corporal's heart is set on seeing my papers, he shall see them. (*Moving towards the door*) I left them in the pocket of my coat.

Simone: (*Unexpectedly, from the background*) Not in your *linen* coat?

Stranger: (*Pausing*) Yes. Why?

Simone: (*With apparently growing anxiety*) Your *cream* linen coat? The one you were wearing yesterday?

Stranger: Certainly.

Simone: Merciful Heaven! I sent it to the laundry!

Stranger: To the laundry!

Simone: Yes, monsieur; this morning; in the basket.

Stranger: (*In incredulous anger*) You sent my coat, *with my papers in the pocket*, to the laundry!

Simone: (*Defensive and combatant*) I didn't know monsieur's papers were in the pocket.

Stranger: You didn't know! You didn't know that a packet of documents weighing half a ton were in the pocket. An identity card, a *laisser passer*, a food card, a drink card, an army discharge, a permission to wear civilian clothes, a permission to go farther than ten miles to the east, a permission to go more than ten miles to the west, a permission to—

Simone: (*Breaking in with spirit*) How was I to know the coat was heavy! I picked it up with the rest of the bundle that was lying on the floor.

Stranger: (*Snapping her head off*) My coat was on the back of the chair.

Simone: It was on the floor.

Stranger: On the back of the chair!

Simone: It was on the floor with your dirty shirt and your pajamas, and a towel and what not. I put my arms round the whole thing and then—woof! into the basket with them.

Stranger: I tell you that coat was on the back of the chair. It was quite clean and was not going to the laundry for two weeks yet—if then. I hung it there myself, and—

Madame: My dear boy, what does it matter? The damage is done now. In any case, they will find the papers when they unpack the basket, and return them tomorrow.

Stranger: If someone doesn't steal them. There are a lot of people who would like to lay hold of a complete set of papers, believe me.

Madame: (*Reassuring*) Oh, no. Old Fleureau is the soul of honesty. You have no need to worry about them. They will be back first thing tomorrow, you shall see; and then we shall have much pleasure in sending them to the Administration Office for the Corporal's inspection. Unless, of course, the Corporal insists on your personal appearance at the office.

Corporal: (*Cold and indignant*) I have seen monsieur. All that I want now is to see his papers.

Stranger: You shall see them, Corporal, you shall see them. The whole half-ton of them. You may inspect them at your leisure. Provided, that is, that they come back from the laundry to which this idiot has consigned them.

Madame: (*Again reassuring*) They will come back, never fear. And you must not blame Simone. She is a good child, and does her best.

Simone: (*With an air of belated virtue*) I am not one to pry into pockets.

Madame: Simone, show the Corporal out, if you please.

Simone: (*Natural feeling overcoming her for a moment*) He knows the way out. (*recovering*) Yes, madame.

Madame: And Corporal, try to take your duties a little less literally in future. My countrymen appreciate the spirit rather than the letter.

Corporal: I have my instructions, madame, and I obey them. Good day, madame. Monsieur.

(*He goes, followed by* Simone—*the door closes. There is a moment of silence.*)

Stranger: For a good collaborator, that was a remarkably quick adoption.

Madame: Sit down, young man. I will give you something to drink. I expect your knees are none too well.

Stranger: My knees, madame, are pure gelatine. As for my stomach, it seems to have disappeared.

Madame: (*Offering him the drink she has poured out*) This will recall it, I hope.

Stranger: You are not drinking, madam.

Madame: Thank you, no.

Stranger: Not with strangers. It is certainly no time to drink with strangers. Nevertheless, I drink the health of a collaborator. (*He drinks*) Tell me, madame, what will

happen tomorrow when they find that you have no nephew?

Madame: (*Surprised*) But of course I have a nephew. I tell lies, my friend; but not *silly* lies. My charming nephew has gone to Bonneval for the day. He finds country life dull.

Stranger: Dull? This—this heaven?

Madame: (*Dryly*) He likes to talk and here there is no audience. At Headquarters in Bonneval he finds the audience sympathetic.

Simone: (*Understanding the implication*) Ah.

Madame: He believes in the Brotherhood of Man—if you can credit it.

Stranger: After the last six months?

Madame: His mother was American, so he has half the Balkans in his blood. To say nothing of Italy, Russia and the Levant.

Stranger: (*Half amused*) I see.

Madame: A silly and worthless creature, but useful.

Stranger: Useful?

Madame: I—borrow his cloak.

Stranger: I see.

Madame: Tonight I shall borrow his identity papers, and tomorrow they will go to the office in St. Estèphe.

Stranger: But—he will have to know.

Madame: (*Placidly*) Oh, yes, he will know, of course.

Stranger: And how will you persuade such an enthusiastic collaborator to deceive his friends?

Madame: Oh, that is easy. He is my heir.

Stranger: (*Amused*) Ah.

Madame: He is, also, by the mercy of God, not too unlike you, so that his

141

photograph will not startle the Corporal too much tomorrow. Now tell me what you are doing in my wood.

Stranger: Resting my feet—I am practically walking on my bones. And waiting for tonight.

Madame: Where are you making for? (*As he does not answer immediately*) The coast? (*He nods.*) That is four days away—five if your feet are bad.

Stranger: I know it.

Madame: Have you friends on the way?

Stranger: I have friends at the coast, who will get me a boat. But no one between here and the sea.

Madame: (*Rising*) I must consult my list of addresses. (*Pausing*) What was your service?

Stranger: Army.

Madame: Which Regiment?

Stranger: The 79th.

Madame: (*After the faintest pause*) And your Colonel's name?

Stranger: Delavault was killed in the first week, and Martin took over.

Madame: (*Going to her desk*) A "good collaborator" cannot be too careful. Now I can consult my notebook. A charming colour, is it not? A lovely shade of red.

Stranger: Yes—but what has a red quill pen to do with your notebook?—Ah, you write with it of course—stupid of me.

Madame: Certainly I write with it—but it is also my notebook—look—I only need a hairpin—and then—so—out of my quill pen comes my notebook—a tiny piece of paper—but enough for a list of names.

Stranger: You mean that you keep that list on your desk? (*He sounds disapproving.*)

Madame: Where did you expect me to keep it, young man? In my corset? Did you ever try to get something out of your corset in a hurry? What would you advise as the ideal quality in a hiding place for a list of names?

Stranger: That the thing should be difficult to find, of course.

Madame: Not at all. That it should be easily destroyed in emergency. It is too big for me to swallow—I suspect they do that only in books—and we have no fires to consume it, so I had to think of some other way. I did try to memorize the list, but what I could not be sure of remembering were those that—that had to be scored off. It would be fatal to send someone to an address that—that was no longer available. So I had to keep a written record.

Stranger: And if you neither eat it nor burn it when the moment comes, how do you get rid of it?

Madame: I could, of course, put a match to it, but scraps of freshly burned paper on a desk take a great deal of explaining. If I ceased to be looked on with approval my usefulness would end. It is important therefore that there should be no sign of anxiety on my part; no burned paper, no excuses to leave the room, no nods and becks and winks. I just sit here at my desk and go on with my letters. I tilt my nice big inkwell sideways for a moment and dip the pen into the deep ink at the side. The ink flows into the hollow of the quill, and all is blotted out. (*Consulting the list*) Let me see. It would be good if you could rest your feet for a day or so.

Stranger: (*Ruefully*) It would.

Madame: There is a farm just beyond the Marnay crossroads on the way to St. Estèphe—(*She pauses to consider.*)

Stranger: St. Estèphe is the home of the singleminded Corporal. I don't want to run into him again.

Madame: No, that might be awkward; but that farm of the Cherfils would be ideal. A good hiding-place, and food to spare, and fine people—

Stranger: If your nephew is so friendly with the invader, how is it that the Corporal doesn't know him by sight?

Madame: (*Absently*) The unit at St. Estèphe is a noncommissioned one.

Stranger: Does the Brotherhood of Man exclude sergeants, then?

Madame: Oh, definitely. Brotherhood does not really begin under field rank, I understand.

Stranger: But the Corporal may still meet your nephew somewhere.

Madame: That is a risk one must take. It is not a very grave one. They change the personnel every few weeks, to prevent them becoming too acclimatized. And even if he met my nephew, he is unlikely to ask for the papers of so obviously well-to-do a citizen. If you could bear to go *back* a little—

Stranger: Not a step! It would be like— like denying God. I have got so far, against all the odds, and I am not going a yard back. Not even to rest my feet!

Madame: I understand; but it is a pity. It is a long way to the Cherfils farm—two miles east of the Marnay crossroads it is, on a little hill.

Stranger: I'll get there; don't worry. If not tonight then tomorrow night. I am used to sleeping in the open by now.

Madame: I wish we could have you here, but it is too dangerous. We are liable to be billeted on at any moment, without notice. However, we can give you a good meal, and a bath. We have no coal, so it will be one of those flat-tin-saucer baths. And if you want to be very kind to Simone you might have it somewhere in the kitchen regions and so save her carrying water upstairs.

Stranger: But of course.

Madame: Before the war I had a staff of twelve. Now I have Simone. I dust and Simone sweeps, and between us we keep the dirt at bay. She has no manners but a great heart, the child.

Stranger: The heart of a lion.

Madame: Before I put this back you might memorize these: Forty Avenue Foch, in Crest, the back entrance.

Stranger: Forty Avenue Foch, the back entrance.

Madame: You may find it difficult to get into Crest, by the way. It is a closed area. The pot boy at the Red Lion in Mans.

Stranger: The pot boy.

Madame: Denis the blacksmith at Laloupe. And the next night should take you to the sea and your friends. Are they safely in your mind?

Stranger: Forty Avenue Foch in Crest; the pot boy at the Red Lion in Mans; and Denis the blacksmith at Laloupe. And to be careful getting into Crest.

Madame: Good. Then I can close my notebook—or roll it up, I should say— then—it fits neatly, does it not? Now let us see about some food for you. Perhaps I could find you other clothes. Are these all you—

(*The* Corporal's *voice is heard mingled in fury with the still more furious tones of*

143

Simone. *She is yelling: "Nothing of the sort, I tell you, nothing of the sort!" but no words are clearly distinguishable in the angry row. The door is flung open, and the* Corporal *bursts in dragging a struggling* Simone *by the arm.*)

Simone: (*Screaming with rage and terror*) Let me go, you foul fiend, you murdering foreigner, let me go. (*She tries to kick him.*)

Corporal: (*At the same time*) Stop struggling, you lying deceitful little bit of no-good.

Madame: Will someone explain this extraordinary—

Corporal: This creature—

Madame: Take your hand from my servant's arm, Corporal. She is not going to run away.

Corporal: (*Reacting to the voice of authority and automatically complying*) Your precious servant was overheard telling the gardener that she had never set eyes on this man.

Simone: I did not! Why should I say anything like that?

Corporal: With my own ears I heard her, my own two ears. Will you kindly explain that to me if you can.

Madame: You speak our language very well, Corporal, but perhaps you are not so quick to understand.

Corporal: I understand perfectly.

Madame: What Simone was saying to the gardener, was no doubt what she was announcing to all and sundry at the pitch of her voice this morning.

Corporal: (*Unbelieving*) And what was that?

Madame: That she *wished* she had never set eyes on my nephew.

Corporal: And why should she say that?

Madame: My nephew, Corporal, has many charms, but tidiness is not one of them. As you may have deducted from the episode of the coat. He is apt to leave his room—

Simone: (*On her cue, in a burst of scornful rage*) Cigarette ends, pajamas, towels, bedclothes, books, papers—all over the floor like a *flood*. Every morning I tidy up, and in two hours it is as if a bomb had burst in the room.

Stranger: (*Testily*) I told you already that I was sor—

Simone: (*Interrupting*) As if I had nothing else to do in this enormous house but wait on you.

Stranger: Haven't I said that I—

Simone: And when I have climbed all the way up from the kitchen with your shaving water, you let it get cold; but will you shave in cold? Oh, no! I have to bring up another—

Stranger: I didn't ask you to climb the stairs, did I?

Simone: And do I get a word of thanks for bringing it? Do I indeed? You say: "*Must* you bring it in that hideous jug; it offends my eyes."

Stranger: So it does offend my eyes!

Madame: Enough, enough! We had enough of that this morning. You see, Corporal?

Corporal: I could have sworn—

Madame: A natural mistake, perhaps. But I think you might have used a little more common sense in the matter. (*Coldly*) And a great deal more dignity. I don't like having my servants manhandled.

Corporal: She refused to come.

Simone: Accusing me of things I never said!

Madame: However, now that you are here again you can make yourself useful. My nephew wants to go into Crest the day after tomorrow, and that requires a special pass. Perhaps you would make one out for him.

Corporal: But I—

Madame: You have a little book of permits in your pocket, haven't you?

Corporal: Yes. I—

Madame: Very well. Better make it valid for two days. He is always changing his mind.

Corporal: But it is not for me to grant a pass.

Madame: You sign them, don't you?

Corporal: Yes, but only when someone tells me to.

Madame: Very well, if it will help you, I tell you to.

Corporal: I mean, permission must be granted before a pass is issued.

Madame: And have you any doubt that a permission will be granted to my nephew?

Corporal: No, of course not, madame.

Madame: Then don't be absurd, Corporal. To be absurd twice in five minutes is too often. You may use my desk—and my own special pen. Isn't it a beautiful quill, Corporal?

Corporal: Thank you, madame, no. *We* Germans have come a long way from the geese.

Madame: Yes?

Corporal: I prefer my fountain pen. It is a more efficient implement. (*He writes.*) "For the 15th and the 16th. Holder of identity card number"—What is the number of your identity, monsieur?

Stranger: I have not the faintest idea.

Corporal: You do not know?

Stranger: No. The only numbers I take an interest in are lottery numbers.

Simone: I know the number of monsieur's card.

Madame: (*Afraid that she is going to invent one*) I don't think that likely, Simone.

Simone: (*Aware of what is in her mistress's mind, and reassuring her*) But I really *do* know, madame. It is the year I was born, with two "ones" after it. Many a time I have seen it on the outside of the card.

Corporal: It is good that someone knows.

Simone: It is—192411.

Corporal: 192411. (*He fills in the dates.*)

Madame: (*As he nears the end*) Are you going back to St. Estèphe now, Corporal?

Corporal: Yes, madame.

Madame: Then perhaps you will give my nephew a lift as far as the Marnay crossroads.

Corporal: It is not permitted to take civilians as passengers.

Stranger: But you took me here as a passenger.

Corporal: That was different.

Madame: You mean that when you thought he was a miscreant you took him in your car, but now that you know he is my nephew you refuse?

Corporal: When I brought him here it was on service business.

Madame: (*Gently reasonable*) Corporal, I think you owe me something for your general lack of tact this afternoon. Would it be too much to ask you to consider my nephew a miscreant for the next hour while you drive him as far as the Marnay crossroads?

Corporal: But—

Madame: Take him to the crossroads with you and I shall agree to forget your—your lack of efficiency. I am sure you are actually a very efficient person, and likely to be a sergeant any day now. We won't let a blunder or two stand in your way.

Corporal: If I am caught giving a lift to a civilian, I shall *never* be a sergeant.

Madame: (*Still gentle*) If I report on your conduct this afternoon, tomorrow you will be a private.

Corporal: (*After a long pause*) Is monsieur ready to come now?

Stranger: Quite ready.

Corporal: You will need a coat.

Madame: Simone, get monsieur's coat from the cupboard in the hall. And when you have seen him off, come back here.

Simone: Yes, madame.

(*Exit* Simone)

Corporal: Madame.

Madame: Good day to you, Corporal.

(*Exit* Corporal)

Stranger: Your talent for blackmail is remarkable.

Madame: The place has a yellow barn. You had better wait somewhere till evening, when the dogs are chained up.

Stranger: I wish I had an aunt of your calibre. All mine are authorities on crochet.

Madame: I could wish you were my nephew. Good luck, and be careful. Perhaps one day, you will come back, and dine with me, and tell me the rest of the tale. (*The sound of a running engine comes from outside*)

Stranger: Two years today, perhaps?

Madame: One year today.

Stranger: (*Softly*) Who knows? (*He lifts her hand to his lips.*) Thank you, and *au revoir.* (*Turning at the door*) Being sped on my way by the enemy is a happiness I had not anticipated. I shall never be able to repay you for that. (*He goes out.*) (*Off stage*) Ah, my coat—thank you, Simone. (*Sound of car driving off.* Madame *pours out two glasses. As she finishes,* Simone *comes in, shutting the door correctly behind her and taking two paces into the room*)

Simone: You wanted me, madame?

Madame: You will drink a glass of wine with me, Simone.

Simone: With you, madame!

Madame: You are a good daughter of France and a good servant to me. We shall drink a toast together.

Simone: Yes, madame.

Madame: (*Quietly*) To Freedom.

Simone: (*Repeating*) To Freedom. May I add a bit of my own, madame?

Madame: Certainly.

Simone: (*With immense satisfaction*) And a very bad end to that Corporal!

CURTAIN!

After Reading

1. Select one line spoken by each of the four persons in the play that you feel best conveys the individual's **character**. Justify your choice.

2. For one of the characters in the play, write two **diary** entries. The first entry should represent what the character was feeling before the events in the play and the other should represent his or her feelings the evening after the events. The diary entries should clearly indicate how the character has changed as a result of his or her experiences.

3. There are many examples of **humour**, **dramatic irony**, and **suspense** in this play. Identify one example of each and explain its effect on the **audience**.

4. Sometimes playwrights offer descriptions of the characters at the beginning of the play. For each character in *The Pen of My Aunt*, give at least three characteristics that you think might help a director select the cast.

5. Explain the usefulness of the **stage directions** in the play to the director, actors, and audience.

6. Divide the play into sections for performance by groups in the class. Present the sections in order. After the presentations, evaluate the different interpretations of the characters in the play.

7. Prepare a short **research report** on the role of the French Resistance during World War II to include in the program notes of a production of this play.

Brief Lives: Helen

An Excerpt From *Bachelor Brothers' Bed & Breakfast*

BILL RICHARDSON

"I read <u>Treasure Island</u>. I think about Jim . . ."

Before Reading

Write about your favourite time of year. Use sensory details so that your reader can place himself or herself in that season. Exchange your writing with someone who has written about a different season.

Another sojourn at the Bachelor Brothers' Bed and Breakfast: my seventh January visit. What better place to come to steady the nerves for the year ahead? I return home with my usual reluctance. Back to the flesh-eating cold of the prairie winter! It's been so funny to hear you go on about your few flakes of snow. We won't have weather this mild in Winnipeg until April. May, even. But June makes it worthwhile.

Ever since I was a little girl, I've lived for June. The soft time of year. When June came, the whole world sighed with relief. Then, not even the most freakish weather would bring snow. The two rivers that run through the city, and regularly flooded it,

signed a truce with their banks: they wouldn't challenge them for another year. The lawns shed their winter dinginess and had a short green heyday, before the sun and hot wind scorched them brown. The elm trees that arched over our street turned the colour of mint. There were lilacs. Purple and white. The air was sweet with their breathing. The time of the singing of birds had come.

We grew up slowly back then. My granddaughter, just ten, knows about safe sex. She plays so much Nintendo she has the reflexes of a fighter pilot. She tells me she hates dolls, though I think she still might play with them in her private moments. There are dances at her school, and she has already asked a boy on a date! She falls in love, and with an intensity that astonishes me. Her mother assures me that she is typical. But I despair for her and for her friends. They are being forced into growing like hothouse flowers.

My childhood was so different! On my fourteenth birthday (June 17, another reason I looked forward to that month), my parents arranged for half a dozen girl-friends and me to go on an early evening hayride. Afterwards, we joined other neighbourhood children in a game of hide-and-seek. We had cake and cocoa (or possibly Ovaltine). And then we were allowed to camp out in a big canvas tent my father had pitched in our back yard.

We talked quietly into the night, planning our lives, confessing our small crushes, giggling into our hands. Around three in the morning, we crept from the tent and went for a walk around the neighbourhood in our nightgowns. We shone a flashlight on the darkened houses. We picked some snapdragons from the next-door widow's garden. We felt full of evil. Then we returned to the tent and slept deeply.

I spent my summers reading. Once or twice a week, I took the streetcar to the William St. Library and came home with great armloads of books. I was completely indiscriminate. Anything would do. Jane Austen. The Brontës. *Gone with the Wind*. *The Red Badge of Courage*. Books on self-improvement. "How-to" books. Alone in my room, I would lie on my bed, or sit in a rocker in front of the open, south-facing window—the hot wind blowing across my face—and plough through. Page after page, book after book. I was just passing the time, waiting, waiting, waiting for I didn't know what. For something to happen.

Some books I returned to again and again. I was—am—especially fond of Robert Louis Stevenson. Even *A Child's Garden of Verses* I still read; and not with nostalgia. I love those poems! In September, in 1939, when I was eighteen and studying secretarial and accounting skills at business college, I left a library copy of *Treasure Island* on the streetcar. My borrower's card, with my name and address, was inside. That night, a young man appeared unannounced at the door. I was in my room, practising for a typing speed test. My mother called from downstairs.

"Helen! You have a visitor!"

What must she have thought? Certainly, she couldn't have been more surprised than me when I walked into the living room and saw him, this tall, gangly boy, all limbs and freckles, seated in an armchair and talking to my father. He was my very first gentleman caller.

"How do you do I found your book," he said, all in a nervous rush, pushing it at me with both hands.

"I'll leave you two young people to talk," said my father, rather gracelessly; or so I thought at the time. He liked to tease me about the absence of beaus in my life. This chance visit must have pleased him no end!

A clumsy silence. I had no idea what to say, or how to act. I shielded myself with formality.

"It was very kind of you to return my book, Mr.—"

"Hawkins. Jim Hawkins."

I must have gasped.

"Jim Hawkins? But that's the boy in *Treasure Island*!"

"Don't I know it," he said and laughed.

I began to laugh, too.

And as the whole weight of coincidence and strangeness settled on us, we laughed and laughed and laughed until we were quite literally weak in the knees and had to sit down.

Something had been shaken loose. Now there was nothing between us. We sat and we talked. My mother brought us tea and cookies. He stayed longer and we talked. About what? I can't recall, exactly. I just remember that we spoke with great freedom and abandon. I had never had this kind of easy and immediate communion before; would never have expected to have it with a man. We must have talked about our lives, our families, our notions of the world. We certainly discussed the war, which had just started, and where he expected to go. We talked until my mother appeared again in the living room, to say that it was almost eleven and that if I expected to do well on my test in the morning, I should go to bed.

That was how it started. Jim Hawkins kept calling. He came to see me when he had a day leave from the army training camp. And in January, the day before he got on the train for Montreal, we were married. Nothing was turning out as I'd imagined it. I had envisioned a June wedding: my favourite month, a temperate day, the smell of lilac everywhere. But this was Winnipeg in January. The drifts were six feet high, and you could hardly see through the air, it was so full of frost. The church was freezing, and we both wore our coats. Only our families and one or two friends were with us. The news was as bleak as the weather. All you could smell was danger.

All that night we held each other and talked. Jim slept, finally. I never did. I lay beside him, staring into the dark. I could see nothing but the future, and it was to be so happy! Whatever my gifts, prophecy is not among them. I never saw him again. He was never numbered among the known fallen. He was consigned to the limbo land of the missing, about whom the worst is presumed. For a while, I had vivid imaginings. Gradually, they left me.

It's a commonplace story. A thousand other women my age can tell it. I married again, right after the war. It was a June wedding. The church was full. I had my babies. Now they have theirs. I still love my husband. We still live in Winnipeg. We are fit and active. We belong to a club that walks, all winter long, miles and miles through shopping malls. In February, we go to Palm Springs. We have a timeshare there. But every January, I come here, by myself. My husband understands. I read *Treasure Island*. I think about Jim, about how for a few years I shared his name. I remember who we were, and the wonder of that time. I smile. I haven't cried for him for years.

After Reading

1. Describe Helen's first meeting with Jim Hawkins.

2. Make a list of quotations from the story that create the following feelings: sadness, nostalgia, happiness.

3. a) From paragraph two, label and record two examples of each of the following: **sentence fragment**, **personification**, and **imagery**. For each, explain its effectiveness.

   b) Reread the description you wrote of your favourite season. Try revising your paragraph to include each of the devices above.

4. In the library, look up information on the three authors Helen mentions. Find out whether or not your library carries any books written by these authors. If so, read the first few paragraphs of one of their books and determine the type of reader Helen was as a young woman.

5. The description of the setting of Helen's wedding to Jim might be considered an example of **pathetic fallacy** or **foreshadowing**. Look up these terms and determine why the wedding is an example of each.

6. a) Write a **journal** entry in which you recall a loss or a love in your life. Try to include as much detail as you can.

   b) Underline or highlight strong descriptive words and phrases.

   c) From your underlined parts, create a poem about loss or love.

I Am a Canadian

DUKE REDBIRD

Before Reading

1. What does being a Canadian mean to you?

2. Make a list of Canadian traditions.

I'm a lobster fisherman in Newfoundland
I'm a clambake in P.E.I.
I'm a picnic, I'm a banquet
I'm mother's homemade pie
5   I'm a few drafts in a Legion hall in Fredericton
I'm a kite-flyer in a field in Moncton
I'm a nap on the porch after a hard day's work is done.
I'm a snowball fight in Truro, Nova Scotia
I'm small kids playing jacks and skipping rope
10 I'm a mother who lost a son in the last great war
And I'm a bride with a brand new ring
And a chest of hope
I'm an Easterner
I'm a Westerner
15 I'm from the North
And I'm from the South
I've swam in two big oceans
And I've loved them both
I'm a clown in Quebec during carnival
20 I'm a mass in the Cathedral of St. Paul
I'm a hockey game in the Forum
I'm Rocket Richard and Jean Beliveau

I'm a coach for little league Expos
I'm a baby-sitter for sleep-defying rascals
25 I'm a canoe trip down the Ottawa
I'm a holiday on the Trent
I'm a mortgage, I'm a loan
I'm last week's unpaid rent
I'm Yorkville after dark
30 I'm a walk in the park
I'm Winnipeg gold-eye
I'm a hand-made trout fly
I'm a wheat-field and a sunset
Under a prairie sky
35 I'm Sir John A. MacDonald
I'm Alexander Graham Bell
I'm a pow-wow dancer
And I'm Louis Riel
I'm the Calgary Stampede
40 I'm a feathered Sarcee
I'm Edmonton at night
I'm a bar-room fight
I'm a rigger, I'm a cat
I'm a ten-gallon hat
45 And an unnamed mountain in the interior of B.C.
I'm a maple tree and a totem pole
I'm sunshine showers
And fresh-cut flowers
I'm a ferry boat ride to the Island
50 I'm the Yukon
I'm the North-West Territories
I'm the Arctic Ocean and the Beaufort Sea
I'm the prairies, I'm the Great Lakes,
I'm the Rockies, I'm the Laurentians,
55 I am French
I am English
And I am Metis
But more than this
Above all this
60 I am a Canadian and proud to be free.

After Reading

1. With a partner, cluster the items in this poem into several categories. Compare your categories with the rest of the class.

2. Look up information on at least five famous people or places named in the poem. Describe what each one has contributed to Canada.

3. Make a list of the less than positive images of Canada. Justify their inclusion in the poem.

4. In a well-developed argumentative paragraph, using **definition** as the basic structure, argue for or against the following **thesis**: "I Am a Canadian" is not a poem, but merely a list similar to a grocery list. Be prepared to read your paragraph aloud to the class.

5. Write your own version of "I Am a Canadian". Consider your own feelings, thoughts, and attitudes towards this phrase. Think back to the first Before Reading activity about what being a Canadian means to you. Look at books about Canada, or talk to students or others you know who have lived in other parts of Canada, to help form images of places you haven't travelled to. Include some references to modern Canadian heroes that Duke Redbird has not mentioned.

Coming to Canada

". . . my life is really messed up."

Before Reading

1. Find people in your class who have come to Canada from somewhere else. If everyone in your class was born in Canada, find people whose parents or grandparents have come from other countries. Make a list of the countries represented by your classmates or their families.

2. With a partner, make a list of habits, sayings, traditions, and behaviours that you think are "Canadian" and may seem strange to young people new to Canada.

Too Much Freedom?

BELINDA BINHUA WANG (China)

I like the political freedom in Canadian society. Anyone can openly discuss international or domestic politics and politicians. This was not the case in my motherland, China. I also enjoy personal privacy in this society with regard to lifestyle and personal belongings such as bank accounts.

However, I feel that in some respects Canadians get carried away with freedom of expression. For instance, we, especially the younger generation, are exposed to excessive violence, obscene language, drugs, sex, and infidelity in movies, television programs, magazines, radio, and books. As a result, we may question our family values and weaken in our sense of responsibility towards others and towards society as a whole.

I cannot help but remember my golden years as a teenager in China. Unlike many teens in Canada who are in too much of a hurry to be like adults without fully realizing the implications, I loved my childhood. In those green years I learned many new ideas and enjoyed invaluable experiences in a safe and innocent environment where drugs and sex were never heard of. I grew up in a society with strong moral values and strong family ties. These I believe are very important to keep in my family in Canada.

Here We Go Again

ARMANDO CHO (Brazil)

My native language is Korean. When I moved to Bolivia, I had to learn Spanish, but my parents put me in an American school where we spoke English. Then we moved to Brazil where I continued going to an American school until my parents put me in a Portuguese school. I realized that I was in big trouble. The first year I had to go through hell. Every day after school I had private lessons in Portuguese. Most of the time at home I was doing my homework from school and from my private lessons.

In the second year it got worse because now I had school, private lessons, and swimming lessons. Because I had no time for fun, I became quite serious. Afterwards my parents bought me a computer for entertainment, which for me only meant more studying to do. The following year was even worse. Now I had school, private lessons, swimming lessons, an English course, and piano practice.

Gradually, as I learned Portuguese, my relationships with other kids got better. I wasn't so shy anymore, and I got out more. I took up guitar lessons and Tae-Kwon-Do. I was happy.

Then my parents told me we were going to Canada to start a new life. Now my life is really messed up. I can't speak English well. I can't speak Korean, my native language. I am forgetting Portuguese. I certainly don't feel comfortable living in Canada. I have no close friends.

In the Christmas holidays, I went back to Brazil. There I didn't feel like an outsider. The strangest feeling was that I went back in time, and I was twelve again. Everything had changed, but I couldn't admit that. However I had to face the truth and know that those golden years of my childhood would be only memories from now on.

On my way back from Brazil, in the airplane, I started to realize that those years of my childhood were the best years of my life and nobody could take that away.

Donuts

VICTOR CHAN (Hong Kong)

My first morning in Canada I woke up early and my family decided to go out to have a Canadian breakfast in order to understand more about Canadian customs. Down the street, a pleasant smell invited us into a shop. I went to the counter and ordered coffee for my family while they picked out their choices on the shelves. This was the first time I had used English to communicate with Canadians, but I was very confident.

"My I have five doo-nuts, please," I said to the girl with great confidence.

"Do" and "nut" are very simple words in English.

The girl looked puzzled and she could not understand what I was saying. After some gestures, she said to me, "Do you mean those donuts on the shelves?"

I was very embarrassed at that moment since I knew that I had mispronounced "donut," and I felt shy and afraid to look at the girl again. I realized then I was far from fluent in English. The whole day was spoiled. From that moment on, I was self-conscious about my English.

I Want to Go Back

HARIS BLENTICH (Yugoslavia)

I have gone through many disagreements and conflicts with my parents throughout my life. But since coming to Canada these disagreements have intensified and become a habit. The reason for this is that since coming to Canada I have become closed into my own thoughts and shy because of lack of self-assurance in my knowledge of the English language. But my father does not want me to be sad and lonely and thus tries to persuade me to join various clubs and meet friends just as I did in Yugoslavia. The following is a typical conflict on this matter between my father and me:

"I'm so bored," I said. "I have nothing to do."

My father replied, "Well, why don't you call up some of your friends and go to the movies or something?"

"I don't have their telephone numbers," I said, trying to protect myself.

"Oh, I'm sure you do. It's just that you don't want to call them! What's the matter? You didn't behave like this in Yugoslavia. You were always surrounded by friends!"

"It is not the same as it was in Yugoslavia. I don't even know why we came to this country. We were perfectly happy before we came here. I can hardly wait to go back."

Trying to calm me, father spoke in a gentler tone: "This is an excellent opportunity to learn English perfectly and see some of the world."

"See some of the world! See some of the world! What can I see here? A bunch of skyscrapers. Besides, I would've seen it all sooner or later."

Seeing that it was not easy to convince me to enjoy life in Canada, Father, now with anger in his voice, spoke: "Some day you'll be grateful I brought you here! You must live here and now. Life is as you make it."

I ran to my room, and slammed the door.

I continue to lead my "beautiful" life, counting off the months and years I still have to live in Canada.

After Reading

1. a) Using the Glossary, write down the definition of **slang**, **colloquialism**, and **idiom**. Review the rules that help you spell words correctly. (See The Reference Shelf, pages 243–247.)

    b) With this information fresh in your mind, and thinking back on any personal experiences you may have had, write a letter to a new Canadian student in which you explain why English is such a hard language to learn, and you encourage him or her not to give up. Have a peer read your draft, checking specifically for errors in spelling and grammar.

2. Belinda Binhua Wang refers to her early teen years as "green" and her later teen years as "golden". With a partner, discover the meaning of these colour **symbols**. Then create a chart with three headings: Colour, Meaning, Other Culture's Meaning. Under Colour, list colours that you are interested in researching. Then look up their meaning in a dictionary of symbols. For other cultures, these colours may represent different things. Research at least two cultural meanings.

3. In "Here We Go Again" and "Donuts", communication is a major barrier for these teenagers.

    a) Summarize how their inability to speak a particular language affected each of them.

    b) Write a **journal** entry in which you talk about the fairness or unfairness of parents moving their families to new countries with different languages. Be prepared to share your opinions with others.

4. Belinda Binhua Wang says, "Canadians get carried away with freedom of expression". With your classmates, set up a **debate** in which you agree or disagree with this statement.

5. With a partner, write a **dialogue** that takes place six months later between the father and son in "I Want to Go Back". Indicate changes that may have occurred in the son's attitude and feelings toward Canada. Be prepared to present your dialogue to the class.

The Other Family

HIMANI BANNERJI

"I, you and your father are dark-skinned, dark-haired."

Before Reading

1. In your **journal**, write down the fears you think your parents have about your future.

2. Quickly make a sketch of your family. Compare it to the drawings of the others in your class. How many different family sizes, configurations, and cultures are represented in your class?

When the little girl came home it was already getting dark. The winter twilight had transformed the sheer blue sky of the day into the colour of steel, on which were etched a few stars, the bare winter trees and the dark wedges of the house tops. A few lit windows cast a faint glow on the snow outside. The mother stood at her window and watched the little hooded figure walking toward the house. The child looked like a shadow, her blue coat blended into the shadows of the evening. This child, her own, how small and insubstantial she seemed, and how alone, walking home through a pavement covered with ice and snow! It felt unreal. So different-

ent was this childhood from her own, so far away from the sun, the trees and the peopled streets of her own country! What did I do, she thought, I took her away from her own people and her own language, and now here she comes walking alone, through an alien street in a country named Canada.

As she contemplated the solitary, moving figure, her own solitude rushed over her like a tide. She had drifted away from a world that she had lived in and understood, and now she stood here at the same distance from her home as from the homes which she glimpsed while walking past the sparkling clean windows of the sandblasted houses. And now the door bell rang, and here was her daughter scraping the snow off her boots on the doormat.

Dinner time was a good time. A time of warmth, of putting hot, steaming food onto the table. A time to chat about the important things of the day, a time to show each other what they had acquired. Sometimes, however, her mother would be absent-minded, worried perhaps about work, unsettled perhaps by letters that had arrived from home, scraping her feelings into a state of rawness. This was such an evening. She had served herself and her child, started a conversation about their two cats and fallen into a silence after a few minutes.

"You aren't listening to me, Mother."

The complaining voice got through to her, and she looked at the indignant face demanding attention from the other side of the table. She gathered herself together.

"So what did he do, when you gave him dried food?"

"Oh, I don't quite remember, I think he scratched the ground near his bowl and left."

The child laughed.

"That was smart of him! So why don't we buy tinned food for them?"

"Maybe we should," she said, and tried to change the topic.

"So what did you do in your school today?"

"Oh, we drew pictures like we do every day. We never study anything—not like you said you did in your school. We drew a family—our family. Want to see it?"

"Sure, and let's go to the living room, OK? This is messy." Scraping of chairs and the lighting of the lamps in the other room. They both made a rush for the most comfortable chair, both reached it at the same time and made a compromise.

"How about you sit in my lap? No? OK, sit next to me then and we will squeeze in somehow."

There was a remarkable resemblance between the two faces, except that the face of the child had a greater intensity, given by the wide open eyes. She was fine boned, and had black hair framing her face. Right now she was struggling with the contents of her satchel, apparently trying to feel her way to the paintings.

"Here it is," she said, producing a piece of paper. "Here's the family!"

The mother looked at the picture for a long time. She was very still. Her face had set into an expression of anger and sadness. She was trying very hard not to cry. She didn't want to frighten the child, and yet what she saw made her feel distant from her daughter, as though she was looking at her through the reverse end of a telescope. She couldn't speak at all. The little girl too sat very still, a little recoiled from the body of her mother, as though expecting a blow. Her hands were clenched into fists, but finally it was she who broke the silence.

"What happened?" she said. "Don't you like it?"

"Listen," said the mother, "this is not your family. I, you and your father are dark-skinned, dark-haired. I don't have a blond wig hidden in my closet, my eyes are black, not blue, and your father's beard is black, not red, and you, do you have a white skin, a button nose with freckles, blue eyes and blond hair tied into a pony tail? You said you drew our family. This is not it, is it?"

The child was now feeling distinctly cornered. At first she was startled and frightened by her mother's response, but now she was prepared to be defiant. She had the greatest authority behind her, and she now summoned it to her help.

"I drew it from a book," she said, "all our books have this same picture of the family. You can go and see it for yourself. And everyone else drew it too. You can ask our teacher tomorrow. She liked it, so there!"

The little girl was clutching at her last straw.

"But you? Where are you in this picture?" demanded her mother, by now thoroughly aroused. "Where are we? Is this the family you would like to have? Don't you want us anymore? You want to be a *mem-sahib*, a white girl?"

But even as she lashed out these questions the mother regretted them. She could see that she made no sense to the child. She could feel the unfairness of it all. She was sorry that she was putting such a heavy burden on such young shoulders.

"First I bring her here," she thought, "and then I try to make her feel guilty for wanting to be the same as the others." But something had taken hold of her this evening. Panic at the thought of losing her child, despair and guilt galvanized her into speech she regretted, and she looked with anger at her only child, who it seemed wanted to be white, who had rejected her dark mother. Someday this child would be ashamed of her, she thought, someday would move out into the world of those others. Someday they would be enemies. Confusing thoughts ran through her head like images on an uncontrollable television screen, in the chaos of which she heard her ultimate justification flung at her by her daughter—they wanted me to draw the family, didn't they? "They" wanted "her" to draw "the family." The way her daughter pronounced the words "they" or "the family" indicated that she knew what she was talking about. The simple pronoun "they" definitely stood for authority, for that uncontrollable yet organized world immediately outside, of which the school was the ultimate expression. It surrounded their own private space. "They" had power, "they" could crush little people like her anytime "they" wanted to, and in "their" world that was the picture of the family. Whether her mother liked it or not, whether she looked like the little girl in it or not, made not one jot of difference. That was, yes, that was the right picture. As these thoughts passed through her mind, her anger ebbed away. Abandoning her fury and distance, the mother bowed her head at the image of this family and burst into sobs.

"What will happen to you?" she said. "What did I do to you?"

She cried a great deal and said many incoherent things. The little girl was patient, quietly absorbing her mother's change of mood. She had a thoughtful look on her face, and bit her nails from time to time. She did not protest any more, but nor did she cry. After a while her mother took her to bed and tucked her in, and sat in the kitchen with the fearful vision of her daughter always outside of the window of the blond family, never the centre of her own life, always rejecting herself, and her life transformed into a gigantic peep show. She wept very bitterly because she had caused this destruction, and because she had hated her child in her own fear of rejection, and because she had sowed guilt into her mind.

When her mother went to bed and closed the door, the child, who had been waiting for long, left the bed. She crossed the corridor on her tiptoes, past the row of shoes, the silent gathering of the overcoats and the mirror with the wavy surface, and went into the washroom. Behind the door was another mirror, of full length, and clear. Deliberately and slowly the child took off the top of her pyjamas and surveyed herself with grave scrutiny. She saw the brownness of her skin, the wide, staring, dark eyes, the black hair now tousled from the pillows, the scar on her nose and the brownish pink of her mouth. She stood a while lost in this act of contemplation, until the sound of soft padded feet neared the door, and a whiskered face peeped in. She stooped and picked up the cat and walked back to her own room.

It was snowing again, and little elves with bright coloured coats and snow in their boots had reappeared in the classroom. When finally the coats were hung under pegs with names and boots neatly stowed away, the little girl approached her teacher. She had her painting from the day before in her hand.

"I have brought it back," she said.

"Why?" asked her teacher, "don't you like it any more?"

The little girl was looking around very intently.

"It's not finished yet," she said. "The books I looked at didn't have something. Can I finish it now?"

"Go ahead," said the teacher, moving on to get the colours from the cupboard.

The little girl was looking at the classroom. It was full of children of all colours, of all kinds of shapes of noses and of different colours of hair. She sat on the floor, placed the incomplete picture on a big piece of newspaper and started to paint. She worked long at it—and with great concentration. Finally it was finished. She went back to her teacher.

"It's finished now," she said, "I drew the rest."

The teacher reached out for the picture and spread it neatly on a desk. There they were, the blond family arranged in a semicircle with a dip in the middle, but next to them, arranged alike, stood another group—a man, a woman, and a child, but they were dark-skinned, dark-haired, the woman wore clothes from her own country, and the little girl in the middle had a scar on her nose.

"Do you like it?"

"Who are they?" asked the teacher, though she should have known. But the little girl didn't mind answering this question one bit.

"It's the other family," she said.

After Reading

1. We learn a great deal about the mother's feelings for Canada through what she feels about her daughter. Recreate the chart below to **summarize** the mother's feelings toward her adopted culture. For the second column, use quotations from the text whenever possible.

Page	Mother's Feelings About Daughter	Mother's Feelings for Canada

2. a) In your notebook, write point-form answers to the following questions, referring directly to the story to support your answers:
    - How does the little girl feel about the picture that she has drawn when she first shows it to her mother?
    - How does the girl feel when her mother expresses her disapproval?
    - How does the little girl feel about her picture the next day at school?
    - Compare the way the little girl feels about herself before she shows the picture to her mother with how she feels afterwards.

    What do you think the author is trying to tell us in this story about parents and children?

    b) From the point-form notes you have made, write a paragraph in which you state one **theme** in "The Other Family". Support your choice of theme with clear references to the story.

3. a) Identify the type of **narrator** used in this story.

    b) The second last paragraph of the story reads: "'Who are they?' asked the teacher, *though she should have known*." Explain what the italicized words tell us about the way that the narrator views the teacher.

4. Look over the textbooks you use in school. Prepare a research plan to investigate the ways various cultures are represented in what you read in school.

5. Using the opening paragraph as a model, place your own parent or guardian at the window watching you come home from school, and try to create his or her feelings as he or she watches you. You can write it from the present or the past.

Only Her Hairdresser Knows for Sure

CAROL TALBOT

"Sometimes Mom went to really drastic lengths in her battles against our hair."

Before Reading

1. In your **journal**, write a description of your worst haircut.

2. As a class, discuss how hairstyles have been used as a **symbol** of rebellion.

I could write my life story around "hair". Maybe I'll write a chapter, anyway. Being one of the light-skinned ("high yeller") Talbots, my hair has been, in times past, the bane of my existence, but now, in my enlightened days, the badge of my identity. I'll bet you could measure individual black's degrees of radicalism in their lives with a dated record of their age and changing hairstyles. A scientist could make up some interesting graphs, for example, correlating some celebrities' hairstyles with dates and current events. But seeing as I'm not a scientist . . .

"Woe is me," lamented Mom as she struggled to get some control over my unruly locks—"naps", really. Every day she brushed and combed and pulled and tugged order back into Marilyn's and my

hair. We had the "bad" hair. I remember mine seemed to be a special problem when I was a baby. Mom complained that it was so short and fuzzy it defeated all her efforts at organization—you know, she was and is a very organized individual! Maybe that's why in all those baby pictures of me you often just see one big bow on top of the fuzz, a public indication that a noble effort had been made.

Blessed be the day when our hair grew long enough to put into braids. Mom would go as high as four braids, but not on her life would you ever see *her daughters* with all those little parts and braids "like Topsy". I for one had a real sense of superiority over some of those with "badder" hair who had to wear those tight little braids.

Mom had all kinds of strategies to combat that "bad stuff". When our hair was washed (about every two weeks, 'cause the longer we went between washings the more control could be exerted), she would olive oil it (castor oil sometimes, because that would really condition it, make it less kinky, but it was expensive or something), part it in sections (really!—but only at home where nobody could see), and twist it into what we hilariously called "knobs". When it dried she would then put it into one of the braided styles mentioned earlier.

Very occasionally we got "ringlets". These could be achieved by winding the wet hair around rags and then removing the rags carefully when the hair was dry. What a joy to go swinging with those to church! Of course, they only lasted one day, if that, soon reverting to their customary miscellaneous fuzz that must be quickly disguised in the interminable braids.

Sometimes Mom went to really drastic lengths in her battles against our hair. Once I remember her tying pop bottles on the ends to "stretch it". She also tried washing it in "Super Suds"—after all, who knows what such a powerful detergent could do! Another time she went all out and cut our hair off like boys' in hopes that with a fresh start it might come in "good".

Then, round grade six or so, we were judged too old for braids. "Knobs", curlers, short hair, nylon "mojoes", pin-curls, egg shampoos, 100 daily strokes, ponytails were all enlisted in this ongoing war (escalated to the status of war because of the armaments and troops needed). Marilyn and I both were heavily involved with Mom's workings on our heads. I never knew what it was like to go to bed without a head cover until I was twenty.

Finally, Mom decided to resort to Aunt Kathleen's hot comb. New agonies were visited upon us as Mom began to sweat over our heads every second Saturday in the greasy hot and secret ritual of *really* straightening our hair. Gone were the knobs, the braids, and the tugging and the pulling. Instead we now had the dubious improvement of cringing under the hot comb in the unpractised and sometimes dangerous hands of Mom. The back of the neck was the worst. My skin crawled when I *thought* that she was coming too close, and sometimes she was! You can imagine the problems that we sometimes had trying to explain burns in such outlandish places as the top of the ear or nape of the neck.

We were happy with our greasy, umbrella styles. We had passable imitations of the "good stuff" as long as we didn't get caught in the rain. Oh boy! You didn't want to get your hair wet! Water was the *number one menace* to our new hairdos. Even a little too much humidity would slowly set those stiff strands in motion . . . But . . . rain . . . Heaven forbid . . . on an unprotected 'do, well, bye-bye hairdo—instantaneously. Those naps could shoot back "home" so fast your eyeballs could snap. Now we didn't want to let out the little secret of our hair to the white folks out there, especially our school friends. We didn't want to be any different than we could help, so you can understand why we became a little neurotic about carrying those little fold-up rain hats around. We wouldn't go out on a cloudless day in the middle of a drought without our little rainhats stashed somewhere on our persons! You know, that's the main reason I never learned to swim well at high school: I never wanted to get my hair wet!

When I went to university the hair problem was professionally dispatched to the capable hands of a black hairdresser. She did a job so good that truly "only my hairdresser knew for sure."

Then came the sixties. There I was, way up in the northern bush scrabbling for literature on Martin Luther King, the Black Muslims, and the Civil Rights Movement in the States. I read everything I came across and finally I was moved to do it. I let those marvelous chemical straighteners grow out and went "natural".

That was the beginning of the most significant years of my life. My Afro was a public statement of my identity and the knowledge and courage it took to make that statement were the first small steps toward evolving towards a really "black" me.

After Reading

1. Describe the way the author has ordered her information. Suggest other ways in which the information could have been ordered. Decide which order you think is the most effective. (See The Reference Shelf, page 267.)

2. Select two or three words to describe the **tone** of this story and provide evidence to support each word choice.

3. With a partner, discuss how this selection would be different if it was written about a young male.

4. In the **diary** selections on pages 36 to 37, Lucy Maud Montgomery discusses her desire for bangs as a young girl. Using these two **articles** and personal experience to illustrate or support your ideas, write a short **essay** on the importance of hair to a person's self-image.

5. Write your own life story around "hair".

6. Prepare a short **research report** on the occupations in the beauty industry, including the training required, rates of remuneration, and opportunities for employment.

Borders

THOMAS KING

*". . . I'd be proud of being Blackfoot. . . . But you have
to be American or Canadian."*

Before Reading

Canadian and American societies are very similar. Discuss whether it makes
sense to have border-crossing guards and customs checks between the two
countries.

When I was twelve, maybe thirteen, my
mother announced that we were going to
go to Salt Lake City to visit my sister who
had left the reserve, moved across the line,
and found a job. Laetitia had not left
home with my mother's blessing, but over
time my mother had come to be proud of
the fact that Laetitia had done all of this
on her own.

"She did real good," my mother
would say.

Then there were the fine points to
Laetitia's going. She had not, as my
mother liked to tell Mrs. Manyfingers,
gone floating after some man like a bal-
loon on a string. She hadn't snuck out of
the house, either, and gone to Vancouver
or Edmonton or Toronto to chase rainbows down alleys. And she hadn't been
pregnant.

"She did real good."

I was seven or eight when Laetitia left
home. She was seventeen. Our father was
from Rocky Boy on the American side.

"Dad's American," Laetitia told my
mother, "so I can go and come as I
please."

"Send us a postcard."

Laetitia packed her things, and we
headed for the border. Just outside of Milk
River, Laetitia told us to watch for the
water tower.

"Over the next rise. It's the first thing
you see."

"We got a water tower on the reserve," my mother said. "There's a big one in Lethbridge, too."

"You'll be able to see the tops of the flagpoles, too. That's where the border is."

When we got to Coutts, my mother stopped at the convenience store and bought her and Laetitia a cup of coffee. I got an Orange Crush.

"This is real lousy coffee."

"You're just angry because I want to see the world."

"It's the water. From here on down, they got lousy water."

"I can catch the bus from Sweetgrass. You don't have to lift a finger."

"You're going to have to buy your water in bottles if you want good coffee."

There was an old wooden building about a block away, with a tall sign in the yard that said, "Museum." Most of the roof had been blown away. Mom told me to go and see when the place was open. There were boards over the windows and doors. You could tell that the place was closed, and I told Mom so, but she said to go and check anyway. Mom and Laetitia stayed by the car. Neither one of them moved. I sat down on the steps of the museum and watched them, and I don't know that they ever said anything to each other. Finally, Laetitia got her bag out of the trunk and gave Mom a hug.

I wandered back to the car. The wind had come up, and it blew Laetitia's hair across her face. Mom reached out and pulled the strands out of Laetitia's eyes, and Laetitia let her.

"You can still see the mountain from here," my mother told Laetitia in Blackfoot.

"Lots of mountains in Salt Lake," Laetitia told her in English.

"The place is closed," I said. "Just like I told you."

Laetitia tucked her hair into her jacket and dragged her bag down the road to the brick building with the American flag flapping on a pole. When she got to where the guards were waiting, she turned, put the bag down, and waved to us. We waved back. Then my mother turned the car around, and we came home.

We got postcards from Laetitia regular, and, if she wasn't spreading jelly on the truth, she was happy. She found a good job and rented an apartment with a pool.

"And she can't even swim," my mother told Mrs. Manyfingers.

Most of the postcards said we should come down and see the city, but whenever I mentioned this, my mother would stiffen up.

So I was surprised when she bought two new tires for the car and put on her blue dress with the green and yellow flowers. I had to dress up, too, for my mother did not want us crossing the border looking like Americans. We made sandwiches and put them in a big box with pop and potato chips and some apples and bananas and a big jar of water.

"But we can stop at one of those restaurants, too, right?"

"We maybe should take some blankets in case you get sleepy."

"But we can stop at one of those restaurants, too, right?"

The border was actually two towns, though neither one was big enough to amount to anything. Coutts was on the

Canadian side and consisted of the convenience store and gas station, the museum that was closed and boarded up, and a motel. Sweetgrass was on the American side, but all you could see was an overpass that arched across the highway and disappeared into the prairies. Just hearing the names of these towns, you would expect that Sweetgrass, which is a nice name and sounds like it is related to other places such as Medicine Hat and Moose Jaw and Kicking Horse Pass, would be on the Canadian side, and that Coutts, which sounds abrupt and rude, would be on the American side. But this was not the case.

Between the two borders was a duty-free shop where you could buy cigarettes and liquor and flags. Stuff like that.

We left the reserve in the morning and drove until we got to Coutts.

"Last time we stopped here," my mother said, "you had an Orange Crush. You remember that?"

"Sure," I said. "That was when Laetitia took off."

"You want another Orange Crush?"

"That means we're not going to stop at a restaurant, right?"

My mother got a coffee at the convenience store, and we stood around and watched the prairies move in the sunlight. Then we climbed back in the car. My mother straightened the dress across her thighs, leaned against the wheel, and drove all the way to the border in first gear, slowly, as if she were trying to see through a bad storm or riding high on black ice.

The border guard was an old guy. As he walked to the car, he swayed from side to side, his feet set wide apart, the holster on his hip pitching up and down. He leaned into the window, looked into the back seat, and looked at my mother and me.

"Morning, ma'am."

"Good morning."

"Where you heading?"

"Salt Lake City."

"Purpose of your visit?"

"Visit my daughter."

"Citizenship?"

"Blackfoot," my mother told him.

"Ma'am?"

"Blackfoot," my mother repeated.

"Canadian?"

"Blackfoot."

It would have been easier if my mother had just said "Canadian" and been done with it, but I could see she wasn't going to do that. The guard wasn't angry or anything. He smiled and looked towards the building. Then he turned back and nodded.

"Morning, ma'am."

"Good morning."

"Any firearms or tobacco?"

"No."

"Citizenship?"

"Blackfoot."

He told us to sit in the car and wait, and we did. In about five minutes, another guard came out with the first man. They were talking as they came, both men swaying back and forth like two cowboys headed for a bar or a gunfight.

"Morning, ma'am."

"Good morning."

"Cecil tells me you and the boy are Blackfoot."

"That's right."

"Now, I know that we got Blackfeet on the American side and the Canadians got Blackfeet on their side. Just so we can keep our records straight, what side do you come from?"

I knew exactly what my mother was going to say, and I could have told them if they had asked me.

"Canadian side or American side?" asked the guard.

"Blackfoot side," she said.

It didn't take them long to lose their sense of humor, I can tell you that. The one guard stopped smiling altogether and told us to park our car at the side of the building and come in.

We sat on a wood bench for about an hour before anyone came over to talk to us. This time it was a woman. She had a gun, too.

"Hi," she said. "I'm Inspector Pratt. I understand there is a little misunderstanding."

"I'm going to visit my daughter in Salt Lake City," my mother told her. "We don't have any guns or beer."

"It's a legal technicality, that's all."

"My daughter's Blackfoot, too."

The woman opened a briefcase and took out a couple of forms and began to write on one of them. "Everyone who crosses our border has to declare their citizenship. Even Americans. It helps us keep track of the visitors we get from the various countries."

She went on like that for maybe fifteen minutes, and a lot of stuff she told us was interesting.

"I can understand how you feel about having to tell us your citizenship, and here's what I'll do. You tell me, and I won't put it down on the form. No-one will know but you and me."

Her gun was silver. There were several chips in the wood handle and the name "Stella" was scratched into the metal butt.

We were in the border office for about four hours, and we talked to almost everyone there. One of the men bought me a Coke. My mother brought a couple of sandwiches in from the car. I offered part of mine to Stella, but she said she wasn't hungry.

I told Stella that we were Blackfoot and Canadian, but she said that that didn't count because I was a minor. In the end, she told us that if my mother didn't declare her citizenship, we would have to go back to where we came from. My mother stood up and thanked Stella for her time. Then we got back in the car and drove to the Canadian border, which was only about a hundred yards away.

I was disappointed. I hadn't seen Laetitia for a long time, and I had never been to Salt Lake City. When she was still at home, Laetitia would go on and on about Salt Lake City. She had never been there, but her boyfriend Lester Tallbull had spent a year in Salt Lake at a technical school.

"It's a great place," Lester would say. "Nothing but blondes in the whole state."

Whenever he said that, Laetitia would slug him on his shoulder hard enough to make him flinch. He had some brochures on Salt Lake and some maps, and every so often the two of them would spread them out on the table.

"That's the temple. It's right down-town. You got to have a pass to get in."

"Charlotte says anyone can go in and look around."

"When was Charlotte in Salt Lake? Just when the hell was Charlotte in Salt Lake?"

"Last year."

"This is Liberty Park. It's got a zoo. There's good skiing in the mountains."

"Got all the skiing we can use," my mother would say. "People come from all over the world to ski at Banff. Cardston's got a temple, if you like those kinds of things."

"Oh, this one is real big," Lester would say. "They got armed guards and everything."

"Not what Charlotte says."

"What does she know?"

Lester and Laetitia broke up, but I guess the idea of Salt Lake stuck in her mind.

The Canadian border guard was a young woman, and she seemed happy to see us. "Hi," she said. "You folks sure have a great day for a trip. Where you coming from?"

"Standoff."

"Is that in Montana?"

"No."

"Where are you going?"

"Standoff."

The woman's name was Carol and I don't guess she was any older than Laetitia. "Wow, you both Canadians?"

"Blackfoot."

"Really? I have a friend I went to school with who is Blackfoot. Do you know Mike Harley?"

"No."

"He went to school in Lethbridge, but he's really from Browning."

It was a nice conversation and there were no cars behind us, so there was no rush.

"You're not bringing any liquor back, are you?"

"No."

"Any cigarettes or plants or stuff like that?"

"No."

"Citizenship?"

"Blackfoot."

"I know," said the woman, "and I'd be proud of being Blackfoot if I were Blackfoot. But you have to be American or Canadian."

When Laetitia and Lester broke up, Lester took his brochures and maps with him, so Laetitia wrote to someone in Salt Lake City, and, about a month later, she got a big envelope of stuff. We sat at the table and opened up all the brochures, and Laetitia read each one out loud.

"Salt Lake City is the gateway to some of the world's most magnificent skiing.

"Salt Lake City is the home of one of the newest professional basketball fran-chises, the Utah Jazz.

"The Great Salt Lake is one of the natural wonders of the world."

It was kind of exciting seeing all those color brochures on the table and listening to Laetitia read all about how Salt Lake City was one of the best places in the entire world.

"That Salt Lake City place sounds too good to be true," my mother told her.

"It has everything."

"We got everything right here."

"It's boring here."

"People in Salt Lake City are probably sending away for brochures of Calgary and Lethbridge and Pincher Creek right now."

In the end, my mother would say that maybe Laetitia should go to Salt Lake City, and Laetitia would say that maybe she would.

We parked the car to the side of the building and Carol led us into a small room on the second floor. I found a comfortable spot on the couch and flipped through some back issues of *Saturday Night* and *Alberta Report*.

When I woke up, my mother was just coming out of another office. She didn't say a word to me. I followed her down the stairs and out to the car. I thought we were going home, but she turned the car around and drove back towards the American border, which made me think we were going to visit Laetitia in Salt Lake City after all. Instead she pulled into the parking lot of the duty-free store and stopped.

"We going to see Laetitia?"

"No."

"We going home?"

Pride is a good thing to have, you know. Laetitia had a lot of pride, and so did my mother. I figured that someday, I'd have it, too.

"So where are we going?"

Most of that day, we wandered around the duty-free store, which wasn't very large. The manager had a name tag with a tiny American flag on one side and a tiny Canadian flag on the other. His name was Mel. Towards evening, he began suggesting that we should be on our way. I told him we had nowhere to go, that neither the Americans nor the Canadians would let us in. He laughed at that and told us that we should buy something or leave.

The car was not very comfortable, but we did have all that food and it was April, so even if it did snow as it sometimes does on the prairies, we wouldn't freeze. The next morning my mother drove to the American border.

It was a different guard this time, but the questions were the same. We didn't spend as much time in the office as we had the day before. By noon, we were back at the Canadian border. By two we were back in the duty-free shop parking lot.

The second night in the car was not as much fun as the first, but my mother seemed in good spirits, and, all in all, it was as much an adventure as an inconvenience. There wasn't much food left and that was a problem, but we had lots of water as there was a faucet at the side of the duty-free shop.

One Sunday, Laetitia and I were watching television. Mom was over at Mrs. Manyfingers's. Right in the middle of the program, Laetitia turned off the set and said she was going to Salt Lake City, that life around here was too boring. I had wanted to see the rest of the program and really didn't care if Laetitia went to Salt Lake City or not. When Mom got home, I told her what Laetitia had said.

What surprised me was how angry Laetitia got when she found out that I had told Mom.

172

"You got a big mouth."

"That's what you said."

"What I said is none of your business."

"I didn't say anything."

"Well, I'm going for sure, now."

That weekend, Laetitia packed her bags, and we drove her to the border.

Mel turned out to be friendly. When he closed up for the night and found us still parked in the lot, he came over and asked us if our car was broken down or something. My mother thanked him for his concern and told him that we were fine, that things would get straightened out in the morning.

"You're kidding," said Mel. "You'd think they could handle the simple things."

"We got some apples and a banana," I said, "but we're all out of ham sandwiches."

"You know, you read about these things, but you just don't believe it. You just don't believe it."

"Hamburgers would be even better because they got more stuff for energy."

My mother slept in the back seat. I slept in the front because I was smaller and could lie under the steering wheel. Late that night, I heard my mother open the car door. I found her sitting on her blanket leaning against the bumper of the car.

"You see all those stars," she said. "When I was a little girl, my grandmother used to take me and my sisters out on the prairies and tell us stories about all the stars."

"Do you think Mel is going to bring us any hamburgers?"

"Every one of those stars has a story. You see that bunch of stars over there that look like a fish?"

"He didn't say no."

"Coyote went fishing, one day. That's how it all started." We sat out under the stars that night, and my mother told me all sorts of stories. She was serious about it, too. She'd tell them slow, repeating parts as she went, as if she expected me to remember each one.

Early the next morning, the television vans began to arrive, and guys in suits and women in dresses came trotting over to us, dragging microphones and cameras and lights behind them. One of the vans had a table set up with orange juice and sandwiches and fruit. It was for the crew, but when I told them we hadn't eaten for a while, a really skinny blonde woman told us we could eat as much as we wanted.

They mostly talked to my mother. Every so often one of the reporters would come over and ask me questions about how it felt to be an Indian without a country. I told them we had a nice house on the reserve and that my cousins had a couple of horses we rode when we went fishing. Some of the television people went over to the American border, and then they went to the Canadian border.

Around noon, a good-looking guy in a dark blue suit and an orange tie with little ducks on it drove up in a fancy car. He talked to my mother for a while, and, after they were done talking, my mother called me over, and we got into our car. Just as my mother started the engine, Mel came over and gave us a bag of peanut brittle and told us that justice was a damn hard thing to get, but that we shouldn't give up.

I would have preferred lemon drops, but it was nice of Mel anyway.

"Where are we going now?"

"Going to visit Laetitia."

The guard who came out to our car was all smiles. The television lights were so bright they hurt my eyes, and, if you tried to look through the windshield in certain directions, you couldn't see a thing.

"Morning, ma'am."

"Good morning."

"Where you heading?"

"Salt Lake City."

"Purpose of your visit?"

"Visit my daughter."

"Any tobacco, liquor, or firearms?"

"Don't smoke."

"Any plants or fruit?"

"Not any more."

"Citizenship?"

"Blackfoot."

The guard rocked back on his heels and jammed his thumbs into his gun belt. "Thank you," he said, his fingers patting the butt of the revolver. "Have a pleasant trip."

My mother rolled the car forward, and the television people had to scramble out of the way. They ran alongside the car as we pulled away from the border, and, when they couldn't run any farther, they stood in the middle of the highway and waved and waved and waved.

We got to Salt Lake City the next day. Laetitia was happy to see us, and, that first night, she took us out to a restaurant that made really good soups. The list of pies took up a whole page. I had cherry. Mom had chocolate. Laetitia said that she saw us on television the night before and, during the meal, she had us tell her the story over and over again.

Laetitia took us everywhere. We went to a fancy ski resort. We went to the temple. We got to go shopping in a couple of large malls, but they weren't as large as the one in Edmonton, and Mom said so.

After a week or so, I got bored and wasn't at all sad when my mother said we should be heading back home. Laetitia wanted us to stay longer, but Mom said no, that she had things to do back home and that, next time, Laetitia should come up and visit. Laetitia said she was thinking about moving back, and Mom told her to do as she pleased, and Laetitia said that she would.

On the way home, we stopped at the duty-free shop, and my mother gave Mel a green hat that said "Salt Lake" across the front. Mel was a funny guy. He took the hat and blew his nose and told my mother that she was an inspiration to us all. He gave us some more peanut brittle and came out into the parking lot and waved at us all the way to the Canadian border.

It was almost evening when we left Coutts. I watched the border through the rear window until all you could see were the tops of the flagpoles and the blue water tower, and then they rolled over a hill and disappeared.

After Reading

1. State the **theme** of this story. Write a paragraph supporting your choice.

2. In a small group, discuss who is the hero and who is the villain of this story. Be prepared to report your ideas and conclusions to the class.

3. There are two parallel stories presented in "Borders". One is the story of the border crossing incident and the other, presented in **flashbacks**, deals with Laetitia and her boyfriend, Lester. Explain the relationship of the two stories.

4. At one point in the story, the **narrator** says: "Pride is a good thing to have, you know. Laetitia had a lot of pride, and so did my mother. I figured that someday, I'd have it, too." Write two paragraphs, one explaining the nature of Laetitia's pride and the other, the mother's pride. Give examples from the text to support your points. Write a third paragraph presenting any evidence from the text that suggests the narrator already has his pride.

5. a) Write a **monologue** consistent with the way the **characters** and events are presented in the story, on one of the following:
   - the mother explaining why she insisted on identifying her nationality as Blackfoot rather than Canadian or American
   - Mel presenting his version of what happened after the mother and her son have returned to Canada
   - a member of the press reflecting on his or her role in the border incident
   - the man in the "dark blue suit and an orange tie with little ducks on it" describing his role in the incident
   - a Canadian and an American border guard explaining why they cannot be held responsible for the incident

   b) Perform several monologues as a drama that presents the incident from the **point of view** of the different personal narratives.

6. Writers frequently use real events as an inspiration or basis for a **fictional** story. Select an incident from a television or **newspaper news report** and write a **short story** providing details of **plot**, **character**, and **setting** that contribute to a theme.

7. Look up information about Salt Lake City, Utah on the Internet. Gather additional information on the places mentioned in the story, and prepare a brief **report**.

Lamb to the Slaughter

ROALD DAHL

". . . she could hear them speaking among themselves, their voices thick and sloppy because their mouths were full of meat."

Before Reading

1. With your class, predict what this story could be about.

2. Read the first paragraph. Describe the **mood** in this paragraph and how the writer creates that mood.

The room was warm and clean, the curtains drawn, the two table lamps alight—hers and the one by the empty chair opposite. On the sideboard behind her, two tall glasses. Fresh ice cubes in the ice bucket.

Mary Maloney was waiting for her husband to come home from work.

Now and again she would glance up at the clock, but without anxiety, merely to please herself with the thought that each minute gone by made it nearer the time when he would come. There was a slow smiling air about her, and about everything she did. The drop of the head as she bent over her sewing was curiously tranquil. Her skin—for this was her sixth month with child—had acquired a wonderful translucent quality, the mouth was soft, and the eyes, with their new placid look, seemed larger, darker than before.

When the clock said ten minutes to five, she began to listen, and a few moments later, punctually as always, she heard the tires on the gravel outside, and the car door slamming, the footsteps passing the window, the key turning in the lock. She laid aside her sewing, stood up, and went forward to kiss him as he came in.

"Hullo darling," she said.

"Hullo," he answered.

She took his coat and hung it in the closet. Then she walked over and made the drinks. Soon she was back again in her chair with the sewing, and he was in the other, opposite, holding the tall glass with both his hands, rocking it so the ice cubes tinkled against the side.

For her, this was always a blissful time of day. She knew he didn't want to speak much until the first drink was finished, and she, on her side, was content to sit quietly, enjoying his company after the long hours alone in the house. She loved to luxuriate in the presence of this man, and to feel—almost as a sunbather feels the sun—that warm male glow that came out of him to her when they were alone together. She loved him for the way he sat loosely in a chair, for the way he came in a door, or moved slowly across the room with long strides. She loved the intent, far look in his eyes when they rested on her, the funny shape of the mouth, and especially the way he remained silent about his tiredness, sitting still with himself until some of it went away.

"Tired, darling?"

"Yes," he said. "I'm tired." And as he spoke, he did an unusual thing. He lifted his glass and drained it in one swallow although there was still half of it, at least half of it left. She wasn't really watching him, but she knew what he had done because she heard the ice cubes falling back against the bottom of the empty glass when he lowered his arm. He paused a moment, leaning forward in the chair, then got up and went slowly over to fetch himself another.

"I'll get it!" she cried, jumping up.

"Sit down," he said.

"Darling, shall I get your slippers?"

"No."

She watched him as he began to sip the drink. "I think it's a shame," she said, "that when a policeman gets to be as senior as you, they keep him walking about on his feet all day long."

He didn't answer, so she bent her head again and went on with her sewing; but each time he lifted the drink to his lips, she heard the ice cubes clinking against the side of the glass.

"Darling," she said. "Would you like me to get you some cheese? I haven't made any supper because it's Thursday."

"No," he said.

"If you're too tired to eat out," she went on, "it's still not too late. There's plenty of meat and stuff in the freezer, and you can have it right here and not even move out of the chair."

Her eyes waited on him for an answer, a smile, a little nod, but he made no sign.

"Anyway," she went on, "I'll get you some cheese and crackers first."

"I don't want it," he said.

She moved uneasily in her chair, the large eyes still watching his face. "But you must have supper. I can easily do it here. I'd like to do it. We can have lamb chops. Or pork. Anything you want. Everything's in the freezer."

"Forget it," he said.

"But darling, you *must* eat! I'll fix it anyway, and then you can have it or not, as you like."

She stood up and placed her sewing on the table by the lamp.

"Sit down," he said. "Just for a minute, sit down."

It wasn't till then that she began to get frightened.

"Go on," he said. "Sit down."

She lowered herself back slowly into the chair, watching him all the time with those large, bewildered eyes. He had finished the second drink and was staring down into the glass, frowning.

"Listen," he said. "I've got something to tell you."

"What is it, darling? What's the matter?"

He had now become absolutely motionless, and he kept his head down so that the light from the lamp beside him fell across the upper part of his face, leaving the chin and mouth in shadow. She noticed that there was a little muscle moving near the corner of his left eye.

"This is going to be a bit of a shock to you, I'm afraid," he said. "But I've thought about it a good deal and I've decided the only thing to do is tell you right away. I hope you won't blame me too much."

And he told her. It didn't take long, four or five minutes at most, and she sat very still through it all, watching him with a kind of dazed horror as he went further and further away from her with each word.

"So there it is," he added. "And I know it's kind of a bad time to be telling you, but there simply wasn't any other way. Of course I'll give you money and see you're looked after. But there needn't really be any fuss. I hope not anyway. It wouldn't be very good for my job."

Her first instinct was not to believe any of it, or reject it all. It occurred to her that perhaps he hadn't even spoken, that she herself had imagined the whole thing. Maybe, if she went about her business and acted as though she hadn't been listening, then later, when she sort of woke up again, she might find none of it had ever happened.

"I'll get the supper," she managed to whisper, and this time he didn't stop her.

When she walked across the room she couldn't feel her feet touching the floor. She couldn't feel anything at all—except a slight nausea and a desire to vomit. Everything was automatic now—down the steps to the cellar, the light switch, the deep freeze, the hand inside the cabinet taking hold of the first object it met. She lifted it out, and looked at it. It was wrapped in paper, so she took off the paper and looked at it again.

A leg of lamb.

All right then, they would have lamb for supper. She carried it upstairs, holding the thin bone-end of it with both her hands, and as she went through the living room, she saw him standing over by the window with his back to her, and she stopped.

"For goodness sake," he said, hearing her, but not turning around. "Don't make supper for me. I'm going out."

At that point, Mary Maloney simply walked up behind him and without any pause she swung the big frozen leg of lamb high in the air and brought it down as hard as she could on the back of his head.

She might just as well have hit him with a steel club.

She stepped back a pace, waiting, and the funny thing was that he remained standing there for at least four or five seconds, gently swaying. Then he crashed to the carpet.

The violence of the crash, the noise, the small table overturning, helped bring her out of the shock. She came out slowly, feeling cold and surprised, and she stood for a while blinking at the body, still holding the ridiculous piece of meat tight with both hands.

All right, she told herself. So I've killed him.

It was extraordinary now, how clear her mind became all of a sudden. She began thinking very fast. As the wife of a detective, she knew quite well what the penalty would be. That was fine. It made no difference to her. In fact, it would be a relief. On the other hand, what about the child? What were the laws about murderers with unborn children. Did they kill them both—mother and child? Or did they wait until the tenth month? What did they do?

Mary Maloney didn't know. And she certainly wasn't prepared to take a chance.

She carried the meat into the kitchen, placed it in a pan, turned the oven on high, and shoved it inside. Then she washed her hands and ran upstairs to the bedroom. She sat down before the mirror, tidied her hair, touched up her lips and face. She tried a smile. It came out rather peculiar. She tried again.

"Hullo Sam," she said brightly, aloud.

The voice sounded peculiar too.

"I want some potatoes please, Sam. Yes, and I think a can of peas."

That was better. Both the smile and the voice were coming out better now.

She rehearsed it several times more. Then she ran downstairs, took her coat, went out the back door, down the garden, into the street.

It wasn't six o'clock yet and the lights were still on in the grocery shop.

"Hullo Sam," she said brightly, smiling at the man behind the counter.

"Why, good evening, Mrs. Maloney. How're *you*?"

"I want some potatoes please, Sam. Yes, and I think a can of peas."

The man turned and reached up behind him on the shelf for the peas.

"Patrick's decided he's tired and doesn't want to eat out tonight," she told him. "We usually go out Thursdays, you know, and now he's caught me without any vegetables in the house."

"Then how about meat, Mrs. Maloney?"

"No, I've got meat, thanks. I got a nice leg of lamb from the freezer."

"Oh."

"I don't much like cooking it frozen, Sam, but I'm taking a chance on it this time. You think it'll be all right?"

"Personally," the grocer said, "I don't believe it makes any difference. You want these Idaho potatoes?"

"Oh, yes, that'll be fine. Two of those."

"Anything else?" The grocer cocked his head on one side, looking at her pleasantly. "How about afterwards? What are you going to give him for afterwards?"

"Well—what would you suggest, Sam?"

The man glanced around his shop. "How about a nice big slice of cheesecake? I know he likes that."

"Perfect," she said. "He loves it."

179

And when it was all wrapped and she had paid, she put on her brightest smile and said, "Thank you, Sam. Goodnight."

"Goodnight, Mrs. Maloney. And thank *you*."

And now, she told herself as she hurried back, all she was doing now, she was returning home to her husband and he was waiting for his supper; and she must cook it good, and make it as tasty as possible because the poor man was tired; and if, when she entered into the house, she happened to find anything unusual, or tragic, or terrible, then naturally it would be a shock and she'd become frantic with grief and horror. Mind you, she wasn't *expecting* to find anything. She was just going home with vegetables. Mrs. Patrick Maloney going home with the vegetables on Thursday evening to cook supper for her husband.

That's the way, she told herself. Do everything right and natural. Keep things absolutely natural and there'll be no need for any acting at all.

Therefore, when she entered the kitchen by the back door, she was humming a little tune to herself and smiling.

"Patrick!" she called. "How are you, darling?"

She put the parcel down on the table and went through into the living room; and when she saw him lying there on the floor with his legs doubled up and one arm twisted back underneath his body, it really was rather a shock. All the old love and longing for him welled up inside her, and she ran over to him, knelt down beside him, and began to cry her heart out. It was easy. No acting was necessary.

A few minutes later she got up and went to the phone. She knew the number of the police station, and when the man at the other end answered, she cried to him, "Quick! Come quick! Patrick's dead!"

"Who's speaking?"

"Mrs. Maloney. Mrs. Patrick Maloney."

"You mean Patrick Maloney's dead?"

"I think so," she sobbed. "He's lying on the floor and I think he's dead."

"Be right over," the man said.

The car came very quickly, and when she opened the front door, two policemen walked in. She knew them both—she knew nearly all the men at that precinct—and she fell right into Jack Noonan's arms, weeping hysterically. He put her gently into a chair, then went over to join the other one, who was called O'Malley, kneeling by the body.

"Is he dead?" she cried.

"I'm afraid he is. What happened?"

Briefly, she told her story about going out to the grocer and coming back to find him on the floor. While she was talking, crying and talking, Noonan discovered a small patch of congealed blood on the dead man's head. He showed it to O'Malley who got up at once and hurried to the phone.

Soon, other men began to come into the house. First a doctor, then two detectives, one of whom she knew by name. Later, a police photographer arrived and took pictures, and a man who knew about fingerprints. There was a great deal of whispering and muttering beside the corpse, and the detectives kept asking a lot of questions. But they always treated her kindly. She told her story again, this time right from the beginning, when Patrick had come in, and she was sewing, and he was tired, so tired he hadn't wanted to go out for supper. She told how she'd put the meat in the oven—"it's there now, cooking"—and how she'd slipped out to the grocer for vegetables, and come back to find him lying on the floor.

"Which grocer?" one of the detectives asked.

She told him, and he turned and whispered something to the other detective who immediately went outside into the street.

In fifteen minutes he was back with a page of notes, and there was more whispering, and through her sobbing she heard a few of the whispered phrases—". . . acted quite normal . . . very cheerful . . . wanted to give him a good supper . . . peas . . . cheesecake . . . impossible that she . . ."

After a while, the photographer and the doctor departed and two other men came in and took the corpse away on a stretcher. Then, the fingerprint man went away. The two detectives remained, and so did the two policemen. They were exceptionally nice to her, and Jack Noonan asked if she wouldn't rather go somewhere else, to her sister's house perhaps, or to his own wife who would take care of her and put her up for the night.

No, she said. She didn't feel she could move even a yard at the moment. Would they mind awfully if she stayed just where she was until she felt better. She didn't feel too good at the moment, she really didn't.

Then hadn't she better lie down on the bed? Jack Noonan asked.

No, she said. She'd like to stay right where she was, in his chair. A little later perhaps, when she felt better, she would move.

So they left her there while they went about their business searching the house. Occasionally one of the detectives asked her another question. Sometimes Jack Noonan spoke to her gently as he passed by. Her husband, he told her, had been killed by a blow on the back of the head administered with a heavy blunt instrument, almost certainly a large piece of metal. They were looking for the weapon. The murderer may have taken it with him, but on the other hand he may've thrown it away or hidden it somewhere on the premises.

"It's the old story," he said. "Get the weapon, and you've got the man."

Later, one of the detectives came up and sat beside her. Did she know, he asked, of anything in the house that could've been used as the weapon? Would she mind having a look around to see if anything was missing—a very big wrench, for example, or a heavy metal vase.

They didn't have any metal vases, she said.

"Or a big wrench?"

She didn't think they had a big wrench. But there might be some things like that in the garage.

The search went on. She knew that there were other policemen in the garden all around the house. She could hear their footsteps on the gravel outside, and sometimes she saw the flash of a flashlight through a chink in the curtains. It began to get late, nearly nine she noticed by the clock on the mantle. The four men searching the rooms seemed to be growing weary, a trifle exasperated.

"Jack," she said, the next time Sergeant Noonan went by. "Would you mind giving me a drink?"

"Sure, I'll give you a drink. Some of this?"

"Yes, please. But just a small one. It might make me feel better."

He handed her the glass.

"Why don't you have one yourself," she said. "You must be awfully tired. Please do. You've been very good to me."

"Well," he answered. "It's not strictly allowed, but I might take just a drop to keep me going."

One by one the others came in and were persuaded to take a little drink. They stood around rather awkwardly with the drinks in their hands, uncomfortable in her presence, trying to say consoling things to her. Sergeant Noonan wandered into the kitchen, came out quickly, and said, "Look, Mrs. Maloney. You know that oven of yours is still on, and the meat still inside."

"Oh, *dear* me!" she cried. "So it is!"

"I better turn it off for you, hadn't I?"

"Will you do that, Jack? Thank you so much."

When the sergeant returned the second time, she looked at him with her large, dark, tearful eyes. "Jack Noonan," she said.

"Yes?"

"Would you do me a small favour—you and these others?"

"We can try, Mrs. Maloney."

"Well," she said. "Here you all are, and good friends of dear Patrick's too, and helping to catch the man who killed him. You must be terribly hungry by now because it's long past your suppertime, and I know Patrick would never forgive me, God bless his soul, if I allowed you to remain in his house without offering you decent hospitality. Why don't you eat up that lamb that's in the oven. It'll be cooked just right by now."

"Wouldn't dream of it," Sergeant Noonan said.

"Please," she begged. "Please eat it. Personally I couldn't touch a thing, certainly not what's been in the house when he was here. But it's all right for you. It'd be a favour to me if you'd eat it up. Then you can go on with your work again afterwards."

There was a good deal of hesitating among the four policemen, but they were clearly hungry, and in the end they were persuaded to go into the kitchen and help themselves. The woman stayed where she was, listening to them through the open door, and she could hear them speaking among themselves, their voices thick and sloppy because their mouths were full of meat.

"Have some more, Charlie?"

"No. Better not finish it."

"She *wants* us to finish it. She said so. Be doing her a favour."

"Okay then. Give me some more."

"That's a big club the guy must've used to hit poor Patrick," one of them was saying. "The doc says his skull was smashed all to pieces just like from a sledge hammer."

"That's why it ought to be easy to find."

"Exactly what I say."

"Whoever done it, they're not going to be carrying a thing like that around with them longer than they need."

One of them belched.

"Personally, I think it's right here on the premises."

"Probably right under our very noses. What do you think, Jack?"

And in the other room, Mary Maloney began to giggle.

After Reading

1. a) In your notebook, identify the details the author uses in the first nine paragraphs to develop Mary Maloney's **character**.

    b) Show how these same characteristics help her become the perfect murderer.

2. Roald Dahl is a master of subtlety. Write down five small details that a reader might miss on first reading. Explain why these details are important to a deeper understanding of the story.

3. With a partner, explain the significance of the title, "Lamb to the Slaughter".

4. Describe how the author has used **irony** in the story.

5. a) Rewrite one small section of the story using a **first person narrator**. Compare the two narrative styles and determine which is more effective and why.

    b) Imagine you are Mary Maloney. Write an **interior monologue** about your thoughts and feelings after the police have left.

6. Write a review of this story for a school newspaper. Some things you may want to consider are **theme**, **character development**, and story structure.

7. In a small group, write and perform a **script** in which you put Mary Maloney on trial for murder. Use all the clues from the story to try to get a conviction.

Suitcase Lady

CHRISTIE McLAREN

"Her suitcase is full of dreams."

Before Reading

Discuss with a partner why you personally would or would not give money to people begging on the street. Cite instances when you would give money and others when you would not. Discuss also where you think these people came from and the reasons why they are begging.

Night after night, the woman with the red hair and the purple dress sits in the harsh light of a 24-hour doughnut shop on Queen Street West.

Somewhere in her bleary eyes and in the deep lines of her face is a story that probably no one will ever really know. She is taking pains to write something on a notepad and crying steadily.

She calls herself Vicomtesse Antonia The Linds'ays. She's the suitcase lady of Queen Street.

No one knows how many women there are like her in Toronto. They carry their belongings in shopping bags and spend their days and nights scrounging for food. They have no one and nowhere to go.

This night, in a warm corner with a pot of tea and a pack of Player's, the Vicomtesse is in a mood to talk.

Out of her past come a few scraps: a mother named Savaria; the child of a poor family in Montreal; a brief marriage when she was 20; a son in Toronto who is now 40. "We never got along well because I didn't bring him up. I was too poor. He never call me mama."

She looks out the window. She's 60 years old.

With her words she spins herself a cocoon. She talks about drapes and carpets, castles and kings. She often lapses into French. She lets her tea get cold. Her hands are big, rough, farmer's hands. How

184

she ended up in the doughnut shop remains a mystery, maybe even to her.

"Before, I had a kitchen and a room and my own furniture. I had to leave everything and go."

It's two years that she's been on the go, since the rooming houses stopped taking her. "I don't have no place to stay."

So she walks. A sturdy coat covers her dress and worn leather boots are on her feet. But her big legs are bare and chapped and she has a ragged cough.

Yes, she says, her legs get tired. She has swollen ankles and, with no socks in her boots, she has blisters. She says she has socks—in the suitcase—but they make her feet itch.

As for money, "I bum on the street. I don't like it, but I have to. I have to survive. The only pleasure I got is my cigarette." She lights another one. "It's not a life."

She recalls the Saturday, a long time ago, when she made $27, and laughs when she tells about how she had to make the money last through Sunday, too. Now she gets "maybe $7 or $8," and eats "very poor."

When she is asked how people treat her, the answer is very matter-of-fact: "Some give money. Some are very polite and some are rude."

In warm weather, she passes her time at the big square in front of City Hall. When it's cold she takes her suitcase west to the doughnut shop.

The waitresses who bring food to the woman look upon her with compassion. They persuaded their boss that her sitting does no harm.

Where does she sleep? "Any place I can find a place to sleep. In the park, in stores—like here I stay and sit, on Yonge Street." She shrugs. Sometimes she goes into an underground parking garage.

She doesn't look like she knows what sleep is. "This week I sleep three hours in four days. I feel tired but I wash my face with cold water and I feel okay." Some questions make her eyes turn from the window and stare hard. Then they well over with tears. Like the one about loneliness. "I don't talk much to people," she answers. "Just the elderly, sometimes, in the park."

Her suitcase is full of dreams.

Carefully, she unzips it and pulls out a sheaf of papers—"my concertos."

Each page is crammed with neatly written musical notes—the careful writing she does on the doughnut shop table—but the bar lines are missing. Questions about missing bar lines she tosses aside. Each "concerto" has a French name—Tresor, La Tempete, Le Retour—and each one bears the signature of the Vicomtesse. She smiles and points to one. "A very lovely piece of music. I like it."

She digs in her suitcase again, almost shyly, and produces a round plastic box. Out of it emerges a tiara. Like a little girl, she smoothes back her dirty hair and proudly puts it on. No one in the doughnut shop seems to notice.

She cares passionately about the young, the old and the ones who suffer. So who takes care of the suitcase lady?

"God takes care of me, that's for sure," she says, nodding thoughtfully. "But I'm not what you call crazy about religion. I believe always try to do the best to help people—the elderly, and kids, and my country, and my city of Toronto, Ontario."

After Reading

1. Based on information in the **article**, give reasons why the Suitcase Lady has ended up living on the street.

2. Write an **interior monologue** by the Suitcase Lady that presents her story.

3. When a reporter covers a story like this, people often ask why he or she kept filming or writing rather than helping the person in distress. Explain the obligation you feel that a reporter has towards people in the stories they cover. Explain where you would draw the line and expect them to put their reporting job second and human charity first.

4. Compile a list of ways "Suitcase Lady" is like a **newspaper story** and a list of ways it is like a **short story**. Write a paragraph explaining whether it is more like a newspaper story or a short story.

5. Prepare a short **research report** on the issue of homelessness in Canada.

6. Using print and electronic resources, prepare a **docudrama** to present live or on videotape to raise awareness about Canada's homeless people.

7. Write a short **essay** explaining the responsibility of family and neighbours, the government, and charitable organizations in assisting persons like the Suitcase Lady.

Saving the Earth

". . . unless we connect directly with the earth, we will not have the faintest clue why we should save it."

Before Reading

1. Read only the first paragraphs of both "Healing the Planet" and "Fable for Tomorrow". With a partner, record the similarities and the differences between the two. Consider **point of view**, content, **style**, and **tone**.

2. As a class, make a list of television **commercials** that play on your emotions (positively or negatively) to encourage you to buy a product or support a cause.

Healing the Planet

HELEN CALDICOTT

The only cure is love. I have just walked around my garden. It is a sunny, fall day, and white fleecy clouds are scudding across a clear, blue sky. The air is fresh and clear with no taint of chemical smells, and the mountains in the distance are ringed by shining silver clouds. I have just picked a pan full of ripe cherry guavas to make jam, and the house is filling with the delicate aroma of simmering guavas. Figs are ripening on the trees and developing that gorgeous deep red glow at the apex of the fruit. Huge orange-coloured lemons hang from the citrus trees, and lettuces, beetroots, and cabbages are growing in the vegetable garden. The fruit and vegetables are organically grown, and it feels wonderful to eat food that is free of manmade chemicals and poisons.

It is clear to me that unless we connect directly with the earth, we will not have the faintest clue why we should save it. We need to have dirt under our fingernails and to experience that deep, aching sense of physical tiredness after a day's labour in the garden to really understand nature. To

feel the pulse of life, we need to spend days hiking in forests surrounded by millions of invisible insects and thousands of birds and the wonder of evolution. Of course, I realize that I am very fortunate indeed to be able to experience the fullness of nature so directly—literally in my own backyard. For many people—especially those living in urban areas who are unable to travel out of them regularly—such an experience is difficult to come by. Still, I urge all to try in some way to make a direct connection with the natural world.

Only if we understand the beauty of nature will we love it, and only if we become alerted to learn about the planet's disease processes can we decide to live our lives with a proper sense of ecological responsibility. And finally, only if we love nature, learn about its ills, and live accordingly will we be inspired to participate in needed legislative activities to save the earth. So my prescription for action to save the planet is, Love, learn, live, and legislate.

We must, then, with dedication and commitment, study the harm we humans have imposed upon our beloved earth. But this is not enough. The etiology of the dis-

ease processes that beset the earth is a byproduct of the collective human psyche and of the dynamics of society, communities, governments, and corporations that result from the innate human condition.

We have become addicted to our way of life and to our way of thinking. We must drive our cars, use our clothes dryers, smoke our cigarettes, drink our alcohol, earn a profit, look good, behave in a socially acceptable fashion, and never speak out of turn or speak the truth, for fear of rejection.

The problem with addicted people, communities, corporations, or countries is that they tend to lie, cheat, or steal to get their "fix." Corporations are addicted to profit and governments to power, and as Henry Kissinger once said, "Power is the ultimate aphrodisiac."

The only way to break addictive behaviour is to love and cherish something more than your addiction. When a mother and a father look into the eyes of their newborn baby, do they need a glass of beer or a cigarette to make them feel better? When you smell a rose or a gardenia, do you think of work or do you forget for a brief, blissful moment everything but the

perfection of the flower? When you see the dogwood flowers hovering like butterflies among the fresh green leaves of spring, do you forget your worries?

Now, try to imagine your life without healthy babies, perfect roses, and dog-woods in spring. It will seem meaningless. We take the perfection of nature for granted, but if we woke up one morning and found all the trees dying, the grass brown, and the temperature 120°F, and if we couldn't venture outside because the sun would cause severe skin burns, we would recognize what we once had but didn't treasure enough to save.

To use a medical analogy: we don't really treasure our good health until we lose it or experience a dreadful accident. When I am injured, I always try immediately after the trauma, psychologically to recapture the moment before, when I was intact and healthy. But it is too late.

It is not too late, though, for our planet. We have ten years of work to do, and we must start now. If we don't, it may be too late for the survival of most species, including possibly, our own.

Fable for Tomorrow

RACHEL CARSON

There was once a town in the heart of America where all life seemed to live in harmony with its surroundings. The town lay in the midst of a checkerboard of prosperous farms, with fields of grain and hillsides of orchards where, in spring, white clouds of bloom drifted above the green fields. In autumn, oak and maple and birch set up a blaze of colour that flamed and flickered across a backdrop of pines. Then foxes barked in the hills and deer silently crossed the fields, half hidden in the mists of the fall mornings.

Along the roads, laurel, viburnum and alder, great ferns and wildflowers delighted the traveller's eye through much of the year. Even in winter the roadsides were places of beauty where countless birds came to feed on the berries and on the seed heads of the dried weeds rising above the snow. The countryside was, in fact, famous for the abundance and variety of its bird life, and when the flood of migrants was pouring through in spring and fall people travelled from great distances to observe them. Others came to fish the streams, which flowed clear and cold out of the hills and contained shady pools where trout lay. So it had been from the days many years ago when the first settlers raised their houses, sank their wells, and built their barns.

Then a strange blight crept over the area and everything began to change. Some evil spell had settled on the community: mysterious maladies swept the flocks of chickens; the cattle and sheep sickened and died. Everywhere was a shadow of death. The farmers spoke of much illness among their families. In the town the doctors had become more and more puzzled by new kinds of sickness appearing among their patients. There had been several sudden and unexplained deaths, not only among adults but even among children, who would be stricken suddenly while at play and die within a few hours.

There was a strange stillness. The birds, for example—where had they gone? Many people spoke of them, puzzled and disturbed. The feeding stations in the backyards were deserted. The few birds seen anywhere were moribund; they trembled violently and could not fly. It was a spring without voices. On the mornings that had once throbbed with the dawn chorus of robins, catbirds, doves, jays, wrens, and scores of other bird voices there was now no sound; only silence lay over the fields and woods and marsh.

On the farms the hens brooded, but no chicks hatched. The farmers complained that they were unable to raise any pigs—the litters were small and the young survived only a few days. The apple trees were coming into bloom but no bees droned among the blossoms, so there was no pollination and there would be no fruit.

The roadsides, once so attractive, were now lined with browned and withered vegetation as though swept by fire. These, too, were silent, deserted by all living things. Even the streams were now lifeless. Anglers no longer visited them, for all the fish had died.

In the gutters under the eaves and between the shingles of the roofs, a white granular powder still showed a few patches; some weeks before it had fallen like snow upon the roofs and the lawns, the fields and streams.

No witchcraft, no enemy action had silenced the rebirth of new life in this stricken world. The people had done it themselves.

This town does not actually exist, but it might easily have a thousand counterparts in America or elsewhere in the world. I know of no community that has experienced all the misfortunes I describe. Yet every one of these disasters has actually happened somewhere, and many real communities have already suffered a substantial number of them. A grim spectre has crept upon us almost unnoticed, and this imagined tragedy may easily become a stark reality we all shall know.

After Reading

1. a) These two pieces appear at first to be two different genres, but by the end, we realize their **purposes** and forms are similar. Identify the genres represented by the opening paragraphs of each work.

   b) Explain how "Fable for Tomorrow" changes by the end.

   c) With the class, discuss the effectiveness of each of these **essay** structures and record the conclusions of the discussion in your notebook.

2. a) Make a list of unfamiliar words from each of these essays. For each word, write a sentence in your own words that will help you remember the meaning.

   b) Choose three words from your list and look up their origins. Record the information you find in your notebook. Be prepared to **report** your findings back to the class.

3. Show how each of these essays tries to **persuade** us to take action by appealing to our emotions. (Consider word choice, imagery, and tone.)

4. Write a series of linked paragraphs in which you agree or disagree with the two authors' predictions for the planet and humankind.

5. a) Name something you think needs to be changed in the world. List various emotions you could appeal to in order to persuade your readers to make this change.

   b) Brainstorm ideas for a **commercial** or a public service announcement you could broadcast on television in which you try to persuade your **audience** to change by appealing to these emotions. Write the first minute of your commercial or public service announcement, focusing on your word choice, **imagery**, and **tone**.

   c) Read it to a partner whose role it is to determine whether or not your emotional appeal has been successful.

UNIT 3

Media

Mister Blink

MICHEL TREMBLAY, TRANSLATED BY MICHAEL BULLOCK

"Vote Blink, candidate of the future!"

Before Reading

As a class, brainstorm a list of the roles played by the media during an election.

Mister Blink was dumbfounded. What kind of a game was this? Who had dared. . . . In front of him, on the wooden wall that ran along Cedar Street, was a huge poster, and from the middle of this poster Mister Blink smiled back at himself. Above his photograph, in violent red lettering a foot high, was an incredible sentence that startled Mister Blink: *Vote Blink, candidate of the future!*

Mister Blink removed his glasses and wiped them nervously. He put them back on his nose and looked at the poster again.

He was frightened. He started to run, and jumped onto the first bus to come by. "Impossible, it's impossible," Mister Blink said to himself. "I was dreaming, I must have been! Me, a candidate?"

For weeks people had been talking about these elections. They would surely be the most important elections of the century. One thing was certain, the two major parties were going to fight it out to the death.

Mister Blink was trembling. He tried to read his paper, but he couldn't concentrate on the little black letters that seemed to swarm like crazed flies.

For weeks people had talked about these elections. "Come on, I must have been mistaken!" The most important elections of the century. Without a doubt the most important elections of the century. "It's a joke." The most important. . . . Suddenly he cried out. In the centre-fold of his paper was the biggest picture he had ever seen in a newspaper, right in the middle, spread over the whole page. There he was. There was Mister Blink, and he was smiling, at himself. *Vote Blink, candidate of the future!* He folded his paper and threw it out the window.

Directly across from him a little boy leaned over to his mother and said, "Mommy, look, the man in the poster!" Recognizing Mister Blink, the little boy's mother jumped up and rushed at the poor man, who thought he would die of fear. "Mister Blink," exclaimed the lady as she seized his hands, "Mister Blink, our saviour!" She kissed Mister Blink's hands, and he seemed about to have a fit. "Come now, dear lady," he blurted out finally, "I am not your saviour." But the woman was already screaming as if she were quite mad, "Long live Mister Blink, our saviour!" All the people in the bus repeated together, "Long live Mister Blink. . . ."

At his neighbourhood drugstore Mister Blink bought a bottle of aspirin. "So, going into politics now, are you?" said the druggist. He wore a blue ribbon pinned to his lapel, with lettering in red. . . .

The super's wife stopped him. "Mister Blink," she said, "you wouldn't by any chance have an extra ticket for your big convention tonight, would you?" Mister Blink almost tripped back down the few steps he had just climbed. Convention? What convention? Come on now, there wasn't any convention! "Oh you are the secretive one! I should have known important things were going on in that head of yours. You can bet you sure surprised us, me and my husband."

That evening Mister Blink had no supper. If he had wanted to eat he would not have been able to. The phone didn't stop ringing. His supporters wanted to know when he would get to the convention hall. Mister Blink thought he would go mad. He took the phone off the hook,

put out the lights in his apartment, put on his pyjamas and went to bed.

The crowd demanded their saviour with great shouting in the street. They even threatened to break down his door if he didn't open it within ten minutes. Then the super's wife said a terrible thing that almost started a riot: "Mister Blink may be sick," she said to a journalist. Ten seconds later the crowd had knocked down his door and was triumphantly carrying off its saviour in his pyjamas. What an original outfit! It was a fine publicity stunt. A few men even went home to slip on their own pyjamas. Women in night-gowns went into the streets and followed the procession, intoning hymns of praise. Mister Blink was stunned and could not budge as he sat on the shoulders of the two most respected journalists in the country.

The convention was a smash. Mister Blink did not speak.

The new party, the people's party, Mister Blink's party burst upon the political scene like a bombshell. The old parties got only catcalls. Slavery was abolished, thanks to Mister Blink. B-L-I-N-K. Blink! Blink! Blink! Hurrah! No more tax hikes, Mister Blink would see to that. No more increases in the cost of living. Blink! Blink! Blink!

Only once did Mister Blink attempt to stand and say something. But the crowd cheered so much he was afraid of provoking them and sat down again.

They plied him with champagne, and in the end Mister Blink agreed he was a great hero. As a souvenir of this memorable evening, Mister Blink took home a huge pennant on which, in two-foot letters. . . .

The next day Mister Blink was elected Prime Minister.

After Reading

1. a) Create a chart in which you record Mister Blink's personality traits and the words the writer has used to create that impression of him.

   b) In a paragraph, argue for or against Mister Blink's suitability for his new job.

2. a) List the topics dealt with in the story. Beside each topic, write the **theme** or what the author is trying to say about the topic.

   b) Choose one of the themes and in a well-written paragraph explain how the author has developed this theme in his story.

3. The **narrator** tells us Mister Blink did not speak on the night of the convention. As a class, discuss how "No more tax hikes", "No more increases in the cost of living", and the abolishment of slavery became part of his platform.

4. Find the definition of **satire**. Explain what is being satirized in this story.

5. Explain the role the media had in the election of Mister Blink.

6. As a reporter, write an **interview** that might have taken place with Mister Blink the morning after his election.

7. Research the rules for becoming a political candidate (local, provincial, or federal) in your area. Write a **report** using the information you have found.

R U There?

CONSTANCE L. MELARO

"Dear Anyone Human: Will you please take your head out of the computer long enough to read this? I don't owe you this money!!!"

Before Reading

With a partner, write an exchange of notes (e.g., from a parent to a teacher and vice versa) that gets misinterpreted.

August 17
Dear Madam:
Our records show an outstanding balance of $2.98 on your account. If you have already remitted this amount, kindly disregard this notice.
THIS IS A COMPUTER-GENERATED FORM.
PLEASE DO NOT STAPLE OR MUTILATE.

August 19
Gentlemen:
I do *not* have an outstanding balance. I attached a note with my payment advising you that I had been billed *twice* for the same amount: once under my first name, middle initial, and last name; and then under my two first initials and my last name. (The former is correct.) Please check your records.

September 17
Dear Madam:
Our records show a delinquent balance of $2.98 on your account. Please remit $3.40. This includes a handling charge.
THIS IS A COMPUTER-GENERATED FORM.
PLEASE DO NOT STAPLE OR MUTILATE.

September 19
Dear Machine:
You're not paying attention! I am NOT delinquent in any amount. I do *not* owe this money. I was billed TWICE for the same purchase. PLEASE look into this.

October 17
Dear Madam:
Our records show you to be delinquent for three months. Please remit the new charges plus $4.10. (This includes a handling charge.) May we have your immediate attention in this matter.
THIS IS A COMPUTER-GENERATED FORM.
PLEASE DO NOT STAPLE OR MUTILATE.

October 19
Dear Machine:
MY attention! You want MY attention! Listen here, YOU ARE WRONG!!! I don't owe you $4.10. *CAN YOU UNDERSTAND THAT*? I also DON'T owe you the new charges of $13.46. You billed ME for my MOTHER'S purchase. Please correct this statement AT ONCE!

November 17
Dear Madam:
Our records now show you to be delinquent for four months in the total amount of $17.56 plus $1.87 handling charges. Please remit in full in ten days or your account will be turned over to our Auditing Department for collection.
THIS IS A COMPUTER-GENERATED FORM.
PLEASE DO NOT STAPLE OR MUTILATE.

November 19
Dear Human Machine Programmer—
Dear ANYONE human:
WILL YOU PLEASE TAKE YOUR HEAD OUT OF THE COMPUTER LONG ENOUGH TO READ THIS? I DON'T OWE YOU THIS MONEY!!! I DON'T OWE YOU *ANY* MONEY. *NONE.*

December 17
Dear Madam:
Is there some question about your statement? Our records show no payment on your account since August. Please call DI7-9601 and ask for Miss Gilbert at your earliest convenience.
THIS IS A COMPUTER-GENERATED FORM.
PLEASE DO NOT STAPLE OR MUTILATE.

December 18

. . . Deck the halls with boughs of holly . . .

"Good afternoon. Carver's hopes you enjoyed its recorded program of carols. May I help you?"

"Hello. Yes . . . My bill is . . . should I wait for a 'beep' before I talk?"

"About your bill?"

"Yes. Yes, it's my bill. There's . . ."

"One moment, please. I'll connect you with Adjustments!"

Good afternoon and Merry Christmas. This is a recorded message. All our lines are in service now. If you will please be patient, one of our adjusters will be with you just as soon as a line is free. Meanwhile, Carver's hopes you will enjoy its program of Christmas carols. . . . Deck the halls with . . .

December 26
Dear Machine:

I tried to call you on December 18. Also the 19th, 20th, 21st, 22nd, the 23rd, and the 24th. But all I got was a recorded message and those Christmas Carols. Please, oh, please! Won't you turn me over to a human? *Any* human?

January 17
Dear Madam:

Our Credit Department has turned your delinquent account over to us for collection. Won't you please remit this amount now? We wish to co-operate with you in every way possible, but this is considerably past due. May we have your check at this time.
Very truly yours,
Henry J. Hooper, Auditor

January 19
Dear Mr. Hooper:

You DOLL! You gorgeous HUMAN doll! I refer you to letters I sent to your department, dated the 19th of September, October, November, December, which should clarify the fact that I owe you nothing.

February 17
Dear Madam:

According to our microfilm records, our billing was in error. Your account is clear; you have no balance. We hope there will be no further inconvenience to you. Though this was our fault, you can help us if, in the future, you will always include your account number when ordering by mail or phone.
Very truly yours,
Henry J. Hooper, Auditor

February 19
Dear Mr. Hooper:
Thank you! Oh, thank you, thank you,
thank you!

March 17
Dear Madam:
Our records show you to be delinquent in
the amount of $2.98, erroneously posted
last August to a non-existent account. May
we have your remittance at this time?
THIS IS A COMPUTER-GENERATED FORM.
PLEASE DO NOT STAPLE OR MUTILATE.

March 19
I give up. You win. Here's a check for
$2.98. Enjoy yourself.

April 17
Dear Madam:
Our records show an overpayment on your
part of $2.98. We are crediting this
amount to your account.
THIS IS A COMPUTER-GENERATED FORM.
PLEASE DO NOT STAPLE OR MUTILATE.

After Reading

1. Write a response to the last automated message sent in this selection.

2. Rewrite the incident in this selection as a **newspaper article**, explaining the loss of good will a company suffers due to a communications breakdown such as this.

3. Stage a **debate** in class based on the following resolution: Be it resolved that modern communications technologies have improved to the point that humans can hardly communicate with each other anymore.

4. Write a **short story** or play presenting a series of exchanges that capture the frustration that can occur with new technologies such as automated banking machines, phone answering systems, or the Internet.

5. In a small group, write a video **script** in which you visit the company and get their reactions to the incident. Perform the script, tape the performance (if equipment is available), and present the video to the class.

Etiquette for a Wired World

ROBERT CRIBB

"We haven't yet worked out the community practices, the acceptable behaviour, the rules of the game."

Before Reading

List all the different means available to you for communicating with your friends and family. Discuss as a class whether there is an increase in our ability to communicate effectively as new communications technologies increase.

You're sitting in your office speaking with a colleague when the telephone rings. Your visitor stops mid-sentence and waits for a sign from you, some split-second gesture, a shift of the eye or movement of the hand that hints at the appropriate protocol.

Do you abort your conversation and pick up, or wave the call off to voice mail? Choose carefully.

The wired, always-in-touch, information overload '90s have created what some technology watchers say is an expanding social etiquette vacuum.

We are techno-boors, they say, adopting high-tech gadgetry without a corresponding code of conduct. We're always accessible but never free, dismissing each other with the press of a button like switching channels on a television. And it's making us less courteous and more isolated.

"We haven't yet worked out the community practices, the acceptable behaviour, the rules of the game," says Liss Jeffrey, associate director of the McLuhan Program in Culture and Technology at the University of Toronto. "We've shifted without coming up with the civil rules to give us livable ways to construct our lives. It's more serious than we understand. These are the building blocks of our community."

Never before have so many technological advancements impinged so much on our social conventions.

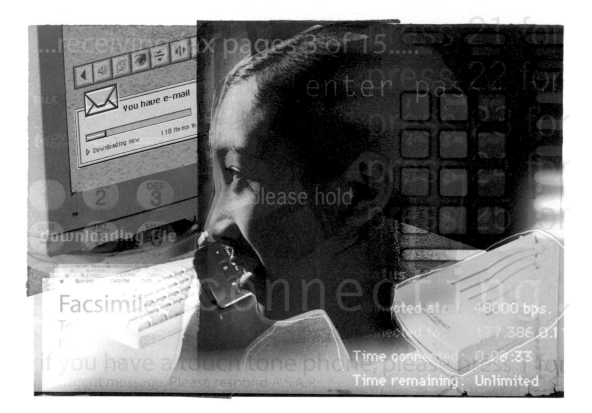

Remember when it was considered improper to answer the telephone during dinner? Or how about the days when you either got a human being or a busy signal when you dialed seven digits.

Reach back to the ancient days, five years ago, when thank-you notes were written on paper.

The blisteringly fast-paced development of communications technology has made such simplicity quaint.

Even teens are supplementing the family telephone with constantly ringing, beeping and vibrating cell phones and pagers. The old busy signal is all but defunct in the new world of multiple "call-management" features.

And e-mail has now surpassed the paper and ink version by volume.

But in adopting all of that high-tech advancement, experts say we've shed our sense of decorum and propriety.

Our common techno-etiquette offences including leaving long, rambling voice mail messages, ignoring e-mails for days, leaving cell phones on to ring in public places, sending e-mails to people who sit a few feet away from us, and perhaps the most controversial electronic etiquette offence, using call waiting.

"It's like someone glancing over your shoulder at a cocktail party in case there's someone else more interesting than you to talk with," says Grant McCracken, a cultural anthropologist in Toronto specializing in popular culture.

Michel Blondeau, special projects director for Toronto software developer

Digital Renaissance, used to have call-waiting. Not anymore.

"It's disruptive. If I'm on the telephone with someone and I'm put on call-waiting, I will hang up. I'm an important person. I'm the centre of my universe. Call me when you have the 10 minutes to talk."

Audrey Glassman, an etiquette expert and author of *Can I Fax a Thank You Note?* tars call-waiting with this spirited pejorative: "It is a technology invented almost solely to be rude. It turns phone calls into a popularity contest. It's profoundly unprofessional."

And yet, we love it.

First launched in 1991, the ubiquitous phone service is one of the most popular features in North America, says Karen Hyponen, a Bell Canada spokesperson.

But despite all the call juggling we're doing, it's nearly impossible to get through the day without being forwarded into at least one voice mail system.

And if you spend time analyzing voice mail messages, you'll understand the etiquette offences of that technology.

Here's a hint: At the tone, be brief.

"It takes a long time for people to get to the point," says Elizabeth Ferrarini, a communications consultant who teaches business communication at Northeastern University in Boston. "Messages are very circuitous. It's incredibly annoying."

When we stop talking and start typing, inverse tendencies seem to emerge. E-mail tends to be curt and reactive, missing the kind of human touch—facial expressions, vocal timbre—that make communication productive, says Blondeau.

"(The Internet is) a very cold medium. Gone are the days when we thought about what we were saying. When you're getting 80 messages a day you need to respond to, it doesn't allow you to move to critical analysis."

It's a broken kind of communication. Ask three questions in an e-mail, for example, and you may well get only one answer, prompting more messaging and growing frustration.

Sit on an e-mail too long before responding (more than a day or two) and you risk giving the impression you are ignoring people.

"People's tolerance for delay has gotten much shorter because e-mail has created the possibility of instant response," says Paul Levinson, a communications professor at New York's Fordham University and author of *The Soft Edge: A Natural History and Future of the Information Revolution*.

"People are operating on different conceptions of etiquette. One person treats e-mail as a conventional letter and doesn't respond right away and the sender sees it as rude."

So what about that ringing phone that interrupted your conversation?

Experts say just let it go.

"The person in your office is the priority," says Ferrarini. "They've taken the time to be there. Be polite."

But even if you already know that interrupting your guest to take a phone call is impolite, chances are you will probably pick up anyway. And you'll leave that cell phone on to ring in the movie theatre and interrupt the next phone conversation you have in order to take another call.

And the reason? Human nature, says Levinson, and the way technology tantalizes our inherent sense of mystery and optimism.

"All of us have these parts of our lives, these unfulfilled dreams, and a ringing phone offers that promise of fulfilment because we don't know who is on the other end," says Levinson.

"Even though 99 times out of 100 it is someone trying to sell you car insurance, all of these disappointments can't extinguish the hope that whoever is calling might be that long lost love or that great job offer—someone who will scratch one of our itches."

After Reading

1. Make a list of the key etiquette offenses identified in this selection when using call-waiting, voice mail, and e-mail.

2. It is suggested in this selection that the rules of etiquette are the "building blocks of our community". Write a short **essay** explaining why you do or do not agree with this assessment.

3. Choose one example of unacceptable behaviour described in the selection and explain how it illustrates Paul Levinson's suggestion in the **article** that the behaviour is a result of "human nature".

4. Review the rules for Internet use in your school and identify which rules address issues of safety and which address etiquette. Identify the issues that are addressed by other rules. Write a brief **report** explaining why certain rules should be dropped or added to the policy.

5. With a partner, create a list of at least five etiquette and five safety rules for the use of cell phones.

6. a) With a partner, list the ten most important technological advances of the twentieth century in order of their importance. Compare your list with that of another pair.

   b) With the same or a different partner, invent a new technological gadget. Present a drawing of the gadget and its features to the class.

Bad Vibrations

SARA JEAN GREEN

"The heavy metal guys . . . are wearing earplugs."

Before Reading

1. With a partner, make a list of loud noises you are exposed to every day.

2. As a class, discuss the differences between skimming, scanning, and in-depth reading. Be sure to talk about when you would use each technique and how each one differs from the others. Use the information on page 253 of The Reference Shelf to help you.

In this crowd, the man in the blue trench coat can't help standing out.

Bearded and bespectacled and a good 50 years older than the young bodies thrashing around him, Dr. Hans Kunov wears head-set-like industrial ear protectors to block out the blood-surging sounds of heavy metal.

Although security guards searched bags and frisked people at the door to make sure cameras and recording equipment weren't smuggled in, no one thought to ask the director of the University of Toronto's Institute of Biomedical Engineering to open his briefcase.

When Metallica takes the stage at The Warehouse, the crowd pushes forward and the mosh pit comes alive. . . . Kunov opens his case and brings out his sound-level meter, an instrument that measures noise intensity in decibels.

Ironically, it's just the heavy metal guys who are wearing earplugs.

The second generation of electrically amplified music listeners has inherited a love of loud music from their boomer parents, the first to plug in to the big concert experience. But it's those very boomer parents who are now realizing there was a price for the adrenaline rush and body buzz that comes with playing it loud.

Boomers Suffer Hearing Loss

The biggest increase in hearing loss is among 40-to-50-year-olds, says Dr. Peter Alberti, senior otolaryngologist (ear, throat and nose specialist) at the Toronto Hospital, General Division, in a research paper to be published in the January issue of *Hearing Instruments*.

There has been "a significant jump" in the number of people whose hearing loss is that of a person at least 10 years older.

Because hearing loss is cumulative and gradual, and because few people get their hearing tested, it's hard for scientists to get a firm grip on the magnitude of the problem. A person's genes and history of concert-going all play a role.

"It all adds up over your life," says Alberti. "Even though there is not a very noticeable difference over time . . . you can lose quite a bit of hearing before you notice it."

Once you lose it, there is no way to get it back.

The Who's lead guitarist, Pete Townshend, is rock's most famous example of a musician with noise-induced hearing loss.

"The real reason I haven't performed live for a long time is that I have severe hearing damage," Townshend told *Rolling Stone* magazine. "It's manifested itself as tinnitus, ringing in the ears at frequencies that I play guitar.

"It hurts, it's painful and it's frustrating."

These days, most rock musicians think it a sign of ultimate stupidity not to protect their hearing.

Metallica drummer Lars Ulrich is quoted by the San Francisco-based Hearing Education and Awareness for Rockers (HEAR) as saying, "Three of the four members of Metallica wear earplugs. Some people think earplugs are for wimps. But if you don't want to hear any records in five or 10 years, that's your decision."

Concert-Goers Are at Risk

But what about concert-goers? Lucas Thompson and Matt Smith, both 16, have been sitting in the lobby for 20 minutes, giving their ears a rest after nearly three hours in front of the speakers listening to Metallica.

"We came out because we were dying in there," says Thompson.

Smith, who looks physically ill, says voices sound muffled and his ears are ringing like crazy. "I've never had it this bad before."

Like most of their peers, and likely, their parents before them, neither wears earplugs at concerts.

"It doesn't sound as good, especially with rumbly bass," Smith says. "I like the music for the sound. I had them in for five minutes, but it sounded like crap."

Industrial workers are not supposed to be exposed to any more than 87 decibels of noise in an eight-hour work day without ear protectors, but there are no rules for concerts.

At a Who concert in Toronto 15 years ago, sound levels soared to 127 decibels, Alberti says. Regular, sustained exposure to 90 decibels may cause permanent damage. Sound becomes painful at around 120 decibels.

"There were thousands of people going into doctors' offices for two weeks after the concert with ringing in their ears. It was unreal."

Back at The Warehouse, as sound levels climb to 115 decibels 10 metres from the stage, Kunov shakes his head. Before he can take readings closer to the speakers, bouncers ask him to leave.

"I have never in my life been exposed to sustained sound levels that high," he says after the concert.

"It's very obvious the auditory systems of those people were overwhelmed. It was one gigantic . . . noise and it didn't do any good for anyone."

Considering his experience as a consultant, measuring noise levels in factories and other loud work environments, Kunov's statement carries added weight.

Young People Could Lose Hearing

It's well accepted in scientific circles that music creates emotive responses. For teenagers and 20-somethings, the organ-massaging vibrations of blaring music produces the ultimate adrenaline high.

"Those kids with ringing in their ears were ignoring an important signal from their own bodies and it will be coming back to haunt them," Kunov says. Ear buzz—or tinnitus—is an early warning sign a person has been overexposed to dangerously high noise levels, he says.

For most people, tinnitus disappears after 24 hours, but continued exposure ups the chances of irreparable harm.

HEAR's founder and executive director Kathy Peck is well acquainted with the pain and frustration of hearing loss.

Bass guitarist for the '80s girl-band The Contractions, Peck says she lost her hearing after opening for Duran Duran in 1984, when a congenital problem worsened with continued exposure to loud music.

Although laser surgery was able to correct some of the damage, Peck still has tinnitus and hyperacusis, a heightened sensitivity to sound that makes a vacuum cleaner sound like a jet plane taking off.

"I think the music industry is in denial," she says.

Even though more musicians are wearing frequency attenuated, individually molded ear protectors, "the industry is terrified of finding out the severity of the impact of music-related hearing loss," says Peck.

Referring to HEAR studies that haven't been published because of a lack of funds, Peck says there is "more and more" noise-induced hearing loss than that caused by old age.

"There are people in their 20s and 30s with the hearing of 60-year-olds because of noise exposure."

And our living environment, with its boomboxes, powerful car audio systems, dance clubs, power tools, video games, jet skis and dirtbikes, is getting louder because of the creation of new artificial sounds coupled with technology that reduces distortion when the volume goes up.

It's impossible to blame a single source.

"It's not just a single concert or a single movie. It's the cumulative effect of noisy jobs, noisy hobbies, noisy recreational activities," says Dr. Margaret Cheesman, a professor and hearing specialist at the University of Western Ontario.

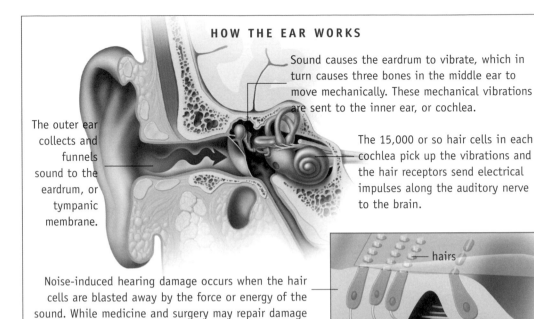

HOW THE EAR WORKS

The outer ear collects and funnels sound to the eardrum, or tympanic membrane.

Sound causes the eardrum to vibrate, which in turn causes three bones in the middle ear to move mechanically. These mechanical vibrations are sent to the inner ear, or cochlea.

The 15,000 or so hair cells in each cochlea pick up the vibrations and the hair receptors send electrical impulses along the auditory nerve to the brain.

hairs

Noise-induced hearing damage occurs when the hair cells are blasted away by the force or energy of the sound. While medicine and surgery may repair damage in the outer and middle ear, nothing can be done to the inner ear—which is about the size of a pea.

nerve

The irony, say audiologists and other hearing specialists, is that what's happening to boomer parents is a sign of what could happen to their children—at a time when deafness caused by childhood diseases such as meningitis and measles has dropped significantly because of immunization.

Geoff Plant, a scientist at the Massachusetts Institute of Technology, is quick to discount the assumption that hearing aids can fix a problem, if it happens.

"It's something like having the radio loud enough but you can't get it on the right station," he says. "We live at a time when people expect technology to solve all their problems but it just doesn't work like that." Surveys in Canada and U.S. indicate kids are increasingly suffering hearing loss caused by headphones with the sound cranked up, says Marshall

Chasin, co-founder and auditory research director of the Musicians' Clinics of Canada.

Loud Music—An Occupational Hazard for Musicians

In its dozen years in Toronto and Hamilton, the clinic has seen about 5,000 musicians.

Any hearing loss can cause learning problems, says Chasin, "but we can't detect any hearing loss from music until someone is in their early teens." It takes about five years of exposure before a hearing test will pick up signs of damage.

Chasin, whose clientele is mostly classical musicians and sound engineers, says most patients walk in the door looking for help with other medical problems, not realizing they've suffered hearing loss.

"All musicians—more than 90 per cent—have the beginnings of hearing loss. But the majority don't realize it at all because it's so gradual and sneaky."

Author of the first book in Canada on the subject, *Musicians And The Prevention Of Hearing Loss* (1996), Chasin says a musician's hearing is affected not only by the instrument he or she plays but also by where they sit or stand on stage.

A violinist is likely to have greater hearing loss in the left ear, which is closest to the violin. String players, who sit in front of the brass and percussion sections, are also more likely to have hearing damage.

Many string instrument players also suffer wrist and arm problems from over-bowing because they can't hear themselves over the other instruments. By attaching a monitor to a bass or cello, musicians can better hear the sounds from their own instruments.

By elevating speakers, the ear is tricked into thinking the sound level is the same, even though the volume is actually lower.

Plexiglas dividers between orchestral sections can act as sound deflectors. Subwoofers, speakers bolted to the bottom of a seat or a plywood board on the floor, can enhance low bass sounds, so the musician doesn't have to play as loudly.

Hearing damage is an occupational hazard few musicians are willing to acknowledge, says a senior member of the Toronto Symphony Orchestra.

"You don't want them thinking there is anything disabling you that will affect your job," says the woman, who asked to be unidentified. "They'll think of you as someone with a handicap.

"It's a really touchy subject. Any kind of hearing loss is a bad thing for a musician."

Although she has no problem tuning her instrument or distinguishing pitches, the woman says her biggest difficulty is hearing conversations, especially when there is background noise.

Even though deflectors are set up behind the string section when a concert is particularly loud, "it is just excruciating sometimes and nothing can really be done about it.

"None of us really likes to wear earplugs because part of the art is playing what is written. We all want to hear (a piece) at its optimal range since that is the way the music was intended to be played."

Classical music audiences, however, are usually well outside the risk levels.

Two days after the Metallica concert, Dr. Hans Kunov takes his briefcase to Roy Thomson Hall.

The night's performance of Mozart's Overture to *Don Giovanni*, Piano Concerto No. 22 and Symphony No. 40, is by a smaller orchestra, the norm in Mozart's time, says Luisa Trisi, a TSO spokesperson.

"Brahms or Mahler would be very loud but Mozart is mainly strings, woodwinds and limited brass," she says.

In this crowd, no one looks twice at the man in the blue trench coat.

Throughout the performance, sound levels hover in the 65 to 75 decibel range. Ironically, the applause from more than 2,000 pairs of hands pushes the noise reading above 85 decibels.

"This is more my type of situation," Kunov says. "You don't get high breathing the air and you can hold a conversation at a decent level."

When Loud Becomes Deafening

How loud is too loud?

On a decibel scale, normal breathing is 10, a whisper is 30, normal conversation is 60, average city traffic noise is around 80, a subway or motorcycle 90, and a pneumatic drill 110.

The Occupational Health and Safety Act warns that exposure to 115 decibels should be for no more than 15 minutes a day; above that, no exposure is permissible.

At 130 decibels, there is a risk of permanent hearing damage after just 75 seconds; at 133 decibels, it drops to 37.5 seconds.

"If you think about the hearing organ like a spiral staircase, then the sensory part—the cells—are like the carpet on that staircase," says professor Norma Slepecky of the Institute for Sensory Research at Syracuse University.

"If you bang one of the those steps really hard, you could blow the entire carpet off. Then it's irretrievable."

Steve Slavin, a self-confessed Deadhead, looks much younger than 30 in his tie-dyed shirt. But he's a concert veteran who figures that in nine years he saw more than 100 shows and circled the Earth three times in pursuit of Jerry Garcia and the Grateful Dead, the Allman Brothers and Hawkwind.

"I used to be a live music junkie," Slavin says.

"I really didn't find Grateful Dead concerts all that deafening, not like The Who or the Allmans, who were always really loud," Slavin says. "At concerts, I always tried to get lawn seats because otherwise, it's like ground zero or something."

He never wears earplugs. And he hasn't had his hearing tested since he was a kid.

Hearing loss? He says he doesn't know.

"But I do seem to say 'What?' an awful lot in conversations."

After Reading

1. Make point-form notes on "Bad Vibrations" using the following subtitles: Dr. Kunov's Research; Dr. Alberti's Findings; Reports From the Musicians and Concert Goers; Kathy Peck and HEAR's Findings; The Effects of Our Environment; Marshall Chasin's Research. Remember, not all the information on these subtitles will be in one place in the article.

2. Write a speech for an **audience** of parents who are opposed to bringing in a live band for a school dance because of their concern about noise levels, and the band's perceived bad influence on young people. (You can support or oppose their views.)

   or

   Write a **letter to the editor** of *The Toronto Star* newspaper in which you respond to the article. (See page 261 for an example of a letter to the editor.)

   For either assignment, brainstorm and organize your ideas before writing. Be sure to adjust your vocabulary, sentence length and complexity, and your **tone** to suit your audience.

3. a) Make a list of the ways the graphic designer has broken up the print to make the article more readable.

   b) Evaluate the effectiveness of the **layout**. Make some suggestions to help create an article that is even more reader friendly.

4. With a partner, describe the intended audience(s) for this article. Be sure to support your opinion with examples of both content and language from the text.

5. In a small group, discuss how the writer has used the following to add interest and variety to a very technical subject: **anecdotes**, references to things/people, quotations, and experts' opinions.

Teens Matter to the Canadian Economy

JO MARNEY

"They have real spending power. . . . They're trend-setters . . . [and] future spenders."

Before Reading

Approximately how much money do you spend every month on clothes, food, entertainment, and so on? Discuss why and how Canadian teens are being targeted by marketers, retailers, and advertisers.

Why is the latest crop of North American teenagers the emerging hot market in the mid-1990s? There are six key reasons:

- They're a growing market as the children of the boomers start to enter adolescence. Currently, they number 2.78 million in Canada alone, a figure that is expected to grow throughout the next 15 years, peaking at more than three million.
- They have real spending power and strong opinions on how to spend it.
- They spend family money, assuming greater responsibility for household shopping than teens did in the past.

- They influence household spending.
- They're trendsetters, not only for one another but the population at large.
- They're future spenders.

But they can't be lumped together and stereotyped. Coca-Cola Ltd. research identified eight distinct teenage groups: preppies, jocks, snowboarder-surfers, rockers, heavy metals, hip-hops, technos and punk-followers.

This new boomer generation differs from the original baby boomers in that they accept mixed races, "non-traditional" families and gender-bending sex roles as mainstream. Family, friends, free time and what the future holds for them are of great importance to them. They're a fun lot, but have their concerns. Power Panel surveys by Winnipeg's *What! A Magazine* reveals that AIDS ranked high in their concern (29%), followed by relationships with the opposite sex (28%), money (26%), choosing a university/college (20%), the economy (20%) and the environment (20%). A U.S. Packaged Facts teen survey characterizes this generation as sophisticated, comfortable with technology, environmentally aware and independent.

It is estimated that teens contribute some $6 billion to the Canadian economy per year. One-third of their money comes from allowances and 57% from their own earnings, according to a Creative Research International Youth target study of young Canadians.

The Power Panel studies reveal that 41% of Canadian teenagers use a bank account that they've opened themselves, and that 58% of the account holders have an automatic banking machine card.

The survey found that two-thirds of Canadian teens do the family grocery shopping at least occasionally. Sixteen percent reported shopping three times a month.

The microwave oven has been around for almost two decades, and today's teens have become the Microwave Generation. The Teenage Marketing and Lifestyle Study by Teenage Research Unlimited of Northbrook, Illinois reported that 47% of 12- to 19-year-olds cook meals for their families and 71% cook for themselves. Looking at the youngest group—the 12- to 15-year-olds—reveals that 48% cook for their families and 70% for themselves.

Keeping up to date in style is important to teenagers. Jeans (the average Canadian teen owns 5.9 pairs), T-shirts and sweats (particularly with sports logos), athletic shoes, denim jackets and blazers are their chosen apparel.

To attract teens, stores need branded merchandise, particularly in denims and athletic shoes, reports a Deloitte & Touche survey. Of the respondents, 97% of boys and 94% of girls said they prefer branded shoes, and 89% of boys and 91% of girls prefer branded jeans. The brands teens consider coolest are Nike, Guess, Levi's, Gap and Sega.

A study found that the preferred stores for buying clothes, in order of preference, are Le Château, Thrifty's, Club Monaco, The Gap, second-hand stores and Levi's. And when it comes to new clothing purchases, Canadian teens are most heavily influenced by: seeing items in stores (71%); by friends (60%); by other kids at school (50%); by their budgets (45%); and by magazine advertising (37%).

Most teens are careful about how they spend their money, but 25% confess to impulse shopping. A study by Canada Market Research reported that, apart from clothing, snacks and soft drinks/juices, teens spend their money on CDs/cassettes/records, going out to movies, video rentals, going to clubs, going to pop/rock concerts, magazines and paperback/hardcover books.

A U.S. Simmons Market Research Bureau teenage study reports that three out of five teens say that advertising helps them to decide what to buy. As to what impresses them most in an advertisement, honesty rates as number one (60%), followed by humor and clear messages (50%), originality (43%) and good music that fits the spot (40%).

The Power Panel surveys found that Canadian teenagers prefer ads that are funny (53%), outrageous or unusual (51%), full of imagery and color (51%) and that make the consumer feel good about the product (51%).

Advertisers are well-advised to remember that teenagers have phoniness sensors and striving to be "cool" is not cool. And, keeping in mind the words of Pope, that "Just as the twig is bent, the tree's inclin'd," forward-thinking companies will actively develop a relationship with teens—the future spenders.

After Reading

1. a) Based on information in this article, select three adjectives that describe the characteristics that advertisers need to be aware of to appeal to young people today. Write a brief **report** that presents evidence to support your choices.

   b) Bring into class print and electronic **advertisements** that appeal to you personally. With a partner, prepare a class presentation analyzing the characteristics of advertisements that work for one or both of you.

2. a) Based on information in this **article**, write a brief **report** for the school newspaper on the role teenagers play in the Canadian economy.

   b) Then create an annotated graphic, including statistics from the article, that visually represents important economic facts about teenagers, their values, and their spending patterns.

3. a) Write a **journal** entry explaining how the economic behaviour and values of teenagers described in the article apply to you. Include at least two ways in which you match the trends and two ways in which you are an exception.

   b) The article states that young people prefer name-brand clothing. Write an **opinion piece** explaining why you believe that teenagers today have or have not bought into the materialistic values of the consumer society.

4. In the last paragraph of the article, the author quotes Alexander Pope, a famous eighteenth-century poet. As a class, discuss the meaning of the quote and its significance to the article.

The Broadcast Code for Advertising to Children

Excerpts from Advertising Standards Canada (ASC)

"Children's advertising should respect and not abuse the power of the child's imagination."

Before Reading

As a class, discuss why it is important to have rules for **advertisements** that are made for young children.

I. BACKGROUND

The purpose of the Code is to serve as a guide to advertisers and agencies in preparing commercial messages which adequately recognize the special characteristics of the children's audience. Children, especially the very young, live in a world that is part imaginary, part real and sometimes they do not distinguish clearly between the two. Children's advertising should respect and not abuse the power of the child's imagination.

Imitation and exploration have always been part of the child's learning process and the broadcast media now form part of that experience. It is recognized, of course, that it remains the primary responsibility of parents "to instruct a child in the way that he/she should go". The Code and the Guidelines that are issued from time to time are designed to help advertisers avoid making that task more difficult.

THE CODE

1. Definitions

(a) "Children's advertising" refers to any paid commercial message that is carried in or immediately adjacent to a children's program. Children's advertising also includes any commercial message that is determined by the broadcaster as being directed to children and is carried in or immediately adjacent to any other program.

(b) Children—"Children" refers to persons under 12 years of age.

(c) A Child Directed Message—"A child directed message" is a commercial message on behalf of a product or service for which children are the only users or form a substantial part of the market as users, and the message (i.e., language, selling points, visuals) is presented in a manner that is directed primarily to children.

(d) Children's Program—A "children's program" is a program that is directed to the under-12 audience, as defined by the broadcaster.

(e) Commercial Message—A "commercial message" has the same meaning as that defined in the Television Broadcasting Regulations, 1987.

(f) Premium—A "premium" is anything offered with or without additional cost, and is conditional upon the purchase of the advertiser's regular product or service.

. . .

3. Factual Presentation

. . .

(b) Written, sound, photographic and other visual presentations must not exaggerate service, product or premium characteristics, such as performance, speed, size, colour, durability, etc.

. . .

5. Avoiding Undue Pressure

(a) Children's advertising must not directly urge children to purchase or urge them to ask their parents to make inquiries or purchases.

(b) Direct response techniques that invite the audience to purchase products or services by mail or telephone are prohibited in children's advertising.

6. Scheduling

(a) The same commercial message or more than one commercial message promoting the same product cannot be aired more than once in a half-hour children's program.

(b) No station or network may carry more than four minutes of commercial messages in any one half-hour of children's programming or more than an average of eight minutes per hour in children's programs of longer duration.

(c) In children's programs only paid commercial messages are included in the four minutes per half-hour limitation.

. . .

8. Price and Purchase Terms

(a) Price and purchase terms, when used, must be clear and complete. When parts or accessories that a child might reasonably suppose to be part of the normal purchase are available only at extra cost, this must be made clear in audio and video.

. . .

(c) The statement in audio, "It has to be put together" or a similar phrase in language easily understood by children must be included when it might normally be assured that the article would be delivered assembled.

(d) When more than one toy is featured in a commercial message it must be made clear in audio and video which toys are sold separately (this includes accessories).

10. Safety

(a) Commercial messages, except specific safety messages, must not portray adults or children in clearly unsafe acts or situations (e.g., the use of flame or fire is not permitted in children's advertising).

(b) Commercial messages must not show products being used in an unsafe or dangerous manner (e.g., tossing a food item into the air and attempting to catch it in the mouth, etc.).

11. Social Values

. . .

(b) Children's advertising must not imply that possession or use of a product makes the owner superior or that without it the child will be open to ridicule or contempt. This prohibition does not apply to true statements regarding educational or health benefits.

After Reading

1. In a short paragraph, explain how a child's imagination could be abused by advertisers.

2. Make point-form notes on the six **definitions** contained in the Code.

3. a) In your notebook, define the words *product* and *premium* as they are used in the Factual Presentation guideline of the code (3).

   b) Rewrite the Factual Presentation guideline. Give examples of how a product or premium might be advertised if this guideline weren't in place.

4. Choose one children's **commercial** you consider good and one you consider poor. Use a **graphic organizer** to gather your thoughts about each one. Referring to your graphic organizer, write an **essay** of at least four paragraphs in which you state your opinions about each commercial. Include specific references to both the commercials and the guidelines to support your opinion.

5. In pairs, write a 15-second commercial for a child's toy. Then explain how your commercial follows the Code's guidelines.

Gender Portrayal Guidelines

Excerpts from Advertising Standards Canada (ASC)

"These guidelines are designed to help . . . develop positive images of men and women and eliminate systemic discrimination based on gender."

Before Reading

1. To assist you when you read this article, look up the following words and write their **definitions** in your notebook: *pervasive, transformations, demeaning, scenario, spectrum, exploitation*.

2. With a partner, think of two **commercials** in which males and females are represented. Write down the characteristics of both the men and the women as they are portrayed in these commercials.

INTRODUCTION

Advertising is first and foremost a business tool, a means of communicating product and service information to potential customers. As such it is a pervasive and powerful mode of communication. Practitioners should recognize and reflect the transformations occurring in our society, not only as a social responsibility but primarily because it makes good business sense to do so.

The social and professional roles of men and women in Canadian society have changed dramatically. Women and men now participate at every level of society and communication is changing to reflect this reality. However, sexual and sex-role stereotyping, demeaning references or images and words that exclude women are still found in everyday dialogue and in the media. Such portrayals are incompatible with the goal of gender equality.

These Guidelines are designed to help creators of advertising develop positive images of men and women and eliminate systemic discrimination based on gender. Advertisers and their agencies are reminded that consultation with the ASC at the storyboard or concept stage can help avoid the expense of producing messages which in their final form may conflict with the Guidelines.

GENDER PORTRAYAL GUIDELINES

I. Authority
Advertising should strive to provide an equal representation of women and men in roles of authority both for the characters within the actual advertising scenario and when representing the advertiser through announcers, voice-overs, experts and on-camera authorities.

2. Decision-Making
Women and men should be portrayed equally as single decision-makers for all purchases including big-ticket items. Where joint decision-making is reflected, men and women should be portrayed as equal participants in the decision-making process whether in the workplace or at home.

3. Sexuality
Advertising should avoid the inappropriate use or exploitation of sexuality of both women and men.

(i) **Sexualization.** There is nothing wrong with positive, relevant sexuality in advertising which portrays a person in control of and celebrating her/his own sexuality. However, people must not be portrayed as primarily sexual or defined by their sexuality. Clothes,

behaviours, positions and poses, camera angles, camera as voyeur, language, audio track and/or product placement can all contribute, implicitly or explicitly, to sexualization.

(ii) **Sexualization of Children.** Boys and girls under 16 must not be portrayed as displaying adult sexual characteristics. Similarly, adult women must not be portrayed as girls or with child-like characteristics while maintaining adult sexual characteristics.

(iii) **Gender Role Stereotype.** Social and sexual interactions must portray women and men as equals and must not reinforce stereotypes, such as male dominant/female submissive.

(iv) **Irrelevant Associations**
a) Using or displaying a woman's sexuality in order to sell a product that has no relation to sexuality is by definition sexually exploitative.
b) Advertising must avoid exploitation of nudity and the irrelevant segmentation of body parts.

(v) **Sexual Harassment.** Advertising must not portray sexual harassment as acceptable or normal behavior in either covert or overt ways, and should avoid representing women as pretty or objects of uncontrolled desire.

(vi) **Objectification and commodization.** People must not be sexually portrayed as objects, toys, animals, or with animal-like characteristics. Nor should products be attributed with negative gender stereotypical characteristics.

4. Violence

Neither sex should be portrayed as exerting domination over the other by means of overt or implied threats, or actual force.

5. Diversity

Advertising should portray both women and men in the full spectrum of diversity and as equally competent in a wide range of activities both inside and outside the home.

6. Language

Advertising should avoid language that misrepresents, offends or excludes women or men.

After Reading

1. Record in your notebook any other words from the guidelines you weren't familiar with. Find their **definitions**.

2. Look back at the two **commercials** you chose before you read the guidelines. For each sub-topic in the guidelines, assess how well your two commercials abide by the guidelines.

3. a) With your class, define *systemic discrimination*.

   b) With a partner, make a list of types of systemic discrimination that can occur (e.g., race discrimination).

   c) In a small group, choose one type of systemic discrimination and, using the same sub-topics as in the Gender Portrayal Guidelines, write some rules you think advertisers should follow to avoid encouraging discrimination.

   d) Collect each group's suggestions and publish them in the classroom.

4. Choose a product to advertise. Create a radio **advertisement** for this product that might have been produced before Advertising Standards Canada (ASC) came into being. Then, create a radio ad for this product reflecting the Gender Portrayal Guidelines. Be ready to perform your second ad for the class and to discuss how this ad differs from the first.

Internet Users Fear Sticky Web of CRTC Regulation

VALERIE LAWTON

"Watchdog's hearings spook 'Netizens' who prize independence."

Before Reading

With a partner, brainstorm a list of positive and negative aspects of the Internet. Compare your list with those of other partners in the class.

OTTAWA—Regulation of cyberspace?

The Canadian Radio-television and Telecommunications Commission, already the country's broadcasting and telecommunications watchdog, is turning its attention to the Internet.

Hearings start today at CRTC headquarters on possible regulation of this new technology.

Many of the so-called Netizens who hang out on the Net have reacted with horror.

Business is also warning that regulation is a threat to the Internet.

But others see an opportunity for the promotion of Canadian culture or sweeping offensive material off the information highway.

The CRTC is studying what, if anything, it should regulate on the Internet. Canadian culture? Privacy? Obscenity? Hate propaganda? Violence? The way women are portrayed? Advertising aimed at children?

It will be the first wide-ranging look at the issue in Canada.

The CRTC insists no decision has been made one way or the other—it just wants to know what people think about the possibility.

Most of the formal submissions made to the CRTC are on the side of no regulation.

And opinions gathered from average folk on an electronic forum for the CRTC have run 10 to one against any new rules.

Passions run strong.

"Get off our backs and get a life," said one man who addressed his note to "CRTC Power Addicts."

Another wrote: "The Internet is a sacred domain of people and computers that should not be violated."

Companies that could be affected if the CRTC decides the Internet is a broadcast medium look at how TV and radio are governed with a sense of dread.

"Creating uncertainty and extra layers of regulation really are unnecessary," said Margo Langford, government programs executive at IBM Canada.

"Right now, our broadcasters have to spend a fortune going before the CRTC and hiring lawyers."

Langford said the reasons for which broadcast regulation was brought in don't apply to the Internet. There's enough room for everyone who wants to be there. And putting up a Web site is cheap.

One of Canada's biggest TV and radio broadcasters—the CBC—has already begun Internet "Webcasting" and doesn't want to face CRTC regulation there too.

"The effect of regulation can be to impede the development of Canadian content on the Web," said CBC president Perrin Beatty.

"If we put a regulatory burden on Canadians that doesn't exist for others outside of the country, we will tend to discourage business in Canada and encourage people to go offshore to operate on the Net."

The government should, however, look at ways other than regulation to encourage the creation of Canadian content for the Internet, he said.

The Independent Film and Video Alliance is one of the leading voices taking the opposite view.

It's proposing a small levy on Internet access companies that would go to help support production of electronic Canadian content.

"I think it's important that Canadians don't miss the boat on that, that we with our resources here stimulate producers, artists," said Peter Sandmark, national co-ordinator of the alliance.

"It's like encouraging entrepreneurship and selling Canadian stories and art and ideas to the world."

The Council of Canadians says the Internet is becoming more and more commercialized—and that spells Americanization.

"The CRTC's role is to ensure that the Internet does not become one massive shopping mall in Canada," said Peter Bleyer, the Ottawa-based group's executive director.

Anti-racism activists, meanwhile, see the hearings as a chance to talk about how to tackle electronic hate propaganda, although some, like B'nai Brith, believe the CRTC isn't qualified to do the job.

Jim Read of the Evangelical Fellowship of Canada is also unsure that the CRTC is the best body to deal with the violent, sexually explicit material he wants off the Web. But he said government needs to start looking at such questions.

The hearings are expected to run for about three weeks and will hear from some 85 groups.

After Reading

1. Make a chart of the special interest groups mentioned in the selection, identifying whether they are in favour of or opposed to the CRTC regulating the Internet. List what or whose interests they represent and the key point(s) in their arguments.

Name of Group	For or Against	Interest(s) Represented by the Group	Argument(s)

2. a) Using the Internet, prepare a **research report** on whether the CRTC has produced any regulations governing the use of the Internet in Canada since the hearings described in the selection.

b) If there are regulations, report on which groups mentioned in the article seem to have influenced the CRTC.

3. **Debate** the following resolution: Be it resolved that use of the Internet in Canada should be regulated.

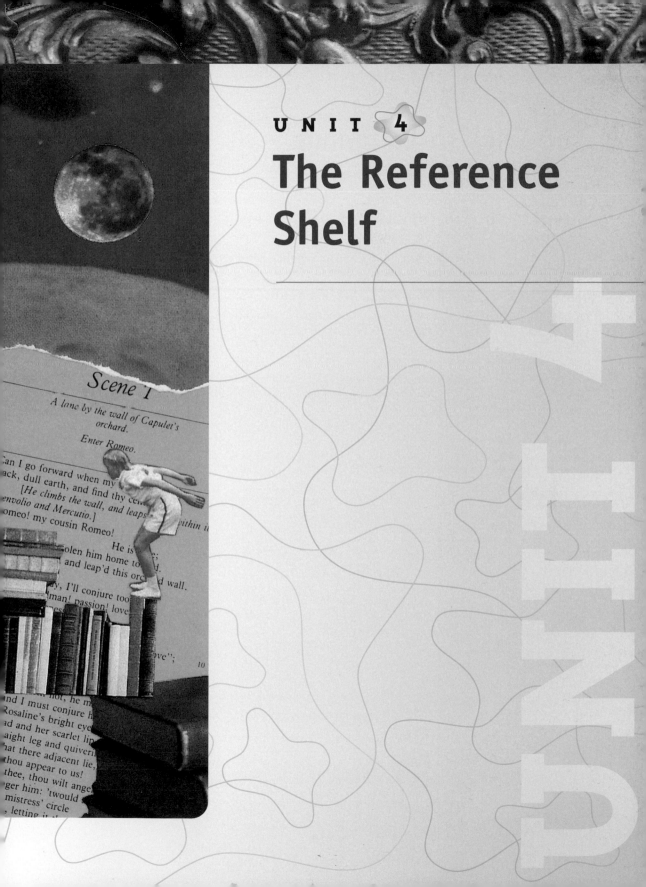

UNIT 4

The English Language

CHANGES TO AND INFLUENCES ON THE ENGLISH LANGUAGE

The world is constantly changing and language changes with it. New words enter our vocabulary from other languages and cultures, from new ideas, and new technologies. Sometimes people invent new words; sometimes words drop out of use because we don't need them in our everyday life. The way we use words also changes as we get older.

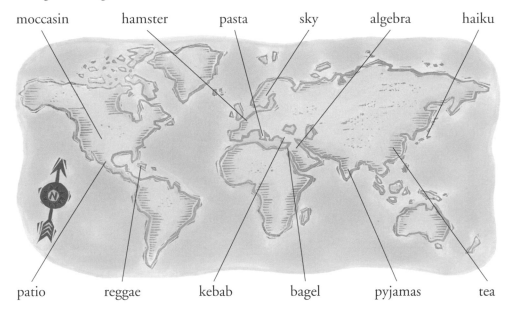

moccasin   hamster   pasta   sky   algebra   haiku

patio   reggae   kebab   bagel   pyjamas   tea

ACTIVITY

Look up the word *etymology* in a dictionary. Check the accuracy of the map above by looking up the "borrowed" words in an etymological dictionary.

Latin Influence on English

Many words in English come from other languages and often their meaning is similar to their meaning in the original language. Once they enter English, these words can change and develop. Quite soon we forget the original language.

For example, the familiar English word *fortune* comes from the Latin *fortuna*. *Fortuna* means luck, usually good luck. We still use the word in this way in English, but sometimes it has a slightly different meaning. For example:

She has just won a fortune on the lottery.

Many of the words we use in English come from (or are derived from) Latin. Look at the following list. Notice any similarities?

Latin	English	Latin	English
adolescens	adolescent	*fragilis*	fragile
adultus	adult	*missa*	mass
angelus	angel	*monasterium*	monastery
candela	candle	*nativus*	native
clima	climate	*severus*	severe
curvus	curve		

ACTIVITY

Complete this chart. Start by placing the following words in the English word column: December, octave, final, navigate, surplus, manuscript. Make sure they line up with their Latin root word.

Latin (root word)	Meaning	English Word	Meaning
centum	a hundred	century	a hundred years
decem			
finis			
manus			
navis			
octo			
plus			

French Influence on English

English has one of the largest vocabularies of all languages, chiefly because of historical events. Early invasions of England by Norse warriors and then by the Normans in 1066 are two examples of how new words were introduced into Britain. In fact, during the rule of the Normans, French became the preferred language of the ruling class, while Anglo-Saxon (and other, older languages) remained the language of "ordinary people". Nowadays, we often have two words for the same thing—one from Anglo-Saxon, and one from French.

ACTIVITIES

1. Read these two sentences. The first contains French-based words and the second uses Anglo-Saxon-based words.

   Immediately upon his return, she offered him a cordial reception and demonstrated her affection with a maternal embrace.

   As soon as he came back, she gave him a hearty welcome and showed her love with a motherly hug.

   Discuss the following questions with a partner:
   - Which of these two sentences seems more formal? Explain why you think this is so.
   - Which would you rather have: *a hearty welcome* or *a cordial reception*? Why?
   - Which of these two phrases seems more genuine and why: *demonstrated her affection with a maternal embrace* or *showed her love with a motherly hug?*

2. We often use French phrases to express a particular idea or feeling. These can become changed with use as they fit into the language. Match the following French phrases to their common meaning:

French Phrase	Common Meaning
au revoir (to *re-see*, literally)	writer's adopted name
nom de plume (name of pen)	a sweet or candy
bon-bon (good-good)	double meaning
double entendre (hear double)	love letter
enfant terrible (terrible child)	until we meet again/goodbye

   continued

228

continued

billet-doux (sweet note)	coolness in danger or difficulty
sang-froid (cold-blood)	someone who behaves in embarrassing ways

3. Using an English dictionary, find out what the following mean:

à la carte	*en route*
joie de vivre	*beau monde*
par excellence	

DEVELOPING YOUR VOCABULARY

A well-developed vocabulary allows you to communicate information, ideas, and feelings accurately, efficiently, and effectively. To develop your vocabulary, you need to read widely, make word lists, do word puzzles (crosswords), play word games (Scrabble), look up unfamiliar words in a dictionary, and look for synonyms (words having the same or similar meaning) of overused words (clichés) in a thesaurus.

LEVELS OF LANGUAGE

Slang is very informal and usually short-lived vocabulary and language patterns used by particular groups or in special informal contexts; it is usually inappropriate to use slang in formal written work, but it is often used in fiction to show character and create mood.

A **colloquialism** is also an informal, conversational expression that is often inappropriate to use in formal written work. Many dictionaries will tell you whether an expression is considered slang or colloquial.

Jargon is specialized vocabulary used by a profession, trade, or group. Jargon must be used carefully in oral and written work. The word has a pejorative meaning, because jargon can often mislead or exclude non-specialists or obscure meaning.

Good writing uses simple, clear language—called plain English—and avoids the use of slang, colloquialisms, and jargon.

1. Read this description of raccoons' behaviour by a biologist and then write a simpler version in plain English.

   "Although solitary under normal prevailing circumstances, raccoons may congregate simultaneously in certain situations of artificially enhanced nutrient resource availability."

2. Now write a plain English version of this extract from a conversation in an office.

   "The major player is Microsoft, and we will need to produce ball-park figures at our next meeting. I will action a report with immediate effect."

Dialect is a local version of language, with its own vocabulary and sentence structure.

ACTIVITY

Here is an extract from a poem by Robert Burns, written in Scottish dialect.

My curse upon your venom'd stang
That shoots my tortured gums alang;
And thr' my lugs gies monie a twang,
Wi' gnawing vengeance;
Tearing my nerves wi' bitter pang,
Like racking engines!

Write down what you think this poem is about, then write it out in your own words. Make a list of the words that you find difficult.

We use **Standard Canadian English** in our schools. This is the oral and written English used by a broad range of Canadian society (including government, medicine, law, science, business, and the media). Standard Canadian English follows accepted rules and practices of grammar, usage, spelling, and punctuation.

Formal and Informal Language and Style

Language is like clothing: often it is fine to dress—or speak—casually. At other times you need to "dress up" your language to fit the occasion. It is a good idea to know when and how to use formal and informal language.

ACTIVITIES

1. a) List the following in order of formality, beginning with the most formal and ending with the least formal:
   - a letter to a friend
   - a conversation with friends
   - a discursive essay
   - an advertisement for a car
   - a school report
   - a letter to the bank manager to arrange a loan
   - a personal diary
   - a leaflet about leisure facilities in your area
   - a tabloid newspaper article
   b) Underline any items you had difficulty placing and discuss your reasons with a partner.

2. Choose appropriate and effective language to write a request or complaint related to one of the items listed above.

PARTS OF SPEECH

Nouns: A **noun** names a person, place, or thing. Nouns are commonly classed as **common**, **proper**, **collective**, **concrete**, and **abstract**.

Noun Type	What It Is	Examples
common	refers to a general name	book, pen, river, woman
proper	refers to a particular name and starts with a capital letter	William Shakespeare, China, Sudbury
collective	stands for a collection of like things—not just one thing	class, flock, herd, jury, pack, team
concrete	names things that can be seen, touched, heard, smelled, and tasted	mirror, table, water
abstract	names things that cannot be seen, touched, heard, smelled, and tasted—can be ideas, qualities, emotions	honesty, justice, love, prejudice

Pronouns: A **pronoun** takes the place of a noun. Pronouns agree with their antecedents (the words to which pronouns refer) in number and gender, but take the case of the role they play in a sentence. Pronouns can be classed as **possessive** or **relative**.

Pronoun Type	What It Is	Examples
possessive	indicates ownership	my (mine), her (hers), your (yours)
relative	introduces subordinate idea	that, which, who, whom, whose This is the woman *whom* we found in the park.

Rewrite the following sentences replacing the nouns (in italics) with one of
these pronouns: *it, she, their, we, they, her*.

  a) Rita was looking forward to being on the basketball team, but *Rita*
     broke her leg.

  b) Look at this watch. *This watch* belonged to my father.

  c) My neighbours go camping every year. This year *my neighbours* went
     camping in British Columbia.

  d) I met Andy and Dean this afternoon and *Andy and Dean and I* went
     swimming.

  e) When you give the book back to Yasmin, ask *Yasmin* if I can borrow
     the book sometime.

  f) Linda and Errol were going to ride *Linda and Errol's* bikes to the
     beach this morning, but *Linda and Errol's bikes* both had punctures.

Adjective: An **adjective** describes a noun or pronoun. Adjectives can be **positive**,
comparative, or **superlative**.

Adjective Type	What It Is	Examples
positive	describes a person or thing	good, fast, beautiful "Her sister-in-law's face, dusted with gold powder, was luminous and breathtaking." (from *Ice Bangles*)
comparative	compares two persons or things	better, faster, more beautiful "A telephone conversation with a passive listener is even more difficult than a face-to-face conversation." (from "Listen Up!")

continued

continued

Adjective Type	What It Is	Examples
		"In fact I find sometimes Zein's more traditional than I am." (from "How We Met")
superlative	compares more than two persons or things	best, fastest, most beautiful "Priscilla was, hands down, the largest student . . ." (from "Priscilla and the Wimps")

ACTIVITY

Here is a piece of writing without any adjectives. Use your own adjectives to make this piece of writing as powerful and descriptive as possible. You can add whole sentences of your own, if you wish.

It is spring. There is a harbour with seagulls flying. A man is walking towards a boat. He is carrying nets and buoys. There is the sound of a foghorn.

Verb: A **verb** identifies the action or state of being in a sentence.
Verbs can be classed as **transitive**, **intransitive**, and **linking** or **copula**.

Verb Type	What It Is	Examples
transitive	has at least one direct object	The woman *left* the bank.
intransitive	has no direct object	The woman *wept*.
linking or copula	has a subjective completion	The young man *is* unhappy.

Add suitable verbs to the following nouns, and using the illustration, write a short piece called On the Way to School.

traffic lights	children	sun
baby in a stroller	cyclist	streetcar
clouds	dog	baby bottles
police cars	shopkeeper	

Verb Tenses: The tense of a verb tells when the action occurs. Tense can also be used to suggest conditions, for example, that an event is possible (*might, could*), ought to happen (*should*), or is likely (*will*). The four most commonly used **tenses** in English are **present**, **past**, **future**, and **conditional**.

ACTIVITIES

1. Write down the tenses of the following sentences—past, present, future, or conditional.
   a) I love chocolates.
   b) We will go to the cinema on Friday.
   c) You should be careful.
   d) They played football all day.
   e) I have written a letter to my sister.
   f) If you drive slowly, you should be safer.

continued

continued

2. We also use certain expressions to help with time, such as *last year* or *after*. Write out these sentences using the correct words or phrases from the list of time expressions to the right.

We'll be going home.	tomorrow
He was always the same.	before I go
I will say goodbye.	afterwards
She felt unhappy about their talk.	whenever I saw him

3. Write three sentences of your own using words or phrases that refer to time.

Voice: If the subject does the action of the verb, as in *the police chased the car*, it is called the **active voice**. If the subject receives the action of the verb, as in *the car was chased by the police*, it is called the **passive voice**.

In both of these examples, the same information is given, but the effect is slightly different.

In writing, the active voice tends to be more direct, hard-hitting, or forceful. Using the passive voice makes writing more formal and a little bit distant.

ACTIVITY

Read these two short passages and discuss with a friend the differences you notice between them. Decide which passage uses the active voice.

The explosion severely damaged the oil rig. Rescue helicopters picked up survivors, some of them badly injured. A Navy destroyer helped the rescue team.

The oil rig was severely damaged by the explosion. Survivors, some of them badly injured, were picked up by rescue helicopters. The rescue team was helped by a Navy destroyer.

Adverbs: An **adverb** describes the how, when, or where of a verb, adjective, or other adverb. In English, adverbs frequently end in *ly*.

Some examples are:

He will talk *proudly*. (how)
He will talk *tomorrow*. (when)
He will talk *here*. (where)

ACTIVITY

Here's an example of a Tom Swifty: *I'm having trouble controlling the chain-saw, Tom said off-handedly*. Make up a few Tom Swifties of your own.

Conjunctions: A **conjunction** is a word that joins words or groups of words used in the same way. Common conjunctions are *and, but, or, so, for, when*. A conjunction can also be a group of words: *as though, except that, in order that, so that, not only…but also*.

Conjunctions can be divided into two classes: **coordinating** and **subordinating**.

Conjunction Type	What It Is	Examples
coordinating	combines words or groups of words used in the same way (principal clauses)	and, but, nor, or, so I was sick *and* I didn't go to school. He asked for apples *or* oranges. She wrote down the number *but* she lost it.
subordinating	combines a main idea (principal clause) and a secondary or less important idea (subordinate clause)	although, if, provided that, whenever, because, unless, while *Though* they didn't win the match, the team was happy to have made it to the finals.

Other common parts of speech include **prepositions**, **interjections**, and **participles**.

Other Parts of Speech	What It Is	Examples
preposition	relates a noun or pronoun to some other words in the sentence	behind, by, in, into, on, to, through, with
interjection	refers to a word or words that express emotion or thought, but are not essential to the sentence	hey, oh dear, oops, well
participle	part verb and part adjective and looks like the *ing* form of the verb	The boy playing the fiddle is from the East Coast. (As an adjective, *playing* describes the boy; as a verb, it takes the object *fiddle*.)

PARTS OF SENTENCES

Words need to be joined together to make sense. Joined together, they are called sentences. It is easy to recognize a sentence: it begins with a capital letter and it ends with a period (or other end punctuation), and it contains at least one verb.

Sentences come in a variety of forms. Some sentences are simple; some are complex. All sentences have a **subject** and a **predicate**. Sentences may also include such elements as an **object**, a **subjective completion**, **prepositional** and **participial phrases**, and **principal** and **subordinate clauses**.

Sentence Part	What It Is	Examples
subject	indicates who or what performs the action of the predicate	*Marion* went to the doctor. Her *checkup* showed that she is not ill.
predicate	indicates what is said about the subject; the key word in the predicate is the verb	The plumber *fixed* the leaking pipe. Mohammed *is* intelligent.
object	receives the action of a transitive verb	The force of the river broke *the dam*.
subjective completion	describes the subject after a linking or copula verb	Ms. Quek is the *teacher*. Joanne is *smart*.
prepositional phrase	acts as adjectives and adverbs describing nouns, pronouns, and verbs	The kitten *in the tree* can't get down.
participial phrase	acts as adjectives and adverbs describing nouns, pronouns, and verbs	The man *swimming the lake* is raising money for charity.
principal clause (independent clause)	refers to the main idea and makes sense on its own	I did not go to school.
subordinate clause (dependent clause)	refers to the secondary idea and does not make sense on its own	I did not go to school *because I had a dentist appointment*.

Draw a table like this:

Main Clause	Subordinate Clause

Look at these sentences. Decide which are the main and subordinate clauses and enter them into the appropriate columns of your table.

a) While he was running for the bus, Joe bumped into an old lady.
b) The teacher, who seemed delighted, congratulated the class.
c) The football game was called off because it began to snow.
d) Even though the sun was shining, the wind was very cold.
e) If the weather brightens up, we will go sailing.

SENTENCE VARIETY

In order to have variety in your writing, it is necessary to know about different sentence kinds, types, and orders.

Sentence Variety	What It Is	Examples
Kind of Sentence:		
assertive	makes statements	The Prime Minister is addressing the United Nations today.
interrogative	asks questions	What is the capital city of Newfoundland?
imperative	makes commands	Hand in your homework.

continued

continued

Sentence Variety	What It Is	Examples
Kind of Sentence:		
exclamatory	expresses emphatic or emotional utterances	Be careful! There's a car coming!
Type of Sentence:		
simple	has one principal clause and a subject and predicate	The priceless antiques were all stolen.
complex	has one principal clause and one or more subordinate clauses, which need a connecting word to relate the subordinate clause(s) to the principal clause	I wanted to go to Sudbury because I had never seen the Big Nickel.
compound	has two or more principal clauses, which need connecting words	Mario joined the others for lunch and then they all went skating.
Sentence Order:		
natural	subject precedes predicate	Mary bought a new dress.
inverted	places the predicate before the subject	At the bottom of the drawer was her wedding ring.
split	sometimes used for effect	"In a house, in a suburb, in a city, there were a man and his wife who loved each other very much and were living happily ever after." (from *Once Upon a Time*)

SENTENCE ERRORS

Writers often make errors. The table below lists some common sentence errors and how they can be corrected.

Sentence Error	What It Is	Examples	How to Fix It
fragment	a group of words, punctuated as a sentence that lacks either a subject or a complete verb	Because I like having my homework done on time. The narrator thinking about the loss of his friend.	Because I like having my homework done on time, I do it as soon as I get home. The narrator is thinking about the loss of his friend.
run-on	too many complete sentences or thoughts joined together as a single sentence	I got a lot of work done today I finished the reading and I went to the library and I started my assignment but I didn't fill in the chart because I couldn't find it.	I got a lot work done today. I finished the reading and I went to the library. I started my assignment but I didn't fill in the chart because I couldn't find it.
comma splice	a comma is used to separate two main clauses or two complete thoughts that are not connected by a connecting word	I liked the story by Nadine Gordimer, it deals with apartheid in South Africa.	I liked the story by Nadine Gordimer. It deals with apartheid in South Africa.

continued

continued

Sentence Error	What It Is	Examples	How to Fix It
subject-verb disagreement	the rule that singular subjects take singular verbs and plural subjects take plural verbs is broken	Janet and Dave is taking skiing lessons this winter.	Janet and Dave are taking skiing lessons this winter.
pronoun-antecedent disagreement	pronouns do not agree with their antecedents in gender (masculine, feminine, or neuter), number (singular or plural), or person (first person, second person, or third person)	Students must submit his/her assignment on time.	Students must submit their assignments on time.

SPELLING RULES

To communicate effectively, you must be able to spell correctly, and the key thing to remember with spelling is: *When in doubt, use the dictionary!*

There are many words that are commonly misspelled. The table on the next page lists some spelling rules for some of these words.

Spelling Rule	Examples	Exceptions
i before *e* except after *c*	diet, pier deceive, receive	neighbour, weigh
When a word ends in a consonant, double the final consonant before adding a suffix (a word ending) that begins with a vowel (*-ing*, *-ent*) only if the word: a) has only one syllable or is accented on the last syllable *and* b) ends in a single consonant preceded by a single vowel.	swim + *ing* = swimming repel + *ent* = repellent	Canadian usage prefers to double the final *l* regardless of accent: travel+er = traveller shovel+ing = shovelling An exception is *unparalleled*. If in doubt, consult a Canadian dictionary.
Drop the silent *e* before adding a suffix that begins with a vowel.	care + *ing* = caring sense + *ible* = sensible	Keep the final *e* in words ending in *ce* or *ge* before a suffix that beings with *a* or *o*: manageable courageous To avoid confusion with other words, keep the final silent *e* in some words: dye + *ing* = dyeing (not dying) singe + *ing* = singeing (not singing)
Keep the final silent *e* before adding a suffix that begins with a consonant.	definite + *ly* = definitely	true + *ly* = truly

continued

continued

Spelling Rule	Examples	Exceptions
When a word ends in *y* preceded by a consonant, change the *y* to *i* before any suffix except one beginning with *i*.	accompany + *ment* = accompan**i**ment plenty + ful = plent**i**ful	Some one-syllable words: shy + *ness* = shyness sky + *ward* = skyward *lady* and *baby* with suffixes: ladylike ladyship babyhood

Rules for Plurals	Examples	Exceptions
To form the plurals of most English nouns, add *s*.	violin/violin**s** night/night**s**	
To form the plurals of other nouns, follow these rules. 1. If the noun ends in *s*, *x*, *z*, *ch*, or *sh*, add *es*. 2. If the noun ends in *y* preceded by a consonant, change the *y* to *i* and add *es*. 3. If the noun ends in *y* preceded by a vowel, add *s*.	dress/dress**es** fox/fox**es** match/match**es** cry/cr**ies** theory/theor**ies** ruby/rub**ies** monkey/monkey**s** buoy/buoy**s**	The plurals of proper nouns: The Murph**ys** The Rile**ys**

continued

Rules for Plurals	Examples	Exceptions
4. For some nouns ending in *f* or *fe*, change the *f* to *v* and add *s* or *es*. Noticing how the plural is pronounced will help you remember whether to change the *f* to *v*.	kerchief/kerchief**s** safe/safe**s** knife/kni**ves**	
5. If the noun ends in *o* preceded by a consonant, add *es*. (The best way to handle plurals of words ending in *o* preceded by a consonant is to check their spelling in a dictionary.)	potato/potato**es** hero/hero**es** tomato/tomato**es**	Nouns for musical terms: piano/piano**s** solo/solo**s** Some nouns have two plural forms: tornado/tornado**s** or tornado**es** zero/zero**s** or zero**es**
6. If the noun ends in *o* preceded by a vowel, add *s*.	patio/patio**s** radio/radio**s** tattoo/tattoo**s**	
7. The plurals of some nouns are irregular.	tooth/teeth man/men mouse/mice	
8. Some nouns have the same form in both the singular and the plural.	deer moose salmon Swiss	
Some nouns borrowed from Latin and Greek form the plural as in the original language.	nucleus/nucl**ei** crisis/cris**es** datum/dat**a**	

continued

continued

Rules for Plurals	Examples	Exceptions
A few Latin and Greek loan words have two plural forms.	vortex/vortic**es** or vorte**xes** gymnasium/gymnas**ia** or gymnasium**s** (Check a dictionary to find the preferred spelling of such plurals.)	
To form the plurals of numerals, most capital letters, symbols, and letters used as words, add an *s*.	Change the *Ns* to *Vs*.	
To prevent confusion, use an apostrophe and an *s* to form the plurals of lowercase letters, certain capital letters, and some letters used as words.	Your *r's* look like *z's*.	
The plurals of decades and centuries may be formed by adding an *s* or an apostrophe and an *s* ('s)	During the 1900's (or 1900s), many new inventions appeared.	

ACTIVITY

Write the correct plural for each of the following: *beach, fly, lie, man, salmon, tooth, tornado, wife.*

COMMONLY CONFUSED WORDS

When we communicate with each other, it is important to use words that express our thoughts clearly. However, some words are frequently confused.

Homophones are words that sound the same but are spelled differently. They are often misspelled unless the writer is very careful. Some examples are *there/their/they're; its/it's; two/to/too.*

ACTIVITIES

1. Use each of the homophones listed above correctly in a sentence.

2. The words listed below are ones that are often used incorrectly. As you read the words on each line, see whether you understand the differences between them. If you are not sure of the differences in their meaning, use a dictionary or talk with a partner or your teacher to find out. For your own writing assignments, keep a list of words that you have not used correctly. The list will be helpful to you for future writing assignments.

a lot, allot	know, no
accept, except	loose, lose
advise, advice	principal, principle
affect, effect	quite, quiet
all ready, already	than, then
all together, altogether	where, we're, wear, were
complement, compliment	whose, who's
farther, further	your, you're
knew, new	

CAPITAL LETTERS

A **capital letter** is used at the beginning of a sentence. A capital letter is also called **upper case**, while a small letter is called **lower case**. Capital letters are used for the following:

For the personal pronoun: *I*

For proper names: James, Canada, Wednesday, Paris, Italian

For the titles of films, books, plays, television programmes, poems, and people: *Romeo and Juliet*, "Hockey Night in Canada"

For certain abbreviations: CBC (Canadian Broadcasting Corporation)

PUNCTUATION

End stops such as **periods** (.), **question marks** (?), and **exclamation marks** (!) are used to end a sentence. Other punctuation marks (**commas, dashes**, and so on) perform different functions.

Periods: You use a period if the sentence makes a statement.

My mother bakes the best chocolate chip cookies.

Exclamation Marks: You use an exclamation mark if the sentence expresses surprise.

What an amazing bike I saw at the shop!

I don't believe it!

ACTIVITY

Working in pairs, discuss the difference in meaning between the two sentences below. Write down your answer.

I like the kitten on my lap particularly. When it purrs it is cozy.

I like the kitten on my lap particularly when it purrs. It is cozy.

Commas: A **comma** (,) is used after an introductory word, phrase, or clause; to separate items in a list; after the introduction to direct speech; and to make the meaning of the sentence clear.

ACTIVITY

> Write out these sentences, inserting commas where appropriate.
> a) At our barbecue we had chicken burgers baked potatoes and marshmallows.
> b) Sean said "It's time to go home."
> c) Mr. Gupta who was born in India enjoyed watching cricket.
> d) After falling down the stairs Jimmy was unable to go on his skiing holiday.
> e) The rusty dilapidated car which belonged to my aunt broke down on the highway.

Dash: A **dash** (—) is used as a strong comma to separate two parts of a sentence or to add emphasis.

Read the following as a script, noting the use of dashes.

The telephone rings. Sue picks it up. There is interference on the line.
Sue: Hello.
Caller: Can I speak to Cheryl, please?
Sue: Sorry—what did you say?
Caller: Can I speak to Cheryl, please?
Sue: Who?
Caller: Cheryl—I want to speak to Cheryl.
Sue: Gerald? There's no Gerald here.
Caller: Not Gerald—Cheryl—CHERYL!
Sue: Oh! Errol! Sorry—Errol doesn't live here.
Caller gives up in desperation.

Apostrophes: An **apostrophe** (') is used to show that one or more letters have been omitted from a word, or to show possession.

1. Rewrite the following passage putting the apostrophes in the right places. Some of the apostrophes show that letters have been omitted, while others show possession.

That couples two children arent like other children. Theyve been so successful at school its amazing. The girls particularly clever. Id like to think Roys going to pass as many exams as shes passed. But I dont think theres much chance of that. Roys interest just isnt in school, thats all it boils down to.

2. Rewrite the following, inserting apostrophes where necessary.
   a) The girls shoes got wet in the puddle but their knapsacks didnt.
   b) I dont know how many of the farmers cows were injured in the accident.
   c) At four oclock itll be time to go to the skating rink.
   d) The womens downhill race didnt take place because it was foggy.
   e) The lone owls hooting could be heard across the wood.

Colon: A **colon** is used to introduce a list, example, or explanation. The colon is also used in dialogue to indicate that a character is speaking.

ACTIVITY

Write out these sentences, inserting colons where appropriate.

Assemble the following ingredients one cup of flour, two eggs, and half a cup of milk.

She used this excuse to explain her lateness her dog hid her school bag.

It is truly said "Man does not live by bread alone."

Quotation Marks: Quotation marks are used to indicate direct speech and the titles of short poems, stories, articles. **Direct speech** requires quotation marks; **indirect speech** does not. For example:

Direct: "Do you have a looney?" Dad said. "I need one for the parking meter."

Indirect: My dad asked me for a looney for the parking meter.

Italics/Underlining: Italics or **underlining** are used to indicate the titles of books, full-length plays, newspapers, and magazines. For example:

We read an article called "Teens Have Power at the Cash Register" in the *National Post*.

Parentheses: Parentheses are used to separate non-essential explanatory words in a sentence. For example:

Canadians were proscribed to fight in World War I (1914–1918).

Mark your responses on the bubble sheet clearly with an HB pencil. (Do not use ink.)

Ellipses: Ellipses dots (. . .) are used by writers to show that part of a quotation has been left out, or to indicate a pause in dialogue. For example:

The Prime Minister, who was in China at the time, said the report was nonsense.

with ellipses becomes

The Prime Minister . . . said the report was nonsense.

Lomov: My heart . . . my foot's asleep . . . I can't . . .

Reading and Researching

READING STRATEGIES

When reading, there are several strategies you can use to help you get the most out of the printed page. You need to select strategies appropriate to the complexity of the material and the form in which it is presented. Reading strategies include such things as

- consulting the table of contents, index, and glossary to assess the relevance of the text
- previewing the vocabulary
- scanning the text to predict the content based on the titles and illustrations
- setting goals and creating key questions to be answered by the text
- skimming the text to find relevant information
- adjusting your reading to suit your purpose and the complexity of the text
- visualizing places, people, and events in the text; connecting personal experiences and prior knowledge to the information and ideas in the text
- self-questioning to monitor your comprehension
- rereading to check your first impressions
- restating information, ideas, and plot in your own words
- comparing your response to and understanding of the text with that of classmates to clarify meaning

Direct and Implied Ideas in Texts

In text, some ideas are stated directly or explicitly. Other ideas are implicit—they must be inferred by the reader. The theme of a short story or the qualities of the characters, for instance, are rarely stated directly, but can be inferred from details provided in the story.

Backgrounds of Readers and Writers Influence Meaning of Texts

With some texts (e.g., a bus schedule), every reader will get the same information and understanding. With most texts, however, readers will not get exactly the same meaning because of differences in personal experiences and prior knowledge. For instance, a student who has experienced a canoe trip in northern Ontario will understand *Silent Words* by Ruby Slipperjack (page 72) in a different way than a student without that experience. Readers' personal experiences and prior knowledge affect their understanding of and preferences for texts. This is why class and group discussions of texts, which draw on a wide range of experience and knowledge, help to refine your comprehension of what you have read.

Similarly, each writer writes from his or her own personal experience and knowledge. Shakespeare could not write about airplanes because they were not part of his experience. An author's view of people, emotions, and values will reflect his or her own experience and knowledge. For this reason, it is always important that you read critically in order to evaluate the information and ideas in a text. In some cases, you may alter your ideas in light of new information in a text; in other cases, you may disagree with a text because it does not seem valid in light of your experience.

RESEARCH STRATEGIES

In order to find sufficient information on a topic for an oral or written report or presentation, you need to conduct research. In doing research, you should follow these steps:

1. Review what you already know about the topic.

2. Determine what you need to know in order to complete your assignment.

3. Depending on the topic, identify potential sources of information. Start with sources that are apt to give you an overview of the topic. There are many sources of information including print materials (books, encyclopedias, newspapers, magazines), non-print materials (videos, slides, film, television, artworks), electronic sources (CD-ROMs, databases, the Internet), and human resources (personal experience, surveys, interviews, experts). Your library or resource centre is a good place to start.

4. After you have done a search and have gotten a good sense of the scope of your topic, decide if there is enough information available to you on the topic. However, if a great deal of information is available, you may have to limit your focus to one aspect of the topic for your project.

5. Skim and scan the materials to ensure that they are relevant and current for your purposes. Read selected sources slowly and record information carefully from the materials. Put direct quotations in quotation marks, and document the source of the information on the same sheet as the information.

6. Sort and classify the information you have gathered under sub-headings for your project.

RESEARCH DOCUMENTATION

In order to avoid charges of **plagiarism** (using someone else's work and claiming it as your own), it is necessary to cite the sources of information and ideas in your work. There are two ways of doing this.

1. Incorporate borrowed information, ideas, and quotations in your writing with introductory phrases such as:

    The Canadian Encyclopedia reports that Robert Service was born in . . .

    or

    According to Advertising Standards Canada, advertisers "should recognize and reflect the transformations occurring in our society, not only as a social responsibility but primarily because it makes good business sense to do so".

2. At the end of a research report, it is necessary to provide your reader with all the sources you consulted in preparing the report. Sources are listed on a final page titled **Bibliography**, **Works Cited**, or **References**. Here is the Modern Language Association (MLA) format for a few typical sources. (Note: If you don't have a computer or are handwriting your work, you must underline all book titles and magazine or newspaper names that you might otherwise put in italics.)

Books

Author's last name, First name. *Title*. City of publication: Publisher,
    Year of publication.

Richardson, Bill. *Bachelor Brothers' Bed & Breakfast*. Vancouver: Douglas
    & McIntyre, 1993.

Newspaper Articles

Author's last name, First name. "Title of article". *Name of Newspaper*
    Full date: Page(s) of article.

Rushowy, Kristin. "How We Met." *The Toronto Star* 29 Nov. 1998: G3.

Magazine Articles

Author's last name, First name. "Title of article". *Name of Magazine*
    Full date: Page(s) of article.

Marney, Jo. "The Wherefores and Whys of Generation Y". *Marketing Magazine*
    1 Apr. 1996:15.

Encyclopedia Entries

Author's last name, First name. "Title of entry". *Name of Encyclopedia*.
    Year of publication.

Randall, Mary. "The Ozone Layer". *New Encyclopaedia Britannica*. 1999.

The Internet

Author's last name, First name. "Title of Work". Year or full date (if applicable) of
publication. <Internet address> (Date of retrieval).

Ledes, Richard. "Housing Construction: The Challenges of Building Interactive
Narrative". 1996. <http://www.intelligent-agent.com/aug_building.html>
(20 Aug. 1999).

or

Name of organization. "Title of Work". Year or full date (if applicable) of publication. <Internet address> (Date of retrieval).

Advertising Standards Canada. "Broadcast Code for Advertising to Children". 1992.
<http://www.canad.com/asc/kidcode.html> (13 Sept. 1999).

Writing

TONE AND PURPOSE

Language will change with the **purpose** and audience of your writing. The language you choose for a piece of writing helps create the **tone** or attitude, also known as **voice**. Your language can range from very **formal** to **informal**.

The table below shows the characteristics of three levels of language: formal, moderate, and informal.

Levels of Language	Formal	Moderate	Informal
vocabulary	• longer, less common words • few colloquialisms, popular phrases • little slang • few or no contractions • avoids the use of pronouns like *you* and *I*	• large and small words • more popular language • some contractions • occasional use of the pronouns *you* and *I*	• shorter, simpler, everyday words • some slang, more popular words and phrases • contractions • use of the pronouns *you* and *I* is common
sentence and paragraph structure	• longer and more complex sentences and paragraphs	• combination of simple, compound, and complex sentences; average-length sentences and paragraphs	• shorter, simpler sentences and paragraphs

continued

continued

Levels of Language	Formal	Moderate	Informal
tone	• academic and impersonal, often instructional	• varies, depending on purpose and audience	• conversational and casual— sounds like everyday speech

Depending on the purpose of your work, you may choose the form and the level of language that is most suitable. The following table shows some forms, their purposes, and the appropriate level of language used.

Forms of Writing	Purpose	Level of Language
Personal Writing: • diaries • journals • logs • lists • letters/notes	• communicates to self and others • records personal thoughts • reflects on activities, events, or experiences	• informal; short, simple, everyday words • may use colloquial language or slang • may use contractions • may use pronouns *I* and *you* • shorter and simpler sentences and paragraphs; unity and coherence may not always be present
Imaginative Writing: • autobiographies • letters • lyrics • monologues • poetry • scripts • stories	• used for self or others • amuses, entertains, evokes emotions, and provokes thought and reflection	• may range from informal to formal depending on the tone the writer wants to achieve • verbs are generally more vivid and vigorous (less use of the verb *to be*)

continued

continued

Forms of Writing	Purpose	Level of Language
		• nouns are more concrete and specific • the number and variety of modifiers (adjectives and adverbs) increases • may use use figures of speech and other literary devices
Informational Writing: • analyses • biographies • business letters • charts • editorials • essays • instructions • lab reports • news articles • plans • reviews • summaries • surveys • textbooks • travelogues	• asks questions to gather information • records information • summarizes information • informs • describes how to assemble or create • records and reports observations, research, and analysis • interprets information, sometimes using graphics • argues and persuades	• may range from informal to formal depending on the purpose and audience • sentences and paragraphs are generally moderate in complexity • some subject-specific language, but mostly familiar vocabulary • some of this writing may be in point form

AUDIENCE

Before you start writing, you have to know who your **audience** is. Who will be reading what you write? Is the audience known or unknown to you?

The answer will have an impact on the **level of language** and the content of your writing.

Examine the two letter excerpts below. In both, the author is writing to complain about a billboard that has been erected in her neighbourhood.

Letter 1: The writer knows to whom the letter should be directed and she has met that person.

Dear Carolyn:

At the last meeting of the ratepayers' association, my mother was speaking to you about beautifying our neighbourhood. Now, the local plaza has put up a huge sign advertising its stores. The sign is really ugly! Is there anything you can do?

Please call me at 412-1213 at your earliest convenience. I'd like to know about any bylaws that might help keep our neighbourhood beautiful.

Letter 2: The writer does not know the specific person to whom the letter should be sent.

To the Head of the Planning Department:

Recently, the local strip mall erected a sign on its property. Not only is the sign taller than anything else in the neighbourhood, it is unattractive. In our local ratepayers' association, we have been examining ways to beautify our neighbourhood. This sign does just the opposite.

I am writing this letter to request your attendance at our next ratepayers' meeting scheduled for September 30. Please respond by fax (323-3933) or phone (323-7633) at your earliest convenience.

How does the vocabulary differ in each letter? How do the sentence structures and lengths compare?

Who Is Your Audience?

Consider the following characteristics of your audience to help determine the language you will use, the ideas you will include, and the way you will present your ideas.

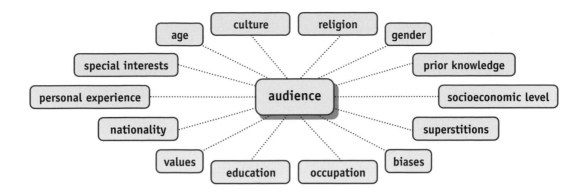

What Impression Do I Want to Make?

Ask yourself the following questions:
- What does my audience expect of me?
- How do I want them to feel about me?
- What do I want this piece of writing to do for my readers?
- What do I want my readers to do as a result of reading my writing?

ACTIVITY

Letter to the Editor:

It was a pleasure to read "Why don't we just make smoking illegal?" by Elvira Cordileone on your Nov. 24 Opinion page.

Cordileone argues that suing tobacco companies is absurd and contradictory when smoking itself is legal.

We, as teenagers, are getting the same kind of two-sided message when it comes to alcohol.

We are bombarded with lessons on never to drink and drive.

My school holds an annual drinking and driving awareness assembly.

Numerous posters with the same message pop up on the walls around the school, especially near Christmastime.

Some use fear to scare us off the bottle, showing brutal consequences of accidents. Others use emotional appeal.

Yet I do not have to look up the statistics to know that it is not working.

The message has become hackneyed and worst of all it does not make sense.

continued

continued

The root of the problem is ignored.

When we are told about horrible accidents involving alcohol, it appears that the message is that it is okay to drink as long as you do not get behind the wheel after that.

Alcohol impairs one's judgment, so how is a person who has been drinking expected to make the right decision about taking a cab instead?

Alcohol causes diseases of the liver and has been linked to some kinds of cancer. It has negative effects on the fetus and has absolutely no nutritional value.

So, why is being familiar with wines considered sophisticated? Why is beer considered a great Canadian tradition?

It is true that it is not easy to change these ideals in one day, but all I am asking is just give us a straight message. Don't tell us not to drink and drive; tell us not to drink at all.

Nida Zaidi
Oakville

1. Identify the audience for this letter to the editor.

2. Discuss the tone, vocabulary, sentence and paragraph length and complexity. Describe where the writing fits on a formal to informal scale.

3. Explain what this writing does for the reader.

4. Identify the action that the writer wants the reader to take.

ORGANIZING YOUR WRITING

Paragraph Development

Depending on the purpose of your writing, there are four different ways to develop your paragraphs: **exposition**, **description**, **narration**, and **process**.

Paragraph Purpose	Structure	Characteristics	Examples of Writing Using These Paragraphs
Exposition: presents information, ideas, and opinions	• topic sentence tells the readers what is going to be discussed • body sentences develop the idea stated in the topic sentence • closing or concluding sentence summarizes ideas in paragraph or draws a logical close	1. uses comparison/ contrast: • presents everything about one idea first and then compares it to another; or • presents one point about one idea and immediately compares it with or contrasts it to another—repeats this pattern until all points are made 2. uses examples/ illustrations: • uses one well-explained example or several small examples to prove point 3. uses transitional words and phrases to help link ideas:	• essays • editorials • newspaper articles • lab reports (See "Etiquette for a Wired World", p. 201.)

continued

continued

Paragraph Purpose	Structure	Characteristics	Examples of Writing Using These Paragraphs
		• to show similarities: *also, and, in like manner, in the same way, similarly* • to show differences: *although, but, however, in comparison, on the contrary, on the other hand, then/now*	
Description: describes events, persons, animals, things, or environments	• may have a topic sentence to let readers know what is going to be described	1. creates an image: • like the eye of a camera, decides how the reader is going to see the described thing • focuses on one aspect of the described object/person and is very detailed about that one part, allowing it to stand for the whole	• fiction • newspaper reports (See *Great Expectations*, p. 20, and *Ice Bangles*, p. 122.)

continued

continued

Paragraph Purpose	Structure	Characteristics	Examples of Writing Using These Paragraphs
		2. creates a feeling or emotion: • shows, but doesn't tell 3. creates an atmosphere or mood: • starts by giving a hint about what will follow • uses similes, metaphors, sense words, onomatopoeia, and strong adjectives and adverbs to help readers feel the mood • uses climactic order to build tension or suspense that is resolved in the final sentence	

continued

continued

Paragraph Purpose	Structure	Characteristics	Examples of Writing Using These Paragraphs
Narration: tells a story	• new paragraph starts with change of speaker, time, place, or action • opening sentence hooks reader and suggests direction for the rest of the paragraph • middle keeps reader's attention and gives reader a reason to read on; should lead to conclusion • ending brings a satisfying conclusion (logical or unexpected)	• maintains unity by creating a single mood and a single point of view • uses dialogue to develop characters • narratives like newspaper stories use 5 Ws + H (who, what, where, when, why, how) to organize ideas • uses a chronological order (beginning to end) or may start at the end and flash back to the beginning to explain the ending	• fiction • newspaper reports (See *The Nest*, p. 80.)
Process: instructs, directs, or explains	• uses step-by-step or chronological order	• uses transitional words often to make sequence clearer (e.g., *a little later, after, at the same time, before, finally, first, next, soon, then*)	• how-to books • recipes • manuals (See *How to Cook Chinese Rice*, p. 48, and *A Bowl of Red*, p. 49.)

As a student, most of your writing may be expository. Two common types of expository writing are essays and reports.

Essays

The word *essay* comes from the French verb *essayer* meaning *to try* or *to try on*. In an essay, a writer "tries on ideas" about a single topic.

Introductory Paragraph: This starts the essay and it may include some general information related to the topic or some background information needed to understand the topic.

The introduction includes the **thesis** or main idea statement, which is the idea you are going to "try on".

Body: It consists of paragraphs that contain proof of the thesis or controlling idea.

Methods of developing expository paragraphs include comparison/contrast and example/illustration, as well as cause/effect, analogy, and definition.

The order can be **chronological** (beginning to end), **sequential** (for instructions), **spatial** (presenting details as you want the audience to see them), or **climactic** (using details, events, or facts in increasing order of importance).

Each paragraph in the body has a point and a proof and must relate back to your thesis or controlling idea.

Conclusion: This restates your thesis and summarizes your evidence.

Reports

Some reports, like lab and science reports, require specific headings. If headings are not given, use the same format as an essay: introduction, body, conclusion.

Introductory Paragraph: This defines your topic and explains the purpose of the report.

Body: This develops the topic in a series of paragraphs, and quotes experts or uses quotations from a variety of sources. Quotations must be accurate and footnotes used to show where the quotations came from.

Visuals such as charts are often used to explain the information.

Conclusion: This summarizes findings and refers back to the introduction.

Bibliography: This lists all the sources that were used, including print, electronic, video, audio, and human resources. (See page 256 for examples of correct bibliographical formats.)

Whether revising your own or someone else's work, here's a simple memory device or mnemonic: RADS. RADS will help you decide whether or not your ideas are complete and in the best possible order. Use RADS to help you examine your entire composition, including each paragraph and sentence.

R   Reorder

- ❏   Are my ideas in the best possible order?
- ❏   Have I considered alternative orders (chronological, sequential, climactic)?
- ❏   Does one idea flow logically into another?
- ❏   Are there any ideas out of place?

A   Add

- ❏   Do I have enough ideas to make my work convincing?
- ❏   Do I need to add more details?
- ❏   Do I need to add some more examples?
- ❏   Have I used enough description including adjectives, adverbs, and interesting verbs?
- ❏   Will my audience be convinced?
- ❏   Could I add some imagery, similes, or metaphors to create a stronger effect?
- ❏   Could I add some transition words to help link my ideas?

D   Delete

- ❏   Do I have any ideas that don't support my main idea?
- ❏   Do I have ideas that don't add to the point I am trying to make?
- ❏   Do I have some ideas that clutter up my work?
- ❏   Is my language too flowery or descriptive for the tone I want to set?
- ❏   Have I repeated ideas?

S   Substitute

- ❏   Are there other ideas I have gathered that might be better than the ones I have?
- ❏   Do I have one weak idea? Should I continue my research to find a better one?
- ❏   Are there words that don't capture the feeling I want to create?
- ❏   Could I use a thesaurus to help find better words?
- ❏   Are there some linking words that are not working?
- ❏   Have I used the appropriate language for my audience?

Proofreading and Editing Your Writing

Good ideas are hard to read if a writer has not proofread and edited his or her work. Check the following before writing your final draft.

Sources

❏ Have I used quotation marks around any words or phrases I have borrowed from other sources?

❏ Have I named the source of those words?

❏ When I have used ideas from other sources, have I given credit to that author?

❏ Have I created a bibliography of all my sources?

Grammar and Usage

❏ Have I checked and corrected any sentence fragments, comma splices, and run-on sentences? (See page 242.)

❏ Have I included a variety of sentence types (simple, complex, compound), sentence lengths, and sentence orders (natural, inverted, split)?
(See page 241.)

❏ Do all my verb tenses agree?

❏ Do all my pronouns agree with their antecedents in number and gender?

❏ Have I used a consistent point of view (not switching from *I* to *you* or *one*)?

❏ If I have used a thesaurus, have I checked the dictionary to be sure the connotation of my new word is correct?

❏ Have I written in the active voice and used the passive only when appropriate? (See page 236.)

❏ Have I written my work sensitively, avoiding racist, sexist, or homophobic language?

Spelling

❏ Have I checked my work for unintended errors such as leaving out letters?

❏ Have I checked all my homophones such as *their/there/they're; know/no?*

❏ Have I checked all my plurals?

❏ Have I checked that I have used apostrophes correctly?

❏ Have I capitalized the correct words (especially in dialogue, scripts, and poetry)?

❏ Have I checked the spelling of specialized vocabulary?

❏ Have I used a dictionary or a spell-check program on my word processor?

Punctuation

❏ Have I used end stops and capitalization appropriately and correctly?
❏ Have I used commas, dashes, and colons appropriately and correctly?
❏ Have I used quotation marks for direct speech and quotations from sources?

PUBLISHING YOUR WRITING

To reach a larger audience, consider these publishing opportunities:
- anthologies of student works
- bulletin board displays
- exchanging writing with another class or another school
- performance of scripts for your own class or other classes
- public readings in class, at other schools, during an arts week, at parents' nights
- reading aloud in class
- school magazine
- school newspaper
- school yearbook

KEEPING A WRITING FOLDER

Set aside one special file folder for keeping all your writing assignments. It's fun and it's useful.
- You can look back and see how much writing you've done over the year.
- You can look back on what has interested you over the year.
- You can see how much you've changed.
- You can keep a list of writing ideas or topics that you can add to and then use when needed.
- You can look back on editors' suggestions and teachers' comments and use them to improve your next piece.
- You have a record of the types of writing you've done.
- You have a record of your marks.

From the work in your writing folder, you can develop a portfolio of your best work. This will help you to

- measure the quality of your work against course expectations and achievement levels
- think, talk, and write about both the process and the product of your work
- set goals for future assignments
- measure your own improvement
- demonstrate the quality of your work

Your portfolio should reflect all areas of English—literature, writing, language, and media. It should also reflect the different areas of achievement—inquiry, communication, application, and knowledge.

Collecting Your Work

Before you choose the items for your portfolio, you might collect your work in your notebook or writing folder. Your teacher and you will have to decide how to store larger projects if you want to keep them as part of your portfolio.

Portfolios are not only for samples of written work. They should include records of your group skills (check sheets, video or audio tapes, photographs, feedback sheets), your process work (planning and progress sheets, conference records, idea gathering, research notes, rough drafts), as well as your final products.

Selecting Your Work

Not everything will go into your portfolio. On a regular basis, you will select what you believe is your best work. Your teacher will give you criteria on which to base this selection.

Reflecting on Your Work

When you have chosen a piece to be included in your portfolio, you will explain why you have chosen it. This means thinking about
- what you have learned
- what criteria have been met in your work
- what you like about the piece
- what you would change if you were to do it again

Here are some prompts you can use to help guide your reflection:
"I learned . . ."
"I feel good about . . ."
"I had this problem . . . and did (or did not) overcome it by . . ."
"This assignment was better than my last because . . ."
"I have improved in the following areas . . ."
"Some things I did well in this piece . . ."
"I could make this even better if . . ."
"What I like about this is . . ."
"My group and I were successful at . . ."
"One place our group could have improved was . . ."
"When I presented I felt . . ."
"Some ways I've tried to make myself less nervous are . . ."
"Artistically, I have accomplished . . ."

Setting Goals

Reflecting on your work is an important step in recognizing your strengths and weaknesses and in setting goals for trying to improve on them. Use the criteria your teacher has given you, and your own reflections, to set two or three specific goals for future work.

Use these goals! Setting goals won't help unless you look at those goals when you are working on your next assignment. Think about how you can accomplish them. When you are getting peer feedback, give your peers your goals so they can help you decide whether or not you have achieved them.

DEVELOPING GOOD HOMEWORK HABITS

Developing good homework habits will help you become better organized and produce better work. For instance:

- Do homework the night it is assigned.
- If you are assigned homework that requires more than one night's work, plan ahead and allow time for that homework.
- Seek help at home, or from friends or teachers.
- Underline or highlight key words in questions.
- Repeat key words in your answers.
- Attempt to answer every question.
- Highlight any questions that give you problems.

Oral Communication Skills

GOOD LISTENING SKILLS

Good listening skills are essential to oral communication (see "Listen Up! Enhancing Our Listening Skills", page 13). Your success at communicating depends on how well you listen to others and receive their messages. Below are some do's and don'ts of listening.

Do's	Don'ts
• make eye contact with the speaker • review what the speaker has said • concentrate • try to recall facts and ideas • take notes • record instructions • ask questions • tune out outside noises • avoid distracting behaviours • use mnemonics (memory devices) • pay attention to non-verbal communication • pick up on the message reinforcers like charts, diagrams, photos, slides	• judge a person by appearance or delivery • fake attention • bring your prejudices to the presentation • avoid difficult ideas/concepts • tune out or let your mind wander • interrupt the speaker • use selective listening • make side comments to others or listen to or pay attention to the behaviour of others and their side comments

Just as it takes time to develop reading and writing skills, discussion and group-work skills must be developed over a period of time through experience and evaluation. The following list of helpful and hindering roles will help you to become aware of the ways people work in groups. You can also use the lists to evaluate your own success as a team player.

Helpful Roles	Hindering Roles
1. Organizing • identifying goals • defining tasks	1. Fragmenting • going off topic • introducing irrelevant information
2. Self-starting • suggesting new ideas • volunteering to tackle a task	2. Resisting • seeing problems where none exist • failing to exercise initiative
3. Information-seeking • asking questions • seeking facts • requesting clarification	3. Withdrawing • appearing shy and insecure • daydreaming • fearing to say the wrong thing
4. Information-providing • offering ideas and their sources	4. Information-withholding • avoiding involvement in discussion
5. Encouraging • responding enthusiastically to others and their ideas • inviting everyone's participation	5. Belittling • undercutting the suggestions of others • discouraging participation
6. Summarizing • summarizing points of discussion • simplifying complicated ideas	6. Smooth-talking • pretending superior knowledge • oversimplifying problems
7. Co-ordinating • keeping discussion on topic • trying to involve everybody	7. Monopolizing • hogging the discussion • interrupting others

continued

continued

Helpful Roles	Hindering Roles
8. Challenging • stimulating discussion by presenting different viewpoints • confronting weak ideas	8. Arguing • indulging in disagreement • disregarding the ideas of others
9. Mediating • working to resolve differences • looking for alternative solutions	9. Fence-sitting • side-stepping the making of decisions
10. Tension-relieving • expressing points with humour • making people feel good about themselves	10. Clowning • disrupting progress • fooling around

Your Voice and Mine 4 by D. Hilker, et al. (Toronto: Holt, Rinehart and Winston of Canada, 1989), pp. 201–202. Reprinted by permission of the publisher.

ORAL PRESENTATIONS

Just as it is important to listen while someone else speaks, whether in a formal or an informal group setting, so it is important that you speak well to effectively convey your message. As a student, you require good speaking skills for your various formal oral activities including:

- debates
- demonstrations
- dramatic and/or choral readings
- group work
- independent study presentations
- performances—role plays, readings, storytelling
- interviews
- meetings
- reports
- seminars
- speeches
- video presentations

A formal oral presentation is one of the most common activities that you will be involved in. Here are some suggestions to help you plan an effective oral presentation.

Planning Your Content

Know Your Subject

- read—books, articles, electronic information
- talk—personal or phone interview, discussion
- view—movies, documentaries, interviews
- record—on tape, on cue cards, in your notebook, on your computer
- organize
  - delete information that is not adding to your presentation
  - add information where you find you have gaps
  - substitute information that might be weak with stronger points
  - order your information in the most logical order, starting with a hook to get your audience interested and ending with a powerful conclusion
  - think of ways to get your audience involved

Fifteen Openers for Oral Presentations That Involve the Audience (And Do Not Use, "My topic is . . .")

1. "What would you do if . . ."

2. "Imagine that you have just . . ."

3. "It is especially fitting (or right, or appropriate) that we will be talking about _____ today because . . ."

4. "For many years I have wondered about . . ." or "For many years I have admired . . ."

5. As _____, a very wise man (woman) once said . . . (use quote) . . ."

6. "Our country (province, town) could become a leader in (example of, authority on) . . . if . . ."

7. "If we continue to _____ at the rate we are going, then . . ."

8. Use a statistic: "Can 99% of the population be wrong . . . (Maybe, yes!)"

continued

---

continued

9. Create a mental picture: "If we stacked the garbage from one household for one year, we would have a pile _____ high."

10. Current reference: "As we have heard Mrs./Mr. _____ say many times . . ."

11. Challenge the question: "How long will it take us to realize . . . ?"

12. Puzzler #1: "What do _____ and _____ have in common?"

13. Puzzler #2: "What is the single most common cause of _____?"

14. Promise #1: "In the next _____ minutes I am going to share with you . . ."

15. Promise #2: "When I finish this presentation, you will be able to . . ." or "When I finish this presentation, you will all look at the _____ with new eyes."

Secrets of Power Presentations by Peter Urs Bender (Toronto: The Achievement Group, 1991). Reprinted with permission.

Know Your Purpose and Audience

- decide how formal your presentation must be
- tailor your language to the audience and the purpose
- time your presentation to the needs of your audience

Prepare Audio-Visual Aids

- think about how you can use audio-visual aids to your advantage
- consider a range of aids: blackboards, flip charts, posters, overheads, audio tapes, video tapes, computer-assisted presentation software, models

Planning Your Presentation

Getting Organized

- order any equipment you'll need well in advance
- create audio-visual aids
- write out your presentation notes clearly so you can refer to them easily
- plan what you will wear

Rehearsing

- practise in front of a mirror
- read or speak slowly
- time yourself
- practise moving during the presentation, for example, from the overhead to the board and out toward the audience when you are making a strong point
- revise your presentation where there are gaps or awkward moments
- practise with the equipment you will be using
- leave time for questions and discussion
- work to make the presentation seamless
- use deep-breathing exercises and other relaxation techniques to put you in a good frame of mind

---

Oral Presentations: Tricks to Involve Your Audience

Your teacher may excuse you for giving a "perfunctory" presentation—one that basically does the job (demonstrates your scholarship) but is somewhat dull and passionless. But your classmates may not. Here are some tricks and techniques you can use to spark up your classroom presentation and get your audience involved in a learning experience.

1. **Nothing Succeeds Like Excess:** Be very well prepared. You should have researched your topic well enough and conferenced well enough with the teacher to be an "expert". You will likely know more about your topic than anyone else in the classroom (including the teacher), so you should feel confident.

2. **Show and Tell:** Bring in something concrete for the presentation. A picture, significant object of some sort, a chart or diagram, a handout—any of these items will provide moral support for you and a point of interest for others in the class.

3. **Showtime:** Bring in a short film, a tape-recorded interview, a set of pictures, or a cassette or CD to provide sound effects. Make sure that your audio-visual support is appropriate to your topic and that it helps you to develop your theme.

4. **Comic Liftoff:** Begin with an amusing story, joke, or anecdote which raises your initial point or topic, or demonstrates most people's attitude

continued

continued

to the topic. Be careful here, considering what may be suitable for the classroom and the sensitivity you need to show to others in terms of race, religion, gender, and so on. Most public libraries have a copy of an anthology of jokes and anecdotes suitable for all occasions published by the Toastmasters' organization, but some of this material may seem old-fashioned and even politically incorrect in today's social climate.

5. **Demonstration:** Begin with a poetry reading, an excerpt read from a source book, or an actual demonstration of some aspect of your topic with the purpose of introducing your initial or main point.

6. **The Five-Minute Workout:** Think of an effective exercise that members of the class could do alone or with a group to understand your topic more profoundly.

7. **The Devil's Advocate:** Spark interest in or discussion around your topic by making an outrageous statement which you know will be contrary to the beliefs of most people in the classroom (e.g., "We would be better people and have a better society if everyone had less education" or "The world would be a better place without TV and telephones"). Throw out your statement with confidence and keep your cool when people start to object. Lead them on by adding fuel to the fire—more "evidence" to back up your initial statement. Ultimately, you can capitulate to the class point of view, but provide them with information which may give them the slant you took.

Oral Presentation Checklist

Name: _____ Topic: _____

Date of Presentation: _____ Time: _____

Content, Planning, and Organizing

❏ I have a clear introduction which does not say "My topic is . . ."
❏ My thesis is definite and I have a clear statement of it.

continued

continued

❏ My research is evident through frequent, appropriate references to sources (primary and secondary), and even a display of sources.

❏ My presentation is a unified, coherent piece of work with a logical sequence.

❏ My notes, overheads, display items, and so on are organized and easy to reach.

❏ My knowledge is broad enough to handle questions and discussion.

❏ The "audience" will recognize that I have put a legitimate amount of thinking, planning, and overall work into this presentation.

❏ I have an effective conclusion which will signal "the end" to the audience.

Delivery: Oral and Teaching Skills

❏ I have some "device" or tactic to involve the audience immediately in my presentation.

❏ I have practised to have a clear, well-paced, audible delivery.

❏ I will aim to present enthusiastically in order to hold audience interest throughout the presentation.

❏ I have created a timeline for my presentation and will pace myself accordingly.

❏ I have attempted to be creative in my approach to add novelty and interest—to share with or teach my classmates (and teacher) something that they did not know before, or to demonstrate a fresh approach.

Adapted from *Contacts: Teaching Literacy and Communication Across the Curriculum* by Catherine Costello, et al. (Toronto: Ontario Secondary School Teachers' Federation, 1997), pp. 182–183.

The Presentation

- test all equipment before the presentation
- speak confidently
- if you make a mistake, carry on (We all make mistakes.)
- smile and enjoy yourself

Dealing with Stress Before Oral Presentations

Signs of Stress

Some of you may be comfortable speaking in front of an audience and many of you may not be. Some may experience stress and have these signs:
- dry mouth (and tongue sticking to the roof of the mouth)
- trembling
- paleness
- sudden bursts of energy
- goose bumps

Avoiding Stress

To avoid stress before a presentation, consider doing some of these:
- first, choose a subject you are interested in
- prepare well
- practise
- take several deep breaths before you begin
- hum with your mouth closed but your teeth open to limber up and relax your vocal cords
- shrug your shoulders tightly and hold that position for five seconds; then relax, blowing out your breath at the same time
- remember to breathe (even though it sounds silly—not breathing is a common cause of anxiety)
- think about each person in the audience as an individual
- speak much more slowly than you think is normal
- concentrate on what you are saying
- make your audience laugh
- keep a glass of water handy and take time to drink some to keep your mouth moist

What Can We Learn from Debating?

Content
- general knowledge
- current issues, public affairs
- formality
- awareness of the world
- vocabulary, jargon of debate
- depth of thought

Skills
- listening
- logical thinking
- quick thinking
- communication skills
- an urbane manner (an elevated speaking level)
- argumentation
- accepting criticism
- teamwork/collaboration/sharing
- organizing (structure and sequence)
- time management
- adaptability, flexibility
- higher-level thinking: analysis, synthesis, evaluation
- risk-taking
- researching
- competitiveness
- intuition
- self-assessment
- sense of humour

Values
- respect for others
- self-confidence
- openness to other points of view
- appreciation for negotiation
- commitment to non-adversarial conflict resolution
- acceptance of others

- open-mindedness and tolerance
- loyalty
- substance over style (both being necessary)
- role playing

Debate Procedure

The Chair introduces the topic, introduces the speakers, explains the time limits, and announces the judges' decisions. It is up to the Chair to maintain the tone of the debate.

The First Speaker for the Affirmative   **4 minutes**

Give a brief introduction to the topic, define any necessary terms, note any points agreed on by all debaters, note any issues to be excluded, state clearly and briefly all the affirmative points, and prove the point you have chosen to deal with.

The First Speaker for the Negative   **3 minutes**

State agreements and disagreements with the interpretation of the topic by the first speaker, state the arguments for the negative side, indicate who will prove each argument, refute briefly the arguments of the first speaker, and present your own arguments.

The Second Speaker for the Affirmative   **3 minutes**

Refute the arguments of the first speaker for the negative and state your own arguments and proof.

The Second Speaker for the Negative   **4 minutes**

Refute any arguments for the affirmative as yet unanswered, state your own arguments and proof, and sum up the arguments for the negative side.

The First Speaker for the Affirmative   **1 minute**

Do not introduce any new arguments; refute arguments already made and sum up the affirmative arguments.

Debate Terminology

refute: to prove a statement or argument to be wrong or false

point of order: a question to the chair regarding proper following of rules

point of personal privilege: a question to the chair regarding a misrepresentation of your argument

The Media

ELEMENTS OF VISUAL PRODUCTION: TELEVISION, VIDEO, FILM[1]

People who make television programs, videos, films, and other visual productions must deal with two main things: picture elements (what the production looks like) and sound elements (how the production will sound).

Picture Elements

- original live-action or dramatized footage
- stock footage: archival footage or footage from other films
- interviews
- re-enactments
- still photos
- documents, titles, headlines, cartoons, other graphics
- blue screen (for special effects)
- special effects

Sound Elements

- sound recorded at the same time as visuals (on-the-street interviews, at a live concert)
- sound recorded on its own and dubbed onto the film/tape
- voice-over: voices or commentary recorded separately from filmed visuals and then dubbed onto the film/tape
- narration: scripted voice-over spoken by a narrator, the filmmaker, or a participant
- sound effects
- music
- silence

---

[1] Information based on Arlene Moscovitch, *Constructing Reality: Exploring Issues in Documentary* (Montreal: National Film Board of Canada, 1993).

1. a) As a class, list as many specific types of videos, television programs, and films as you can, such as music videos, docudramas, and feature films.

   b) With a partner, choose five types from the class list and record the picture and sound elements most likely to appear in each one.

2. As a class, create a bulletin board display naming a variety of films, television shows, and videos, and the sound and picture elements used for each one.

FILM AND EDITING TECHNIQUES

Most programs are filmed using a variety of camera shots, movements, and angles. The filmmaker or film editor then edits the film, taking out or rearranging the shots in a way that best tells the story.

Camera Shots

- **long shots:** include a lot of detail about where the action is taking place
- **medium shots:** show us things in greater detail than long shots
- **close-up shots:** include the most detail, especially expressions on people's faces

Camera Movement

- **pan:** the camera swivels side to side on the tripod
- **tilt:** the camera moves up and down
- **dolly:** the camera moves with or away from the action

Camera Angle

- **eye level:** as is suggested, the camera is held at eye level, just as we would see something
- **bird's-eye:** the camera is held above the action and looks down on the action
- **worm's-eye:** the camera is held below the action and looks up at what it is filming

Editing Terminology

- **cuts:** the editor cuts out parts of the film that are poorly shot or not effective

- **cutaways:** to shorten time, a filmmaker cuts out non-essential shots. The audience may see a student getting to the front door of the school in one shot and then sitting in class in the next shot. To prevent the audience from thinking this is too strange, the filmmaker inserts a shot that prepares the audience for the leap in time. It might be a close-up of a book on a desk or a note on the blackboard. The audience understands the next sequence will be in the classroom

- **inserts:** to lengthen time and, usually, to build suspense, the filmmaker inserts shots. For example, if a student is caught cheating on an exam in real life, the consequences may happen quickly. In a film, to lengthen that moment, the filmmaker may insert a close-up of the reaction on the face of a student sitting behind the cheater or insert a series of shots that go between the face of the student and that of the teacher.

Meet the Media by Jack Livesley, et al. (Toronto: Globe/Modern Curriculum Press, 1990). Reprinted with permission.

ACTIVITIES

1. Create a chart on which you can record camera angles, shots, and movements. Watch your favourite television show. For the first two-minute segment, record the camera angles used. For the second two-minute segment, record the shots. For the third two-minute segment, record the camera movement.

2. Record a two-minute segment from a television show or a movie. Replay it and record the camera angles, shots, and movements. In your notebook, explain the effect the different techniques have on the viewer.

3. Either in class or at home, play a video or a movie and explain how the filmmaker has used editing to compress or extend time, and to create tension and mood.

CREATING A VISUAL PRESENTATION: POSTERS, COLLAGES, STORYBOARDS[2]

Just as writers gather information, organize it, and create drafts before their final version, visual artists plan each and every thing they draw or create on computer. If you are creating a visual product that requires drawing or putting together pictures and type, then here are a few helpful hints.

Research

- If you need some background images, look through books and magazines to get ideas for these images.
- Photocopy the pages you like. (Never cut up a book that isn't your own!)
- Take photographs yourself.
- If you want to draw animals, go to the zoo or a pet store or rent a video with animals in it.

Create Thumbnail Sketches

- Thumbnail sketches are just for composition purposes. Do them quickly inside a frame that is the same proportion as the final work. They shouldn't contain any detail.
- Produce as many thumbnail sketches as possible so you will be sure to include your best and most creative ideas (which sometimes come later rather than sooner).
- Experiment with colour and value.
- Avoid tracing your research pictures. Try to change the angle or view of your subject. (Remember, most pictures and drawings, including cartoons, are the property of the artist.)

Here's an example of a television ad using a form of the thumbnail sketch called a storyboard frame. Each storyboard frame shows a key shot in the ad and includes a place to describe the action and audio that will accompany the shot.

---

[2]Information based on Mark Thurman, *How to Plan Your Drawings* (Markham: Pembroke Publishers Ltd., 1992).

Before

Production Title: Monkey Ad for VISA Canada
Production Team: Leo Burnett Co. Ltd., Toronto, ON

Shot size:_____ Shot size:_____ Shot size:_____

Action:_____ Action:_____ Action:_____

_____ _____ _____

_____ _____ _____

Audio: _____ Audio: _____ Audio: _____

_____ _____ _____

After

Photos courtesy Leo Burnett Co. Ltd. and VISA Canada Association.

ACTIVITIES

1. For each frame, explain the effect the director of the commercial was trying to achieve with the specific camera angles and shots.

2. This commercial has a monkey retrieving a dropped wallet for a man. Later we see the monkey has kept the VISA card. What message do you think the designers of this ad were trying to send to the viewers about VISA?

3. Explain the advantages of creating a storyboard for any script before shooting it.

Choose a Focus

What do you want to put in the foreground, middle ground, and background of your visual presentation?

Create Rough Sketches

- Once you have your subject matter and your thumbnail sketches, you need to put them all together in a final rough layout, larger than the thumbnails but still in proportion to the final.
- Decide on your focus. Will it be the characters, the setting, an object, or the action?
- If you need more room, draw outside the border and then draw a new border, ensuring proportions are maintained.
- Ensure you create a definite centre of interest and subordinate the less important information to the special emphasis you've created.

Final Copy

- When you're pleased with your design, create a final, full-sized version of your masterpiece.

VISUAL LITERACY: UNDERSTANDING THE LANGUAGE OF ADVERTISEMENTS

Advertisements

Advertisements are everywhere—on billboards, in the subway, in newspapers and magazines, to name just a few places. What is the function of an advertisement?
- to sell a product or increase sales
- to sell an image
- to perform a public service
- to promote an event

How are advertisements created? Here is what one advertising agency had to say in an interview about how an advertising campaign is designed.

How do you make advertisements?

Many people think that advertisers simply sit and think up good ideas. Before we can even start to plan an advertising campaign, we have to collect a mountain of information. We call this "market research"—this means finding out who the likely buyers are, their needs and habits, and the amount of money they can afford to spend. After we've got this information, we start making decisions about the actual advertising campaign.

What sorts of decisions?

First we have to decide which media we will use. This will depend on the amount of money the client has to spend. Television advertising is very expensive, but it is very effective. Radio is cheaper and so are newspapers, but they are not as effective. If we decide to use radio or television we have to buy time. Different times of the day cost different amounts of money. Then we have to decide what approach we will take. For example, if we are planning a 60-second TV commercial we would have to decide whether it should be serious or funny, whether we would use a famous person in it, whether we would use music, jingles or a voice-over, whether we would shoot it on location or in a studio. These are just a few of the many decisions that are made in planning the advertisement.

Who decides what the advertisement will look like?

The people in the creative department of the agency; the copywriters and the art directors have this responsibility. Together they plan the words and pictures that will appear in the final advertisement. Advertising is the art of persuasion, so an effective advertisement will get the audience's attention and contain something that will appeal to the target audience. There are many sorts of appeals that can be made. We could appeal to the audience's sense of fun and show people enjoying themselves while using the product. We could appeal to their pocketbooks by demonstrating how cheap the product is, or we could appeal to their sense of adventure by showing exotic places. Whatever we decide, the final advertisement will have to make some link between the product and something people like or would like to have.

Meet the Media by Jack Livesley, et al. (Toronto: Globe/Modern Curriculum Press, 1990), p. 26. Reprinted with permission.

1. Look over several magazines. Find companies that use ads to sell a product, sell an image, perform a public service, and promote an event. Record the name of the company and the type of ad it uses.

2. Find a product that uses a famous person in its ad. Explain why the celebrity is an appropriate spokesperson for the product or service.

3. Find ads that promise you one of the following lifestyles:
   • rich and famous
   • sporty
   • party
   List the ads and what they promise.

4. Health and safety are important to most people. Find ads that promise a healthier and safer world for you. List the products that tend to do this the most.

5. a) Examine the advertisement below. Identify the product.
   b) What ideas, emotions, and messages does the ad use to persuade the audience to buy the company's products?

Not all ads or movies appeal to all audiences. That's because they were not designed for all audiences. Moviemakers and advertisers know how to create visual images to appeal to different audiences. As you learned from the interview with the advertising agency, advertisers must first do market research before they can create an ad. They carry out careful research to understand their audiences' likes and dislikes, fears and wishes. Some researchers study demographics, that is, they collect and study social and economic statistics. Other researchers study psychographics, that is, the likes and dislikes of different segments of society. These researchers put their findings together to get a good picture of their audience.

ACTIVITIES

1. a) In a small group, find several magazines that are aimed at different audiences. Look at the subjects covered in the articles to help you decide on the age, gender, and interests of the audience.

   b) Examine the ads in the magazines and infer from them the likes, dislikes, fears, and wishes of the demographic. Present your findings to the class.

2. Look at two or three advertisements for the same type of product (e.g., hair care, cars, snack food). Make a chart of the various ways the ads grab and hold your attention.

Glossary

advertisement: A public notice in newspapers and magazines, on posters and billboards, in broadcasts (radio and television), and so on, designed to increase sales or draw attention to or promote organizations, goods or services, events, or ideas. Refer to page 291 for information on how advertisements are created. See also **commercial**.

alliteration: A group of words that begin with the same sound. Alliterations can help make the writing memorable and reinforce meaning. Several alliterations in "The Highwayman"—"ghostly galleon" and "clattered and clashed"—draw attention to the images and enhance the sound of the language in the poem.

allusion: An indirect reference to a familiar figure, place, or event that is known from literature, history, myth, religion, or some other field of knowledge. For example, "Priscilla and the Wimps" uses a biblical allusion to describe the school as Monk's "Garden of Eden" and Priscilla as "the serpent" in the Eden. The downfall of Monk and his Kobras, brought about by Priscilla, parallels the downfall of Adam and Eve in their Garden of Eden.

anecdote: A short account of an interesting or amusing incident or event. For example, Lucy Maud Montgomery includes a few anecdotes in her journal about her childhood and people she knew. In "Only Her Hairdresser Knows for Sure . . ." the narrator shares anecdotes of her mother's battles with her daughters' hair.

anthology: A published collection of literary material including poems, short stories, novels, non-fiction selections, or other material.

article: See **essay/magazine article/supported piece** and **newspaper article/report/story**.

atmosphere (or **mood**): The prevailing feeling in a literary work created through word choice, descriptive details, and evocative imagery. The vivid description of the marriage scene in *Ice Bangles* creates a festive atmosphere.

audience: The group of people for whom a piece of writing, film, television program, and so on, is intended. See pages 259–262 for more on audience.

author: A person who writes short stories, novels, non-fiction selections, or any other written material.

autobiography: The story of a person's life written by that person.

biography: The story of a person's life written by someone other than the person.

brochure: A printed booklet, or pages that are folded into panels, used to advertise or give information about a business, product, place, and so on. It often contains colourful graphics or pictures. See also **pamphlet**.

business letter: A letter written to or from a business. The writing style is formal and it is usually typed or neatly written on 8 1/2 x 11 paper. It has six elements: the return address and the date; the name and address of the person or organization to whom you are writing; the salutation (e.g., Dear Sir or Madam; Dear Mr., Mrs., or Ms.; or To Whom It May Concern:); the body; the closing (e.g., "Yours sincerely," or "Yours truly,"); and your signature and typed name (if your letter is typed).

character: Refers to 1) an individual in a story, narrative poem, or play, and 2) the qualities of the individual. The latter are usually revealed through dialogue, description, and action. In "Cats", for example, the character of Sylvia as a complainer and fickle-minded woman, prone to jealousy, is revealed through her letters.

A **character description** is a sketch of a character's qualities that uses nouns and adjectives to name the character's qualities, and examples and quotations from the story, play, poem, and so on, as evidence of those qualities. A character description does not normally describe the character's physical appearance unless it reveals some aspect of his or her qualities or personality.

Character development is a technique used by a writer, poet, or playwright to 1) add details to and reveal more of a character's personality as the story progresses, and 2) to show how a character changes during the work. Depending on their type, characters may or may not develop or change. Characters may be classified as realistic or stereotyped, static or dynamic.

A **realistic character** has several sides to his or her nature. Fatimeh in *Ice Bangles* is an example of a fully developed character.

A **stereotyped character** is a familiar figure with certain characteristics that are fixed, predictable, and unrealistic. Stereotyped characters are often used to add humour to a comedy. Stepan Chubukov in *A Marriage Proposal* could be considered a stereotype of a middle-aged father anxious to see his daughter married off.

A **static character** does not change in the course of the narrative. Laura in "On the Sidewalk, Bleeding" is a static character.

A **dynamic character**, often the protagonist, goes through a significant change. Mary Maloney in "Lamb to the Slaughter", for example, changes from a perfect, subservient wife to a cunning woman who murders her husband *and* gleefully conceals her crime. Andy in "On the Sidewalk, Bleeding" is also a dynamic character in that he changes his view of himself and his relationship to the gang.

collage: A combination of various items and materials that makes a visual statement about an idea or a theme.

colloquial expression or **language:** Informal or conversational language; it is considered inappropriate to use colloquial language in formal writing, but it can be an essential part of fiction writing. The conversation between Laurie and his parents in "Charles" uses many colloquial expressions.

commercial: A television or radio advertisement. See also **advertisement**.

conflict: A struggle between opposing characters, forces, or emotions, usually between the protagonist and someone or something else. The central conflict in "The Other Family" is between the narrator of East Indian descent and the white culture into which she has brought her daughter. Many writers use the conflict created by cultural differences as part of their stories.

debate: A discussion or argument that presents both sides of a topic. A debate can be formal, such as a televised debate between politicians. Formal debates take place in public, are guided by rules, and are overseen by a moderator. See pages 283–284 for more information on debates.

definition: A statement or explanation used to clarify the meaning of words or concepts.

dialect: A local version of language, which has its own vocabulary and sentence structure. *Great Expectations* contains several examples of dialect. See page 230 for more information on dialect. See also **idiom**.

dialogue: A conversation between two or more characters. Dialogue is often used by writers and dramatists to reveal charac-ter and conflict. Laurie's character in "Charles" is developed through dialogue as a precocious, insolent, and misbehaving child who calls his father "dumb".

diary: A book used to write down an account of each day's events, and the ideas and feelings associated with them. See also **journal**.

diction: The deliberate choice of words to create a specific style, atmosphere, or tone. Dickens in the excerpt from *Great Expectations* uses words like *terrible, fearful, coarse, glared,* and *growled* to convey the image of the convict as a savage man, arousing in the reader the same fright that Pip feels.

direct speech: The exact words spoken by a character. Direct speech is almost always enclosed in quotation marks.

docudrama: A drama that is based on facts and actual incidents.

drama: A story written in the form of dialogue intended to be acted out in front of an audience. It consists of plot complication and resolution, character revelation, conflict, setting, and theme. *Twelfth Night, The Pen of My Aunt,* and *A Marriage Proposal* are all dramas.

dramatic irony: See **irony**.

dramatic reading: Reading a piece of literature aloud using vocal intonation and emphasis to convey the meaning of the work.

dynamic character: See **character**.

Elizabethan English: The English spoken during the reign of Queen Elizabeth I in the sixteenth century, exemplified in the works of Shakespeare. See pages 226–229 for information on the evolution of the English language.

essay/magazine article/supported opinion piece: Non-fiction prose that examines a single topic from a point of view. It requires an introductory paragraph stating the main or controlling idea, several paragraphs developing the topic, and a concluding paragraph. The title identifies the topic. Formal essays are usually serious and impersonal in tone. Personal or informal essays reveal the personality and feelings of the author and are conversational in tone. "Listen Up!" and "Teens Matter to the Canadian Economy" are examples of this type of non-fiction writing. See page 267 for more details on essays. Essays can be informational, persuasive, or argumentative.

A **persuasive essay** uses supporting details and attempts to persuade the reader to the writer's point of view.

An **argumentative essay** argues for or against a question or a position on a topic, issue, and so on.

fable: A story meant to teach a lesson. It often includes talking animals.

fairy tale: A fantasy story written primarily for children and frequently about princesses, princes, and witches with supernatural powers. "Once Upon a Time" uses elements of a fairy tale.

fiction: Prose writing that is based on imagination rather than fact.

first person narration: See **point of view**.

flashback: A device that shifts the narrative from the present to the past, usually to reveal a change in character or illustrate an important point.

folk tale: A story originating among the common people (the "folk") and handed down, usually orally, from generation to generation. "Talk" is a folk talc.

foreshadowing: Refers to clues that hint at what is going to happen later in the plot. Foreshadowing is used to arouse the reader's curiosity, build suspense, and help prepare the reader to accept events that occur later in the story. The appearance of the white cat with pink eyes in *The Jade Peony* foreshadows the grandmother's death.

free verse: See **poetry**.

glossary: A list of special, technical, or difficult words with definitions or comments.

graphic organizer: A chart, graph, Venn diagram, or other visual means used to record, organize, classify, analyze, and assess information.

headline: The title of a newspaper article, which reveals the topic of the article. It is written in a complete sentence and is usually short and attention grabbing. For example, "It's War!" or "Teens Speak Out Against Drugs". (See also **newspaper article/report/story**.)

humour: Written, oral, or media work containing material which is intended to amuse the reader or provoke laughter. "The Mistake" and *A Marriage Proposal* use humour.

icon: An image representing or symbolizing a type of person, place, thing, or idea. Many computers use icons to identify commands or to show the location of information.

idiom: A widely used expression that is not meant to be taken literally. Idioms are particular to cultures and to small groups within cultures. In English, there are many idiomatic expressions, such as *hit it off, let your hair down, give a piece of my mind,* and *bite your tongue.* See also **dialect**.

image/imagery: A picture created by a writer using concrete details, adjectives, and figures of speech, which gives readers a vivid impression of what or who is being described. The convict in *Great Expectations* is described as "A fearful man, all in coarse grey, with a great iron on his leg. . . ." Similes, metaphors, and symbols are all specific kinds of imagery.

incremental refrain: See **refrain**.

interior monologue: See **monologue**.

interview: A recorded discussion, usually structured in a question-answer format. Examples of interviews are those between an employer and a job applicant, a reporter and a politician, an immigration officer and a new immigrant. See "An Interview With Michael Ondaatje" on page 61 and the advertising section on page 291 for examples of interviews.

irony: A literary device that creates a contrast or discrepancy between what is said and what is meant or between expectations and reality. There are three common types of irony.

    Dramatic irony occurs when the writer or dramatist reveals something important to the reader or audience that a character in the plot does not know. For example, the audience in *Twelfth Night* knows that Cesario is Viola, a woman, but the Duke is unaware of this.

    Situational irony occurs when what actually happens is different from what is expected. "Mistaken" gives an example of such an irony.

    Verbal irony occurs when a character says one thing literally, but really means something else. When a student has neglected to do his homework and the teacher says, "I can see you are making every effort to do well in this course", the teacher is speaking ironically.

journal: A notebook that contains personal reflections and responses to writing, events, incidents, people, and so on. See also **diary**.

layout: A plan or design of a page of a book, advertisement, newspaper, or other printed material that shows the placement of the words and illustrations or photos. Layouts can be done by hand or by using computer design software.

letter to the editor: A letter written to a newspaper or magazine in response to a story or article in a previous issue. It usually contains the opinion of the letter writer. See pages 261–262 for an example of a letter to the editor.

memoir: An autobiographical account or a record of a person's experiences.

metaphor: A figure of speech that makes a comparison between two seemingly unlike things without using connective words such as *like* or *as*. An example is "The moon was a ghostly galleon" from "The Highwayman".

monologue: A speech by one person telling a story, revealing character, or describing a humorous or dramatic situation.
    An **interior monologue** is a form of writing that reveals the inner thoughts of a character. See also **soliloquy**.

montage of shots: The editing of several shots to create a sequence or episode in a film or video.

mood: See **atmosphere**.

moral: The implied or stated lesson of a story. The moral of "Fable for Tomorrow" is that if humans do not take care of this planet, we will face the tragedy that the writer has created in her story. See also **fable**.

motif: A word, idea, object, image, metaphor, or character that recurs in a work or several literary works. For example, *Great Expectations* and *Silent Words* both share a common motif of coming of age and answering the question "Who am I?"

myth: A traditional story that often contains heroic acts and explains a belief, a cultural practice, or a natural phenomenon. Like folk tales, myths are passed down from generation to generation within a culture. Many cultures, for example, have myths that explain their origins.

narrator: The person or character who tells the story.

newspaper article/report/story: Non-fiction prose that informs readers about an event or issue. It has titles in the form of brief sentences (see **headlines**). The most important information appears first in a newspaper article so that the reader can stop reading once he or she has sufficient information on the topic.

onomatopoeia: The formation or use of words with meanings that are connected to their sounds. The word *buzz* suggests the noise of a bee. In *Silent Words*, the protagonist "listened to the swishing of the water . . . birds chirping . . . ducks quacking . . . croaking frogs . . . buzzing flies . . . seagulls squawking . . . splash of fish . . ."

open-ended question: A type of carefully worded question used by an interviewer to solicit a longer response from the interviewee than a yes or no answer that reveals little. See "An Interview With Michael Ondaatje".

opinion piece: See **essay/magazine article/supported opinion piece**.

pamphlet: A short, unbound printed work with a paper cover used to advertise or provide information about a place, person, organization, product, and so on. See also **brochure**.

pathetic fallacy: A literary device in which nature or inanimate things are described in a way that is sympathetic to or prophetic about events and the emotions of the characters. In "Brief Lives: Helen", wintry and bleak January is the time of the year when she married and lost her husband and later it became the time when she went away on her own to reminisce.

personification: A metaphor in which human attributes are given to inanimate objects.

perspective: The viewpoint or bias of a writer or character. "Healing the Planet" reveals the perspective of its author, environmentalist Helen Caldicott.

persuasive essay: See **essay**.

plot: Plot is a series of events and the thoughtful interrelations of these events, their causes and effects, and so on; the main story in a narrative or drama. The plot of "Lamb to the Slaughter" tells how the perfect wife, Mary Maloney, ends up

murdering her husband and cleverly covering up her crime.

poetry: A unique form of writing about experiences, thoughts, and feelings, frequently divided into lines and stanzas, which uses compressed language, figures of speech, and imagery to appeal to readers' emotions and imagination. There are a variety of poetic structures with different requirements of length, rhyme, rhythm, stanza formation, and so on.

A **narrative poem**, such as "The Cremation of Sam McGee", tells a story.

A **lyric poem**, such as "Bearhug", conveys a central idea or emotion.

Free verse is a type of poetry that has no regular metre or rhyme scheme. "Mistaken" is written in free verse.

A **prose poem** is written in prose but uses poetic devices like rhythm, imagery, and figures of speech to convey a single idea. "The Page" is a prose poem.

point of view: The perspective from which a story is told. There are three common points of view.

In the **first person point of view**, the story is told by the protagonist, a minor character, or an interested bystander using the pronouns *I* or *we*. *The Jade Peony* is written in the first person from the point of view of Sek-Lung, the protagonist. The first person narrator in "Borders" is a secondary character; in "Priscilla and the Wimps", it is an unknown bystander.

The **third person omniscient point of view** is an all-seeing, all-knowing perspective. It reveals the thoughts and emotions of several characters using *he, she,* and *they*. "The Nest" has a third person omniscient narrator.

Third person limited point of view also uses the pronouns *he, she,* and *they,* but tells the story from the perspective of one of the characters. "Lamb to the Slaughter" is written in the third person, but the point of view is restricted to revealing only Mary Maloney's thoughts and feelings.

prose poem: See **poetry**.

protagonist: The main character in a literary work on whom the audience's interest focuses. The main character may or may not be the narrator.

purpose: The aim or goal of any piece of writing, including articles, advertisements, brochures, and so on. See pages 257–259 for more information on purpose.

refrain: A phrase or verse repeated regularly in a poem or song.

In an **incremental refrain**, a new line or lines are added each time the refrain is repeated. These new lines become part of the refrain. See "Talk" for an example.

repetition: Words or phrases that are repeated to create emphasis, atmosphere, rhythm, or imagery. An example is "The highwayman came riding—riding—riding" in "The Highwayman".

report: An oral or written account or opinion formally expressed, based on findings from investigation or inquiry.

research report: A form of non-fiction writing intended to inform an audience about a particular topic. It contains factual information that is carefully researched.

review: A form of writing that discusses the good and bad points of a book, film, work of art, and so on. It usually provides a synopsis or description of the work and focuses on a few key aspects, using evidence to support arguments.

rhyme: Repetition of vowel sounds and all sounds following them in words at the end of the lines of a poem. *[B]low* and *row* and *sky* and *fly* are rhyming words in "In Flanders Fields".

rhyme scheme is the pattern of end rhymes. A rhyme scheme is indicated by assigning each new end rhyme a different letter of the alphabet. For example, the rhyme scheme of the first stanza of "In Flanders Fields" is *aabba: blow, row, sky, fly, below.*

rhythm: A pattern of sound created by stressed and unstressed syllables. Shakespeare creates the rhythm of his lines by alternating unstressed and stressed syllables.

role play: Assuming and acting the role of a character, fictitious or real, and using dialogue and/or gestures, appropriate to the individual, to present the character to an audience.

satire: A literary work that ridicules human vices and follies, often with the purpose of teaching a lesson or encouraging change. "Mister Blink" is a satire on political elections.

script: The text written for a play, video, film, radio or television broadcast. It includes dialogue, sound effects, stage directions, and so on.

sentence fragment: A group of words, punctuated as a sentence, that lacks either a subject or a complete verb.

serial: A story presented one part at a time in a magazine, on radio or television, and so on. Television programs that present a story in installments are called serials.

setting: The place and time of a story, play, or poem. The setting of *The Speling Konferens* is "a room somewhere in the Parliament buildings".

short story: A short fictional prose narrative having only one major character, plot, setting, and theme. The short story usually focuses on a single conflict, character, or emotional effect.

simile: A figure of speech that makes a comparison between two seemingly unlike things using a connective word such as *like* or *as*. An example is "Talk of your cold! Through the parka's fold it stabbed like a driven nail" in "The Cremation of Sam McGee".

slang: Very informal and trendy vocabulary and language patterns used by particular groups or in special informal contexts;

it is usually inappropriate to use slang in formal written work, but it can contribute to character and mood in fiction.

soliloquy: A speech made by an actor to him- or herself. It divulges information to the audience, reveals a character's true motives, and so on. See **monologue**.

stage directions: The directions in a play, used to describe the stage setting and to tell actors when to exit or enter the stage, how to deliver their lines, and so on. Stage directions may appear in brackets or italics to set them off from the dialogue.

Standard Canadian English: The oral and written English used by a broad range of Canadian society (in education, government, medicine, law, science, business, and the media). Accepted rules and practices of grammar, usage, spelling, and punctuation are followed.

stanza: A set number of lines grouped together to form units in poetry.

stereotyped character: See **character**.

storyboard: A series of panels with sketches and dialogue, representing the shots in an advertisement, film, television program, and so on, used to plan a work on film or video. See page 289 for an example of a storyboard.

storytelling: The oral telling of stories, using intonation, volume, pace, and so on, to capture the meaning and tone of the words of the story for an audience.

style: The particular way in which a writer expresses him- or herself in writing. It is the sum effect of the author's choice of voice, vocabulary, and sentence structure, and use of devices, such as imagery, onomatopoeia, and rhythm.

summary: A brief account giving the main points of a story or article. See also **synopsis**.

surprise ending: The conclusion of a story or poem that goes against expectations. "Charles" has a surprising ending when his mother discovers that the "Charles" Laurie had been talking about is actually himself.

suspense: The condition of being uncertain about an outcome, used by writers to create tension, excitement, or anxiety. In "On the Sidewalk, Bleeding", readers are kept in suspense as to whether Andy will die or be saved.

symbol: A person, place, thing, or event that stands both for itself and for something beyond itself. The wall that surrounds the family home in "Once Upon a Time" is a symbol of the division between the white and black races in South Africa; the jade peony in Wayson Choy's novel symbolizes the grandmother's promise that she will be with her grandson always—even after her death.

synopsis: A brief statement giving an overview of a book, story, play, and so on. See also **summary**.

tableau: The representation of a particular moment in time by actors frozen in a position depicting interrelationships or a point in a story.

theme: A statement of the central idea of a work, usually implied rather than directly stated. One theme of "Listen Up!" is that developing good listening skills is important for effective communication.

thesis: A main or controlling idea or statement about a topic that a writer proposes and supports in an essay. "The wired, always-in-touch, information overload '90s have created what some technology watchers say is an expanding social etiquette vacuum" is the thesis statement in "Etiquette for a Wired World".

tone: The attitude a writer expresses towards his or her subject. The tone of writing may be formal or informal, personal or impersonal, angry or cheerful, bitter or hopeful, and so on.

topic: The subject that is being written or talked about. The subject of "Bad Vibrations" is loud music and the resulting hearing problems in certain groups of people. (Note: Topic and thesis are often confused: **topic** is the subject matter; **thesis** is the statement about the topic.)

topic sentence: A sentence that states the subject of the paragraph.

Index

The Page by Margaret Atwood from *Murder in the Dark: Short Fictions and Prose Poems* by Margaret Atwood. Used by permission, McClelland & Stewart, Inc. The Canadian Publishers. **The Speling Konferens** by Ken Weber. Reprinted by permission of the author. **Talk** from *Scholastic Scope*, April 2, 1993. Copyright © 1993 by Scholastic Inc. Reprinted by permission of Scholastic Inc. **Listen Up!** by Audrey Greer. Reprinted by permission of Warren Sheppell Consultants Corp. **The Highwayman** by Alfred Noyes. Reprinted by permission of Hugh Noyes on behalf of the author's estate. **The Cremation of Sam McGee** by Robert Service from *Songs of a Sourdough*. Reprinted by permission of the author's estate. From **The Selected Journals of L.M. Montgomery, Volume II: 1910-1921**, edited by Mary Rubio and Elizabeth Waterson (Toronto: Oxford University Press, 1987). Copyright © 1987 University of Guelph. Reprinted by permission of the Editors and Oxford University Press Canada. **Cats** by Norma Harrs from *Where Dreams Have Gone*. Copyright © 1997 by Norma Harrs. Reprinted by permission of the author. **How to Cook Chinese Rice** by Andy Quan from *Queeries: An Anthology of Gay Male Prose*. (Vancouver: Arsenal Pulp Press, 1993). Adapted by permission of the publisher. **A Bowl of Red** by Joe Fiorito from *Comfort Me with Apples* by Joe Fiorito. Nuage Editions, Winnipeg, 1994. Copyright © 1994 Joe Fiorito. Reprinted by permission of the author. **Starvin' Guy Chicken Pie** from *Looneyspoons: Low-Fat Food Made Fun!* Copyright © 1996 by Granet Publishing. Reprinted by permission of the publisher. **Once Upon a Time** by Nadine Gordimer. Copyright © 1991 by Felix Licensing, B.V. **Bearhug** by Michael Ondaatje from *The Cinnamon Peeler* by Michael Ondaatje. Copyright © 1984 by Michael Ondaatje. Reprinted by permission of the author. **An Interview with Michael Ondaatje** by Tania Charzewski from *The Reader's Showcase*. Reprinted with permission of the author. **Charles** from *The Lottery* by Shirley Jackson. Copyright © 1948, 1949 by Shirley Jackson and copyright © renewed 1976, 1977 Laurence Hyman, Barry Hyman, Mrs. Sarah Webster and Mrs. Joanne Schnurer. Reprinted by permission of Farrar, Straus & Giroux, Inc. **Stones** by Sandra Birdsell from *Agassiz Stories*, Turnstone Press, 1987. Originally Published in Night Travellers, Turnstone Press, 1982. **Silent Words** by Ruby Slipperjack. Reprinted with permission from *Silent Words*. Copyright © 1992 by Ruby Slipperjack. Published by Fifth House Ltd. Calgary. **The Nest** by Robert Zacks. Reprinted by permission of McIntosh and Otis. Copyright © 1975. From **The Jade Peony** by Wayson Choy. Copyright © 1995 by Wayson Choy. Reprinted with permission of the author. **As I Grew Older** by Langston Hughes from *Collected Poems* by Langston Hughes. Copyright © 1994 by the estate of Langston Hughes. Reprinted by permission of Alfred A. Knopf, Inc. **Priscilla and the Wimps** by Richard Peck from *Sixteen Short Stories by Outstanding Writers for Young Adults*, edited by Donald R. Gallo. Copyright © 1984 by Richard Peck. Used by permission of Dell Publishing, a division of Random House, Inc. **On the Sidewalk, Bleeding** by Evan Hunter. Originally published in *Happy New Year, Herbie and Other Stories*. Copyright © 1957, 1985 by Evan Hunter. Reprinted by permission of the author. **Mistaken** by Vikram Seth from *All You Who Sleep Tonight*. Reprinted by permission of Alfred A. Knopf Inc. Copyright © 1987, 1990 by Vikram Seth. **How We Met** by Kristin Rushowy from *The Toronto Star*, November 29, 1998, p. G3. Reprinted by permission of the author. **A Marriage Proposal** by Anton Chekhov from *The Brute and Other Faces* compiled by Eric Bentley. Reprinted by permission of Applause Theater Books Publishers. **Ice Bangles** by Nazneen Sadiq from *Ice Bangles*. Copyright © 1988 by Nazneen Sadiq. Published with permission by James Lorimer & Company Publishers. Reprinted by permission. **The Mistake** by Isaac Asimov. Based on a story entitled "The Immortal Bard". Copyright 1953 by Palmer Publications, Inc. from *Earth is Room Enough* by Isaac Asimov. Used by permission of Doubleday, a division of Random House, Inc. **The Pen of My Aunt** by Josephine Tey (Gordon Daviot). Reprinted by permission of David Higham Associates. **Helen** by Bill Richardson from *Bachelor Brothers' Bed & Breakfast*. Copyright © 1993 by Bill Richardson, published by Douglas & McIntyre. Reprinted by permission of the publisher. **I Am a Canadian** by Duke Redbird. Copyright © Duke Redbird.

PHOTOGRAPHS

ILLUSTRATORS